MW01030174

PATRIOTISM AND FRATERNALISM IN THE KNIGHTS OF COLUMBUS

PATRIOTISM AND FRATERNALISM IN THE KNIGHTS OF COLUMBUS

A History of the Fourth Degree

Christopher J. Kauffman

A Herder & Herder Book
The Crossroad Publishing Company
New York

The Crossroad Publishing Company
481 Eighth Avenue, New York, NY 10001

Copyright © 2001 by The Knights of Columbus

All rights reserved. No part of this book may be reproduced, stored in a retrieval system, or transmitted, in any form or by any means, electronic, mechanical, photocopying, recording, or otherwise, without the written permission of The Crossroad Publishing Company.

Printed in the United States of America

Library of Congress Cataloging-in-Publication Data

Kauffman, Christopher J., 1936–
Patriotism and fraternalism in the Knights of Columbus : a history of the fourth degree / Christopher J. Kauffman.
p. cm.
"A herder & herder book."
Includes bibliographical references and index.
ISBN 0-8245-1885-3 (hardcover : alk. paper)
1. Knights of Columbus. Fourth Degree—History.
2. Anti-Catholicism—United States—History. I. Title.
HS1538.K65 K38 2000
267'.242—dc21 00-011652

1 2 3 4 5 6 7 8 9 10 05 04 03 02 01

This book is dedicated with appreciation
to special persons
who represent
Fraternalism, Family, and Friendship.

To Past Supreme Knight Virgil C. Dechant
and to Supreme Chaplain Bishop Thomas V. Daily,
for making their mark on the history
of the Church.

To the memory of my granddad, Chris O'Brien,
for modeling political loyalty and religious meaning.
And to my grandson, Michael R. Kauffman Marinelli,
for making play and poetry real for me.

To John and Dorli Bokel,
for making friendship vital
and for revealing blessings of the
twenty-five years of their marriage.

Contents

Acknowledgments

IT HAS BEEN A GRATIFYING EXPERIENCE to situate the Knights' commitment to patriotism, embodied in the Fourth Degree, within various religious, social, and political contexts. To research and write this history entailed visits to several archives and consultation with historians, theologians, and leading Knights. Associates, friends, and family have offered advice, encouragement, and inspiration.

My association with the Knights over the years has been professionally and personally a good experience. I am grateful to the Order for a grant which allowed me to complete this book during two summers and while on sabbatical from the Catholic University. Past Supreme Knight Virgil C. Dechant brought his enthusiasm for history to this project. It was he who initiated the Knights' museum at the international headquarters in New Haven, Connecticut, which recently opened in a separate building expertly designed by professionals in several areas. Its curator, Mary Lou Cummings, has been a valuable resource person over the years. The Knights of Columbus Archives is an integral and vital part of the museum. Susan Brosnan, the archivist, provided me with historical materials, illustrated by the many ACK (Archives of the K. of C.) designations in the notes for each of the five chapters. Most valuable was her proofreading of the entire manuscript with a command of history, the sources, and the contents of the text. Without her critical eye this work would never have achieved its level of accuracy and clarity. Thanks so much, Susan, for your close reading of the manuscript. Thanks also to Charles H. Lindberg, the staff member of the Fraternal Services Department responsible for the Fourth Degree, for photocopying the relevant material from over forty years of Supreme Knights' reports.

Charles H. Foos, former Supreme Master of the Fourth Degree, and recently appointed Supreme Secretary, was also enthusiastically committed to this history. He not only provided me with historical material, but he also read the text, which resulted in the correction of names, dates, and places. I have relied on Charles Foos as the liaison person in New Haven. He is a man I could call upon whenever I needed his expertise during the writing phase of the project. I am grateful for his responses rendered with interest and commitment. Mr. Dechant and Mr. Foos blended their interest in the project with an understanding of the scholarly freedom inherent in the historical enterprise.

Carl A. Anderson, former Supreme Secretary, succeeded Virgil Dechant as Supreme Knight on October 1, 2000. He and Nestor Barber, Supreme Master who succeeded Charles Foos, will preside at the festivities at the close of the centennial year of the Fourth Degree, February 22, 2001. I am grateful to Mr. Anderson and Mr. Barber, who share a keen interest in the pubication of this work.

I interviewed former Supreme Master Hilary Schmittzehe, who shared his insights on the reforms undertaken to assure uniformity among the Honor Guard and Color Corps of the Fourth Degree. Thanks so much, Hilary. Major William R. Smith, USA (Ret.) sent me a copy of his detailed history of the Fourth Degree's "Sword of the [Fourth Degree of the] Knights, A Pictorial History Order of the Knights of Columbus." Thank you, Major Smith, for sharing with me your fine study.

Francis M. Feeley, Vice Supreme Master of Calvert Province, has expressed deep interest in this history. At the Catholic University, I presented two lectures on topics included in this book. I am grateful to Timothy Meagher, Archivist of the University, for sponsoring a lecture. In the audience were Fourth Degree Knights from Washington Assembly, including the State Deputy, Harry T. Jackson, Jr. I appreciate their responses and enjoyed discussing Fourth Degree history with them. The second was the Annual Lecture of the Catholic Daughters of the Americas (CDA), sponsored by the university in honor of the CDA's endowment of the Chair In American Catholic History, a chair which I have occupied since 1992. Of course, I share the university's gratitude for the CDA endowment. These lectures allowed me to sharpen my historical perspective on the governing idea of this book.

There is an abundance of photographical material at the headquarters in New Haven, which Karen Buchanan has organized with professionalism and keen interest. I am grateful to Ms. Buchanan, Photo Archivist, for the illustrations that so well depict several historical trends in this book. John R.

Cummings, Director of the Graphics Department and the photographer of the Knights of Columbus, placed the photos on electronic disks. Thanks, John, for your collaboration with Karen on the visual material for this book.

There is a notable symbiosis between historians and archivists. I have noted Susan Brosnan's archival support. I also gratefully acknowledge the assistance of Sharon Sumpter and Kevin Cawley at the University of Notre Dame Archives. Ms. Sumpter was particularly helpful in preparing material for my arrival, while Mr. Cawley responded to my research needs during my research at the archives. Both archivists represented expertise and personal commitment.

At the Archives of the Archdiocese of Chicago, Julie Satzik was very helpful. Though I came away with only a few documents, I am grateful to her for her assistance and diligent search for relevant material. While in Chicago, I consulted with Ellen Skerett, an expert on various historical spheres of Chicago Catholicism. She and her husband, John O'Malley, were gracious hosts at a gathering in their home. Thanks, Ellen, for your command of history and your easeful hospitality.

Thanks also to Sylvia Linda Rael, Archivist and Library Director of the Archdiocese of Denver, for sending me material relevant to the first Supreme Master, John Reddin. I am also grateful to Monsignor Francis J. Weber, Archivist of the Archdiocese of Los Angeles, who kindly sent me two articles he wrote on Joseph Scott for the *Encyclopedia of California Catholic History,* which were very informative.

William Colbert, Archivist of the American Irish Historical Society in New York City, led me to important files in this valuable collection. I am grateful for his permission to photocopy the relevant material that allowed me to elucidate the significance of Edward F. McSweeney, the chairman of the Fourth Degree's Historical Commission.

I extend my thanks to the three research assistants at The Catholic University of America, who brought to their work interest and concern: Patrick McNamara, presently Assistant Archivist for the Diocese of Brooklyn, photocopied bibliography and searched for relevant historiography; Daniel Conkle, a graduate student in church history, was a great help in the Library of Congress; Charles Kaczynski, a graduate student in history, discovered significant material in the Wilson Papers located in the Manuscript Division of the Library of Congress.

In the Introduction I listed many historians whose works are related to topics in this book. A few of them are also participants in our Clio group, historians of American Catholicism in the Baltimore-D.C. area who are valuable colleagues: Dorothy Brown, Emmett Curran, William Dinges, Maureen Harp, Elizabeth McKeown, Timothy Meagher, William Portier, and Leslie Woodcock Tentler. Many historians have been influential over the years, particularly Scott Appleby, Joseph P. Chinnici, Jay P. Dolan, James Fisher, Philip Gleason, James Hennesey, S.J., Martin E. Marty, Thomas W. Spalding, C.F.X., and Joseph M. White. To them I extend my gratitude for their work and friendship.

No scholar has matched the influence of Justus George Lawler. Not only has he been the editor par excellence of everything I have written over the past thirty years, but his own work, including the two incarnations of *Continuum,* have deepened my appreciation of the intersection of religion, literature, and history. Most importantly, George is an old friend whose favorite line has in my mind achieved the status of a maxim: "One should always remember to cultivate irony." Thanks, George!

The Sulpician provincials Fathers Edward Frazier, Gerald Brown, and Ronald Witherup, S.S., the present provincial, have graciously allowed me the use of an office at the Sulpician Archives, where I have been located since 1982, when I began research on their history, *Tradition and Transformation.* It is here where I wrote this book on the Fourth Degree during summers and while on a sabbatical year. John Bowen, S.S., Archivist Emeritus, has proofread everything I have written since 1986. Thanks, John, for your friendship over these many years. Robert Shindle, a former Assistant Archivist, has been a fine colleague. The Associate Archivist, Janine Bruce, is not only a professional archivist, but during her free time she deciphered my handwriting and placed it in the computer with skill and concern. Many thanks, Janine, for your patience, expertise, persistence, and cooperation.

Gwendolin Herder, the publisher of Crossroad Publishing Company, expressed keen interest in my work that has been very encouraging; Alison Donohue, Managing Editor, has guided the manuscript to its book form with professional expertise and personal concern. The HK Scriptorium designed this book with more than simply business interest, but with pride and commitment. I am, therefore, gratified by Crossroad's publication of this book.

I am grateful for the collegiality of my friends in the Church History Department at The Catholic University of America who have consistently expressed interest in my work: Jacques Gres-Gayer, Jane Merdinger, Nelson Minnich, and Robert Trisco.

The pages of my "book of life" reveal the deep imprint of Helen Schaberg Kauffman, spouse-partner over these thirty-four years of marriage. Our children, Jane, Christopher, and Kathryn Ann, are poems in progress: Jane with Robert Marinelli and our grandson, Michael; Katie with Luis Maldonado, and Kiffer with the many characters he brings to life in the theater. The title of my personal story is: "Life's Loves."

INTRODUCTION

IN MY INTRODUCTION TO THE FIRST EDITION of *Faith and Fraternalism,* I elaborated on a password by which a Knight identified himself as a member in good standing: "diligence, devotion, and defense." This example of alliterative fraternal coinage was minted in 1895 when the American Protective Association (APA) was reaching the apex of its national popularity as the predominant anti-Catholic society of the period. Diligence conveys the qualities necessary for responsible membership in the Order: reliability, perseverance, temperance, commitment, and loyalty. A diligent Knight would project patriotic images of responsible citizenship and respectability to the guardians of Americanism ever suspicious of the loyalty of immigrant Catholics. "Devotion" conveyed the essential disposition toward the Order, church, and society. A devoted Knight pledged his fealty as a practical Catholic to respond to brothers in distress, to be faithfully engaged in pious societies, to attend mass on Sundays and Holy Days, and, in accord with the model established by the founder, Father Michael J. McGivney, perform corporal and spiritual works of mercy. A devoted Catholic is correspondingly a dedicated patriot because, as George Washington said on more than one occasion, religion is essential for good citizenship. "Defense" called a Knight to be conscious of the enemies of anti-Catholicism and nativism. The devoted Knights eagerly defended the faith not with vindictive rhetoric but with the respectful civil discourse of patriotic gentlemen exemplifying virtues essential for the vitality of the republic. Hence, the password "diligence, devotion, and defense" represents a stance that is thematic to this book.

Two other Knights' passwords substantiate the significance of this conflict: "Christopher Columbus" and "Commodore Barry." These two were chosen not because of their Italian or Irish nationality but rather because each represented the Catholic contribution to the making of America. This conscious assertion of Catholic citizenship and patriotism was steeped in historical memory to counter the distorted images of the church past and present.

The principal repository for documenting this history is the Archives of the Knights of Columbus in New Haven. Besides the record group, the Fourth Degree, which includes the reports of the Supreme Assembly from 1900 to the present, there are those on the bogus oath, the Historical Commission, and an extensive collection of the Luke E. Hart papers, 1922–1964. The Order's monthly publications, *The Columbiad* (1893–1920) and *Columbia* (1920–), are important as a primary and a secondary sources.

Since John H. Reddin of Denver, Colorado, was the Supreme Master of the Fourth Degree for thirty years (1910–1940), his papers, though not extensive, are significant, particularly the history of the degree he published in 1931. The archives also contain materials on each of the Supreme Masters; those papers on Timothy Galvin (1940–1945) and William Mulligan (1945–1964) are relatively slim. Mulligan tended to defer to the Supreme Knights as the Order's spokesmen for the ideals of patriotism. When Luke E. Hart became Supreme Knight in 1953, he and the other principal officers took up residence in the central office in New Haven because of the complexity of administering programs for hundreds of thousands of members and millions of dollars of insurance. Though the Masters of the Fourth Degree continued to represent patriotism within the Fourth Degree, the papers, reports, and speeches of Supreme Knights are valuable sources for discerning the salient patterns of patriotism from the 1950s to the turn of the century.

The Noll Papers in the Archives of the University of Notre Dame yielded significant material on anti-Catholicism. Bishop John Noll of Fort Wayne, Indiana, was the founder of *Our Sunday Visitor* and an avid collector of such pamphlets. It was in his papers that I also found the *Newsletter of the Americans and Others United for the Separation of Church and State*, covered in chapter 4. Notre Dame also has the papers of Thomas F. Mahony of Longmont, Colorado, which are important because they reveal a social-reform dimension during the Knights' antisocialist campaigns during the 1920s and 1930s. I visited the Archives of the Archdiocese of Chicago, where I found a useful letter from Father John Noll before he became bishop, and material for general background. The Archives of the Irish American Historical Society, located in New York City, house the papers of

Daniel Cohalen, president of the Friends of Irish Freedom; Edward F. McSweeney's correspondence with Cohalen and others is significant, as it added a new dimension to his role as the founder and chairman of the Fourth Degree's Historical Commission, one that published such works as W. E. B. DuBois's *A Gift of the Black: The Negroes in the Making of America.*

The Woodrow Wilson Papers, located in the Manuscript Division of the Library of Congress, include several letters on the bogus oath of the Fourth Degree, as well as a valuable letter from Patrick Henry Callahan, the chairman of the Knights' Commission on Religious Prejudices. The Archives of the Catholic University of America yielded background material for chapter 3, but they were very valuable for documenting chapters in *Faith and Fraternalism.*

Among the books on patriotism, John Bodnar's work has made a significant impact. His book *Remaking America: Public Memory, Commemoration and Patriotism* enriched my understanding of the complexity of patriotism. Four chapters of his edited work, *Bonds of Affection: Americans Define Their Patriotism,* were related to several topics, especially those in chapter 1. Cecilia Elizabeth O'Leary's chapter included an insightful remark on how patriotism entails conflicts over "historical memory." Since these conflicts were expressed in struggles over symbolic languages and foundation stories, O'Leary's notion was applied to the conflicts between the Order and the forces of anti-Catholicism and nativism.

John Higham's *Strangers in the Land: Patterns of American Nativism, 1860–1925* is generally recognized as a classic in the field. His analysis of anti-Catholicism and nativism was foundational to chapter 2 on the bogus oath and the postwar movements of the 1920s, as well as several topics in chapter 3, "The Tribal Twenties," his descriptive term for the general ethos of that volatile decade. Higham's *Send These to Me: Immigrants in Urban America* contextualized the anti-immigrant restriction projects of Edward F. McSweeney. Cecilia Elizabeth O'Leary's book *A Nation To Die For: The Paradox of American Patriotism* also focused on the abuses of nationalism during the war and in the postwar years. Lynn Dumenil's article on "The Tribal Twenties" helped to sort out the meanings of conflict. For anti-K. of C. activities of the Ku Klux Klan I am particularly indebted to Robert Alan Goldberg's work *The Ku Klux Klan in Colorado.*

For the story of the origins and development of the African-American Catholic fraternal society the Knights of St. Peter Claver, I referred to Cyprian Davis's groundbreaking book, *The History of Black Catholics in the United States.* For material on developments in African-American history of the 1920s, I turned to Steven J. Ochs's book *Desegregating the Altar: The Josephites and the Struggle of Black Priests.* I have consulted works by several other religious historians: Patrick Carey, Joseph Chinnici, Jay P. Dolan, George Q. Flynn, Gerald P. Fogarty, Philip Gleason, Martin E. Marty, Mark Massa, Elizabeth McKeown, and Leslie Woodcock Tentler. But David O'Brien's books, *American Catholicism and Social Reform, Public Catholicism* and *The Renewal of American Catholicism,* were especially valuable, as they related to such wide-ranging topics in this book: the republican Catholicism of John Carroll and John England in chapter 1, the social Catholicism of John A. Ryan in chapter 3, and religious and social developments from the 1930s to the 1960s in chapters 4 and 5.

The works on fraternalism by Mark Carnes and Mary Ann Clawson were incorporated into the introduction to the second edition of *Faith and Fraternalism* (1992); their insights into masculinity were also cited in this work. Since no scholar of fraternalism has considered the Knights of Columbus, I have liberally drawn from my own work to situate this study of the Fourth Degree within the historical context of the Knights.

This book focuses on the national movements of the Knights' patriotism. Local developments enter the narrative as their programs achieved national recognition and as they engaged in the conflicts over historical memory. This was evident in chapter 3 when reports of Provincial Assemblies revealed responses to Ku Klux Klan activity. Since celebrations of the Catholic heritage are at the core of the Fourth Degree's initiation or exemplification ceremonies, which are rooted in the past, preservation of Catholic historical memory is characteristic of the Fourth Degree. In the discussion of the national reorganization of the degree in chapter 2, I listed six Fourth Degree provinces named after Catholic explorers: Champlain, Cabot, Calvert, de Soto, Marquette, and La Salle.

National and international expansion necessitated new provinces with names representing local notables from colonial times to the twentieth century. Since there are twenty-five provinces in the year 2000, I will introduce those that represent the continuity of the American Catholic heritage. Bishop James A. Healy Province, named after the first black bishop in the United States, encompasses Massachusetts, Connecticut, Rhode Island, Vermont, and Maine. The son of an Irish father and a slave mother, James Augustine Healy (1830–1900) was bishop of the Diocese of Portland, Maine. Two of his brothers were also priests. Guadalupe Province, which is predominantly composed of assemblies in Texas and one in Oklahoma, honors Our Lady of Guadalupe, a Marian devotion popular in the Hispanic community. Since the 1960s the Mexican-American community has formed its own councils and then assemblies.

Francis C. Kelley Province, which takes in Newfoundland, New Brunswick, Nova Scotia, and Prince Edward Island, commemorates the founder of the Catholic Church Extension Society (in 1905), dedicated to funding rural parish ministry and featured in chapter 2. Kelley was born in Vernon River, Prince Edward Island. He became bishop of Oklahoma City in 1924, where he remained until his death in 1948. There is also Bishop Francis C. Kelley Assembly in Tulsa, Oklahoma. Two provinces are named after saints: Felipe de Jesús in Mexico and St. Isaac Jogues in New York and northern New Jersey. The Philippines celebrate the first Catholic explorer of the islands, Ferdinand Magellan. The John H. Reddin Province honors the first Supreme Master of the Fourth Degree (1910–1940). Embracing Colorado, Utah, and West Virginia, the province is unique in acknowledging a historical figure in the Order. There is also a John H. Reddin Assembly.

Several historical figures featured in this book are commemorated and honored by local assemblies: Joseph Scott Assembly in Barstow, California; Luke E. Hart Assembly in Defiance, Iowa, and in Clarkston, Washington; and Bishop Peter Muldoon Assembly in Rockford, Illinois. There are several assemblies named after popes, but Pope John XXIII—with seventeen—is by far the most popular pope so honored. Bishops and priests dominate the names of assemblies, but Bishop Charles Greco, longtime Supreme Chaplain from Louisiana, and Father Michael J. McGivney are the most widely commemorated. Priests and bishops are also popular in Quebec, but saints are commemorated as well, such as St. Vianney Assembly in Shipsaw. The founder of the Fourth Degree in the Philippines, Monsignor George J. Willman, S.J., is commemorated by an assembly in Gingoog City.

African-Americans are members in many assemblies, but there are some assemblies well known for their activism, such as Washington Assembly in Washington, D.C., and Charles Carroll of Carrollton in Baltimore, both of which are well represented in civic and church events. The evolution of the Fourth Degree throughout its first century has been a blend of national and local patriotism expressed by Supreme Masters and Supreme Knights and by Sir Knights parading on Main Street during civic and church events. In both spheres they vitalize American Catholic historical memory.

1

The Origins of Catholic Patriotism

I

PATRIOTISM, THE BOND BETWEEN CITIZENS and the nation, has frequently been understood as simply a family relationship of the individual to the country. It is actually more complex than that, since it entails an emotional attachment to the national heritage expressed in foundation stories that tend to blend myth, history, and memory. Such biblical symbols as "a city on a hill," "a new Jerusalem," "a redeemer nation," translate "the newness in America into familiar cultural language."[1]

Historian Cecilia Elizabeth O'Leary elaborates on the strand of patriotism that is thematic to this chapter and a subtext of this book:

> Although patriotic culture might appear timeless and consensual, it requires an on-going negotiation of competing points of view and interests. Nations are held together not by their essential unity but through the articulation, always partial, of different forces. Rather than being "natural" or "God-given," nations are "imagined," patriotic traditions are "invented," and social forces struggle over which historical memories, symbols, and rituals will dominate national discourse.[2]

At the first initiation of the Knights of the Fourth Degree in 1900, the ceremonials expressed Catholic patriotic symbols and historical memories in competition with the symbols of nativism and anti-Catholicism that were infused into the American Protective Association (APA) aimed at excluding

Catholics from full citizenship. Such symbols of "republicanism" as "the little red school house" were regarded by the APA as emblematic of the necessary training for citizenship, in opposition to the "Vatican-dominated" parochial schools with their alleged conspiracy against national institutions and the democratic spirit.[3] The Fourth Degree symbols celebrated the American Catholic heritage: Christopher Columbus was the heroic figure who represented the Catholic baptism of the nation; the *Santa Maria* was a countersymbol to the *Mayflower;* towns named after saints were symbolic of the sacralization of the American topography; Catholic phraseology and vocabulary translated "the newness in America into familiar cultural language." Illustrating the significance of Catholic patriotism and citizenship are the titles of the two Knights who led the initiation or exemplification of the Fourth Degree: Expositor of the Constitution and Defender of the Faith. Thus, the Fourth Degree's Catholic identity was rooted in historical memories, symbols, and rituals.

II

Led by Father Michael J. McGivney, the Knights of Columbus established a death-benefit society in 1882 that was based on two "degrees," unity and charity. As Father McGivney explained in a letter to Catholic pastors in Connecticut: "our object is to unite the men of our faith throughout the Diocese of Hartford, that we may gain strength to aid each other in time of sickness, to provide for a decent burial, and to render pecuniary assistance to the families of deceased members."[4] This commitment of unity to provide charity was prefaced by what the twenty-nine-year-old curate at St. Mary's Parish, New Haven, considered one of the principal purposes of the Knights, "to prevent our people from entering secret societies by offering the same if not better advantages to our members."[5] The initiation rituals or ceremonials were designed to inspire the sense of Catholic brotherhood essential to aid the sick and to provide for a funeral and a financial settlement for the family of the deceased member.

The drama of the initiation ceremonials highlighted the life of Christopher Columbus, while a Third Degree joined unity and charity to the ethos of fraternalism; the three degrees were intended to strengthen the bonds of friendship and foster mutual loyalties among Knights in a society charged with an intense animosity toward Catholics. As one first-generation Knight said, "the social side of the order is perhaps the most beautiful, impressive and magnificent ceremonial . . . and is one of the vital parts."[6] Another early

Knight noted that the ceremonials were in part "exemplification of the life and work of our patron, [Columbus]." He continued on the character of Catholic fraternalism: "let us live, not as bubbles on the waves, which when bursted [*sic*], vanish and leave no trace of their existence, but rather in the language of our ritual; 'Let us live for those who love us, for those we know are true; for the heavens that smile upon us, and the good that we can do.'"[7]

The choice of Columbus as the Order's patron was grounded in the Catholic notion of civil liberty. One of the charter members said that, as Catholic descendants of Columbus, "we were entitled to all the rights and privileges due to such a discovery by one of our faith."[8] Columbus was a cultural symbol infused with the sense of American Catholic peoplehood. The term Knight conveyed a commitment to struggle against nativism and anti-Catholicism not as bitter militants on the offensive but as "Catholic gentlemen in fraternity." This latter phrase was the title of an article by Thomas Harrison Cummings, the first national organizer and first editor of the monthly journal dedicated to the Order's interests, the *Columbiad*. Published in 1893, the year of the Chicago Columbian Exhibition honoring the quadricentennial of Columbus's landing. Cummings's article identified the patriotic stance of Columbianism:

> Like the crew who sailed with Columbus on the first voyage to America, we have men of various races and languages. But by drawing close the bonds of brotherhood, we make for the best type of American citizenship. For the best American is he who exemplifies that this is not a Protestant country, nor a Catholic country, nor a Hebrew country, any more than it is an Anglo-Saxon, or a Latin country, but a country of all races and all creeds, with one great, broad . . . creed of fair play and equal rights for all.[9]

The ceremonial of the Fourth Degree is a variant on the theme of Catholic patriotism: "Proud in the older days was the boast 'I am a Roman citizen'; prouder yet today is the boast 'I am an American citizen'; but the proudest boast of all time is ours to make, 'I am an American Catholic citizen.'"[10]

The ceremonial dramatized Catholic contributions to the making of America with particular attention to Christopher Columbus, to the Catholic Spanish and French explorers and missionaries, to Commodore John Barry of the American Navy, and to Bishop John Carroll of Baltimore. Just as Father Michael J. McGivney, the founder, and James Mullen, the first Supreme Knight, and others chose Columbus as the patron of the Knights, so the founders of the Fourth Degree devised a ceremonial replete with narratives on the compatibility between their American and their Catholic identities. With the rise of the American Protective Association, an organization dedicated to the mid-nineteenth-century Know-Nothings' goal of restricting Catholics from the political and economic life of the nation, the Knights were engaged in a religious competition over the definition of patriotism—engaged, in the words of historian O'Leary, in a "struggle [over] historical memories."[11]

Reverend Josiah Strong, author of *Our Country: Its Progress and Its Crisis* (1885), identified "progress" with Protestant citizenship and the "crisis" with Catholicity. Strong explained the religious basis of republicanism. "In Republican and Protestant America it is believed that church and state exist for the people who are administered by them [i.e., Protestants]—our fundamental ideas of society, therefore, are as radically opposed to Vaticanism as imperialism." Josiah Strong responded to Archbishop John Ireland's mission "to make America Catholic" by simply stating that such a goal was impossible because "every romanist who remained obedient to the Pope would necessarily be disloyal to our free institution."[12] This conflict over the religiously inclusive definition of citizenship of Thomas Cummings and the Knights with the Reverend Josiah Strong's exclusivist notion constitutes the central theme in this study.

The political scientist Rogers M. Smith, explores the significance of Josiah Strong, who blended his fear of Vaticanism with his liberal social-gospel vision and a die-hard Anglo-Saxonism.[13] Strong's first book, preceding *Our Country: Its Progress and Its Crisis,* entitled simply *Our Country,* was published by the American Home Missionary Society, founded in the 1840s during the heyday of Protestantism's Righteous Empire, the title of Martin E. Marty's characterization of the period. Invoking the essential congeniality between Protestantism and republican citizenship, Strong asserted that Catholic "allegiance demanded by the Pope . . . was wholly inconsistent [with] good citizenship."[14] Smith points out that at the birth of citizenship in the United States in the 1770s, it was simply assumed that Protestantism "reinforced republicanism" while "many believed that Catholicism . . . undermined it." Smith captures the significances of what Gordon Wood referred to as "religion and republicanism [working] hand in hand."

> Maintaining a Christian, Anglo-Saxon, male dominated citizenry seemed appropriate if Americans were to fulfill their mission to create a city on a hill, a bastion of Christian [i.e., Protestant] virtue nay freedom, as well as a model Republic. However, there were the optimistic political thinkers, confident in the popularity of republican virtue, who perceived the importance of a "per-

vasive Protestantism" but one that was "usually tempered by tolerance for minority Christian and Jewish sects."[15]

The Fourth Degree ceremonial extols the contributions of the Catholic proprietor of Maryland, Cecil Calvert, for planting the banner of religious toleration, and of Bishop John Carroll of Baltimore, the first bishop in the United States, for having been "one of the grand, staunch patriotic prelates." Indeed, the bishop was committed to republican participation in parish governance by elected lay trustees with the power of the purse but not the authority to select pastors. He was also committed to the benefits of the separation of church and state and to religious liberty. Historian David O'Brien notes that Carroll and "the founding generation had learned that the distinction between religion and public life offered a way of dealing with the realities of freedom, separation, and voluntarism, while securing the church as an institution within the pluralistic framework of American religion." They were also "confident that reasonable people should be able to find common ground in their shared humanity."[16]

In 1789, John Carroll responded to anti-Catholic criticism in a letter in the *Gazette of the United States* that called for the continuation of the religious test for holding office, which was obviously intended to exclude Catholics. This response was made before Carroll had been consecrated a bishop, before the passage of the First Amendment to the Constitution guaranteeing religious liberty, and well before the state of Massachusetts finally disestablished the church in 1820. Carroll reminded the author of the letter that Catholics' "blood flowed as freely (in proportion to their numbers) to cement the fabric of independence as that of any of their fellow-citizens":

> They concurred with perhaps greater unanimity than any other body of men, in recommending and promoting that government, from whose influence America anticipates all the blessings of justice, peace, plenty, good order and civil and religious liberty. What character shall we then give to a system of policy, for the express purpose of divesting of rights legally acquired, those citizens, who are not only unoffending, but whose conduct has been highly meritorious.[17]

Bishop John England of Charleston was equally committed to republicanism. For the governance of his diocese he wrote a constitution that provided lay representation on the parish, district, and diocesan levels. In the preamble he drew parallels between the principle of federalism in the U.S. Constitution and the Catholic arrangement of pope (president), bishop (governor), and priests (mayors), and he designed a bicameral legislature for his diocese. Clearly republicanism was being promoted by bishops, priests, and laity during the period 1790s to 1840s.[18]

Archbishop Carroll supported James Madison's declaration of war against Great Britain in 1812, but in a sermon he stated, "Patriotism can never be separated from justice." He noted Madison's deep reluctance to enter the war, and he responded favorably to the mayor of Baltimore's call that religious leaders participate in a day "of repentance and thanksgiving . . . for the principal deliverance from the dreadful evils which we were threatened by the hostile attack of the British fleet and Army."[19] Patriotism was to be tempered by concerns for justice and religion. Bishops Carroll and England were not merely accommodating to the new republic but were committed to the principles upon which the republic was based. Rogers Smith does not refer to American Catholic republicanism, perhaps because he is principally concerned with an analysis of those ideas articulated by significant intellectuals and politicians who either supported or deviated from the ideals of the republic. When Smith considers the period of Carroll and England, he deals with the "ascriptive citizenship" that was evident in the letter to the *Gazette of the United States*. However, in his discussion of the Whig party's evolution from a "romanticized notion of Anglo-Saxonism [that] gave way in the late 1840s and early 1850s . . . to new nativist faction," Smith does cite "New York's pugnacious Archbishop John Hughes [who] promised to convert every American to Catholicism." Smith also notes that Popes Gregory XVI and Pius IX had "denounced republican institutions," freedom of the press, and the "absurd doctrine . . . liberty of conscience." Smith ends with the dictum: "Paranoid as nativist fears of Catholic conspiracies were, the collision between Catholic beliefs and liberal republican ideology was real." To substantiate this clash Smith cites Hughes's remark that if Protestants don't wish to convert then they "can pack up as quickly as they can and go."[20] Hughes *was* committed to a strategy of contentiousness toward Protestants, whom he considered inherently anti-Catholic, and he was given to vigorous polemic. However, Hughes did not lash out at liberal republicans but rather directed his rage at the nativist and anti-Catholic forces that denied his flock full citizenship. Popes Gregory and Pius were opponents of the republican creed because of the association with the violent anti-Catholicism, the September massacres of priests, and the Reign of Terror of the Jacobin ascendancy during the French Revolution.[21]

The anti-Catholic paranoia of the nativists drew upon a body of what would be called today "hate literature," some of which was financed and actually written by Protestant ministers such as those who paid Maria Monk, a "mentally retarded and deranged Protestant girl" to give her name as author of what was actually a fictional "autobiographical" exposé, *The Awful Disclosures of the Hotel Dieu in Montreal* (1836), "a lurid and detailed account of the sexual lives of priests and nuns."[22] There were other such bizarre tales that had an impact upon the era of religious incivility. Anti-Catholic sentiment reached violent proportions in the 1830s and 1840s. An Ursuline convent (1834) was burned in Charlestown, Massachusetts, by a nativist mob that had earlier attacked an Irish neighborhood in Boston.[23] The Reverend Lyman Beecher had preached against the Catholic menace on "fire and brimstone" corner (well known as a place for incendiary sermons), which had an inflammatory effect upon an already heated atmosphere. The next year Beecher, president of Lane Seminary in Cincinnati, published his *Plea for the West*, a call for united action against the impending crises of Catholic immigrants, presumably imbued with royalism and Vaticanism, who were threatening to take over the Mississippi Valley.[24]

Church burning in Philadelphia was incited by an extremist interpretation of Bishop Francis P. Kenrick's successful appeal for permission from the school board to allow Catholic students to read a version of the Bible approved by their parents. After impassioned criticism that he was actually undermining the legitimacy of scripture, violence erupted for nearly three days; thirteen were killed and fifty injured during the anti-Catholic rioting. The message was simple: Protestantism was as synonymous with republicanism as Catholicism was with disloyalty. Fearing that nativist violence would spread to New York, John Hughes posted guards around the cathedral and warned that "if one church was burned in New York, the city would become a second Moscow."[25] As a result, nativists did not rally, a fact that led Ray Allen Billington, the historian of the *Protestant Crusade*, to conclude that the leadership of Bishop Hughes defused violence and promoted peace.[26]

The Whig Party was divided over slavery and its extension into the territories in the West, but it became united on an agenda of nativism and anti-Catholicism in the late 1840s and early 1850s. Some antislavery Whigs pointed to Catholic obedience to the pope—prince of the papal states and absolute ruler of the church—as comparable to the condition of American slaves in the South. A resolution passed at the Know-Nothing Party convention in Norfolk, Massachusetts, included this statement: "Roman Catholicism and Slavery [are] alike founded and supported on the basis of ignorance and tyranny [they are] therefore, natural allies in every warfare against liberty and enlightment."[27] Many Whigs joined the anti-Catholic American Party, an offshoot of the Order of the Star-Spangled Banner, a lodge-based secret society founded in 1854. Since its members refused to reveal their aims and objectives, it was called the Know-Nothing Party. With intense sectionalism and the contentious issues of slavery inflaming the larger body politic, this nativist party concentrated on such issues as immigrant restrictionism, revision of the naturalization laws by extending the time for applying for citizenship from seven to twenty-one years, and the exclusion of immigrants from ever holding office. With members alienated from both the Whig and the Democratic parties, the Know-Nothings thrived in the mid-1850s until the Republican Party emerged in 1858.[28]

In the 1854–55 elections the Know-Nothing Party gained victories in local, state, and federal elections in eleven states. The designers of the Fourth Degree were well aware of the legacy of Know-Nothingism in Connecticut, New York, and Massachusetts. A Know-Nothing candidate won the mayoral contest in New Haven in 1854. The following year William T. Minor, a loyal party member, was elected governor of Connecticut. One reporter noted that there were 169 Know-Nothing lodges with 22,000 members during the year of Minor's election. The *Hartford Current*, which endorsed the party, published an editorial featuring the standard fare of papal conspiracies: "The individual Catholic votes as the priest dictates; the priest follows the dictates of the prelate and so he controls the elections as shall best serve the interests of the Pope, the establishment of the church, and its subsequent complete rule of the church."[29] In addition to the election of Minor, there were Know-Nothing victories in gubernatorial elections in Massachusetts, Pennsylvania, and Maine, and in forty-eight congressional elections, including eleven in New York; a vast majority of the Pennsylvania and Massachusetts delegations to Congress were of the Know-Nothing Party. Abraham Lincoln rejected the nativist party, fearing that the readers of the Declaration of Independence would soon perceive its wording as "all men are created equal except negroes, and foreigners and Catholics."[30]

III

In her chapter entitled "Teaching Patriotism" in *Bonds of Affection: Americans Define Their Patriotism*, Cynthia M. Koch captures the image of Columbus in several spheres of early-nineteenth-century life. "In the schoolbooks . . . Columbus . . . became an Old Testament patriarch struggling to achieve his mission against ignorance and reaction."[31] This Protestant patriotic lore had its origins in the 1792 tricentennial celebrations of the landfall of Columbus. Jeremy Belknap composed an ode to Columbus that included the latinized form of the name, *Columbia*, comparable to *Germania, Hibernia, Gallia*—all pseudo-mythological figures. *Columbia* was portrayed as the land of liberty that had severed itself from *Britannia;* thus King's College in New York City became Columbia College.[32] The nation's capital in the District of Columbia symbolized the hope of the new nation and a new liberty. Belknap's ode invoked the anti-Catholic "black legend" that portrayed Catholic Spain primarily in terms of the cruelties of the Inquisition, a legend first articulated in England. Columbus presumably transcended the Catholic "superstition" of his era. Indeed, in Belknap's ode to Columbus, sung at the Boston celebration of the tricentennial, the great navigator was depicted as a symbol of the freedom of the new republic.

> Black Superstition's dismal night
> Extinguished Reason's golden ray;
> And Science, driven from the light
> Beneath monastic rubbish lay
> The Crown and Mitre, close allied
> Trampled whole nations to the dust
> Whilst Freedom, wandering far and wide
> And pure Religion, quite was lost.
> Then, guided by th' almighty Hand
> Columbus spread his daring sail,
> Ocean received a new command
> And Zephyrs breathed a gentle gale. . . .
> Sweet Peace and heavenly truth shall shine
> on Fair Columbia's ground
> There Freedom and Religion join
> And Spread their influence all around.[33]

Several of these poetic images illustrate Robert Bellah's notion of civil religion as the creed, code, and cult uniting diverse peoples into a common American identity. There were sacred texts: the Declaration of Independence, the Preamble of the Constitution, the Bill of Rights, the Gettysburg Address, and so on, and special "feast days," such as Thanksgiving, Memorial Day, and the Fourth of July, all celebrated with patriotic hymns, flag-waving rituals, and prayers affirming the nation's role in God's providential design. These manifestations of civil or public religion were significant for a new nation, since they generated patriotic devotions to individuals of great stature and to epic episodes and events, thus enabling the many to become one, *e pluribus unum*.[34]

Columbus was viewed as the prototype of the struggle for liberty. He was portrayed as larger than life, as one who was at the vital sources of the nation, a central figure in the foundation of the civic myth, which Rogers M. Smith writes is "a myth used to explain why persons form a people usually indicating how a political community originated, who is eligible for membership, who is not and why and what the communities' values and aims are."[35] In this sense Belknap's Columbus, "guided by the 'almighty Hand'" brings Sweet Peace and heavenly truth . . . [to] Fair Columbia's ground . . . Freedom and Religion." This is "pure religion" in contrast to the "Black Superstition" of Catholicism.

Enlightened Protestants, however, were "eligible for membership in the political community." Catholics and others (i.e., Jews, blacks, and women) of course were excluded. As Smith observes: "Civic myths may be 'noble lies' . . . [but] may also cloak the exploitations of citizens by their leaders, demonize innocent outsiders and foster invidious inequalities among members of a regime. They may be ugly, ignoble lies."[36] Ascribed citizenship lives in opposition to the ideal of liberal republicanism, human dignity, and self-government, all of which were based on enlightened laws that fostered loyalty among diverse peoples and classes.

The Fourth Degree's Columbianism, indebted to the Order's portrayal of its patron, represents Columbus's entrance into the Catholic "civic myth," which was joined to the Knights' commitment to the founding documents and the heroic figures of American republicanism. There are only two holidays when Fourth Degree initiations, or exemplifications, may be held: George Washington's Birthday and Columbus Day, symbolic of the American-Catholic civic myth so thematic to this book. The republican Catholicism of Bishops John Carroll and John England was congenial to an idealism that ennobled nature and urged moderate lay participation in the affairs of church as well as an active engagement in the civic affairs of town, state, and national governments. Since bishops, priests, and laity were aware of the anti-Catholic attempts to exclude them from citizenship, they no doubt sensed the contradiction between the ideal and the real, that is, "the noble lies." However, it was the invocation or belief in the republican virtues that instilled in Catholic leaders the determination to call upon their Protestant neighbors to live according to American republican principles and to recognize Catholics as loyal citizens dedicated to religious liberty, to equality under the law, and to other civic ideals of the new nation. From the

Declaration of Independence to the election of John F. Kennedy, the force of the Protestant civic myth had compelled Catholics to either separate themselves from the mainstream or to engage in political and religious activities as citizens and patriots. The Knights of Columbus were conscious of their Catholic republican identity steeped in the language of engagement. Father Michael J. McGivney was committed to the temperance movement, a dominant factor in the political life of the nation. A leader of St. Mary's Parish Young Men's Total Abstinence Society, he was particularly well known in the state temperance movement.[37] A charter member of the Order, Cornelius T. Driscoll, was a state chairman of the Catholic Total Abstinence Union, mayor of New Haven, and the first chief legal officer of the Knights.[38]

In a very real sense the local council meeting was an exercise in republican self-government. Besides instructing the Knights on how to organize efficiently in terms of medical examinations for the sickness and death-benefit features and also in terms of accepted rules of order, Father McGivney instructed the local council officers on the need for permanent files, for adhering "strictly to the Laws and Rules of Order, and avoid strife, discord, and personality."[39] In short, he advocated principles and procedures to assure honesty, accountability, reliability and civility grounded in self-government, a pillar of republican virtue.

As mentioned earlier, the Knights' devotion to Columbus was expressed in terms of civil rights based on the political respect due to those who shared the Catholic faith of the great navigator. The American Protective Association, founded in 1887 in Clinton, Iowa, a descendant of the Know-Nothing movement of the 1850s, gained national momentum in the 1890s. The APA was founded by Henry Francis Bowers, a well-known lecturer on the Masonic circuit in Iowa and a thirty-second degree member of Scottish Rite Masonry. Reacting against what they considered to have been the growing strength of the Catholic vote in the rise of the Knights of Labor, Bowers and the founding members formed this new secret society aimed at making democracy safe from "papal imperialism." Besides taking an oath to struggle against all forms of Romanism, members swore not to engage in any business with or to hire any Catholics. The precipitous rise in immigration from southern and eastern Europe fostered a blend of anti-Catholicism and nativist xenophobia clearly evident in the fear of radical unionists who fomented violence such as that at the Haymarket in Chicago in 1887. Because he defended the Knights of Labor and successfully persuaded Pope Leo XIII that the union represented legitimate aspirations and strategies, Cardinal James Gibbons was branded as the friend of radical groups. Unlike the Know-Nothings, the American Protective Association did not form an independent party but rather sought to influence the Republican Party. The APA had a growing influence congruent with the growing prominence of Catholics symbolized by the foundation of The Catholic University of America in 1889, by Pope Leo XIII's appointment of Archbishop Francesco Satolli as the first apostolic delegate to the United States in 1893, and by the ascendancy of Catholic politicians in local, state, and national offices.[40]

As an illustration of the extent to which the APA promoted its own memory in competition with that of Catholics, it published a bogus encyclical of Leo XIII directing American Catholics to initiate a massacre of all heretics on the feast of St. Ignatius Loyola (July 31, 1893).[41] Each member of the APA took a secret oath

> to wage a continuous warfare against ignorance and fanaticism [of the Catholics] . . . to retard and breakdown the power of the pope in this country or any other . . . to never employ Catholics . . . if I can procure the services of a Protestant . . . [to] vote only for Protestants . . . and to place the political positions into the hands of Protestants, to the entire exclusion of the Roman Catholic Church, of the members thereof and the mandate of the Pope.[42]

Catholic newspapers such as the *Connecticut Catholic* noted the rise of the APA but purported not to be terribly alarmed. "There is no danger; America owes much of its present strength and influence in advancement to its Catholic element."[43] As if to respond directly to the APA, Thomas H. Cummings wrote an article for *Donohoe's Magazine*, a Catholic monthly published in Boston, in which he placed the Knights' Americanism in the context of resurgent anti-Catholicism.

> With true American patriotism they [the K. of C.] demand from their members respect for manhood and liberty for the individual, particularly that liberty which is the essence of all liberty and which was first planted on this continent by Roman Catholics, viz.: freedom to worship God according to one's conscience. They ask that no man's social and civil rights be affected by his religious beliefs. Accordingly, the unjust and un-American attempt on the part of a certain coterie of bigoted writers to belittle the character of Columbus simply because he was a Roman Catholic, naturally meets with their dissent and disapproval.[44]

During the 1890s patriotic societies proliferated with particular attention to symbolizing the nation by a devotion to the American flag. The bonds of nationality were reconceived in "hereditary societies." Stuart McConnell notes that by establishment of the "Sons and Daughters of the Revolution (1889, 1890) . . . the Colonial Dames of America (1891) and the Mayflower descendants (1897)—the nation was reinvisioned as a kind of extended family; held together by the blood ties of kinship. True Americanism was limited to those who could prove lineal descent from Revolutionary War patriots, with everyone else treated as sort of a guest."[45]

In an article in the January 1894 *Columbiad*, a Boston monthly published "in the interests of the Knights of Columbus," William J. Coughlin of Lowell Council No. 72 seems to be responding to these exclusive hereditary societies

> . . . as if it were not history that long before that solitary adventurous vessel, the *Mayflower,* of forlorn hope, debarked her sturdy pilgrims by the rock, the towns of St. Augustine in Florida and Santa Fe in New Mexico had been founded and the discoveries of Cortez, Denys, Ponce de Leon . . . and Cartier, supplementary to those of the good Columbus, were surely not less important than the distinguished performance of Drake, Raleigh, and the adventurous Cabot, in whose glory we all aspire to participate.[46]

Coughlin noted that Catholic "patriotism was usurped by a prejudice." He proffered a cosmopolitan rather than an exclusivist image of the Knights.

> Such has been our progress under free institutions that the crude material of the old world is received and converted, as if by magic, into the finished product of modern civilization. . . . The mission of the Knights of Columbus [is] not to disrupt or disunite, but to unify and heal—not to tear down, but to build up. . . . The precepts of fraternity, unity, and charity which we teach are as Catholic as Christianity, and as universal as humanity.[47]

The Knights' rendering of "masculinity" and "manhood" was characteristic of gilded-age rhetoric. The "manly" entailed the cherished bonds forged during the Civil War animating the Grand Army of the Republic. The GAR during peacetime was an impassioned champion of devotion to the American flag, a devotion that represented a "new patriotic language . . . in which the flag emerged as a symbol of abstract nationalism." Stuart McConnell describes the movement from the regimental flags originally associated with local and community organizations to the late 1880s and early 1890s, when the flag "was addressed in the most mystical terms." One GAR chaplain invoked the flag in a prayer: "Give us greater love for the old flag which has seemed to come from the hand of God."[48] The Pledge of Allegiance and patriotic hymns intensified the cult of the flag, while the patriotism of the hereditary societies fostered an American identity congenial to the "ascribed republicanism" coined by Rogers M. Smith, as a republicanism that was inherently nativist and laced with a strong dose of Anglo-Saxonism, of anti-Irishness, and an implicit anti-Catholicism.

These developments were also associated with veterans and the general interest in the masculinity of cadet groups and uniformed drill teams. Mary Ann Clawson, author of a book on fraternalism, associates the effect of "the ultimate experience of male bonding" with the proliferation of fraternal societies in the later third of the nineteenth century.[49] Thomas Cummings extolled the Knights' "kinship and brotherly love" and the "mystic tie of charity and the golden bough of brotherly love." He also stated that "the principles of the Order, if rightly applied and practiced, mean the creation of a new type of Catholic manhood. . . . They stand for what is clean, moral and wholesome in American manhood when that is crowned by the teaching of mother church." The Order promoted "fraternal instincts by which men grow in civilized kindlier emotions of the heart."[50] Hence, the Knights' manliness, according to Cummings, also evoked a feminized domesticity in his description of the gentleman in fraternity, a description that supports the theory of Mark Carnes. Carnes perceives a strong relationship between domesticity and fraternalism; young men were moving out of the home, which was dominated by the feminine ethos of moral and religious values, into the competitive marketplace. "'The family lodge' is a refuge from the marketplace: . . . fraternalism took the same overreaching metaphor of the family but specified a different content, based upon the brotherhood of men."[51] Cummings's "kindly emotions of the heart" were manly fraternal virtues that were parallel to "the ethos of the women's sphere of the domestic hearth."[52] The Knights of Columbus Council, where masculinity flourished, was a refuge from the competition of the marketplace. The uniformed drill teams, popular among patriotic societies, should be understood in the context of the fraternal bonds of wartime, rekindled in the patriotism regnant in the 1890s. The Fourth Degree of the Knights of Columbus has a military character with sword and baldric, which represented a new phase in the development of Catholic manhood identified with patriotism and citizenship, virtues vital for a republicanism from below. However, the APA's attack upon Catholics' loyalty to the nation was the proximate cause for an explicit rendering of Catholic patriotism.

IV

As early as 1886, there had been some discussion of establishing an additional degree to publicly symbolize the nobility of the Catholic presence in

Connecticut's civic society and to draw attention to the Order with a uniform that would attract new members as well as be an assertion of Catholic legitimacy in a nation given to outbursts of anti-Catholic sentiment. The *Connecticut Catholic* reported that Supreme Knight James T. Mullen had proposed the establishment of two commandery degrees, "simple, uniformed membership with no apparent thematic basis, such as patriotism." Mullen had been a leader of the Sarsfield Guards, a Catholic Civil War militia reestablished after the war and incorporated into the Connecticut National Guard. Since this uniformed patriotic society was in his background, he was prompted to propose a separate membership group in its own symbolic dress. Though his recommendation was not adopted, there was at least one New Haven council that did adopt such a "commandery degree."[53] In an editorial of November 6, 1886, in the *Connecticut Catholic* (edited by a Knight), a New Haven representative of the newspaper was quoted as reporting "that the first regular meeting of the proposed uniformed legion will be held on Monday evening, July 12." The author cited an unnamed New Haven newspaper that described the uniform:

> A black Prince Albert Coat, black trousers, black soft felt hat, with an ostrich feather circling the crown similar to that worn by Columbus as represented in his pictures, a reversible cape, black on one side and scarlet on the other, white cross and waist belt, sword and gauntlet. The officers of each commandery will consist of a commander, vice-commander, sub-commander, ensign, and first, second, third, and fourth and fifth orderlies. When five commanderies are established, a battalion will be formed, and officers for the same be appointed by the commanders and ensigns. They representing what would be known in military parlance as the commissioned officers.[54]

The editor of the *Connecticut Catholic*, unsympathetic to this development, interpreted it as contradictory to good governance; one council could dictate the propriety of the new degree to all other councils. He stated that leaders of the New Haven Council, "had no right or authority to speak for others in the State not represented . . . no locality should assume control of the State organization." Since in his estimation the cost of the uniform would be around one hundred dollars, many members would not wish "to go to this extraordinary expense," while some Knights "did not [have the money] anyway." He concluded his opposition to the separate uniform degree on democratic grounds. "It is hardly the proper thing to set up class distinctions in a benevolent society where charity and unity should dwell."[55] The editor's views prevailed, as there is no evidence that the experiment with uniform degree even achieved the level of a commandery, the equivalent to what became a Fourth Degree assembly. According to McConnell's thesis on the language of nationalism, represented in the 1890s rhetoric on the national flag, the Columbus motif of the 1886 "commissioned officers" in the Knights' new degree was too localized and particularized to gain momentum as a national model of patriotism.

The Knights had placed Columbus at the source of the nation's identity as a land of liberty, but the commander's uniform did not convey American national symbols. Such language did not enter the lexicon of Columbianism until the 1890s. Despite its antagonism to a commander degree, the *Connecticut Catholic*, which by 1890 had a special "K of C editor," suggested that the uniformed degree be voluntary.[56] The editor had in mind a representation of the Knights at the 1893 quadricentennial celebration at the World's Fair. The change of location from New York to Chicago precluded a large enough turnout to sponsor a parade. However, there was a large parade in New Haven in 1892 with six thousand Knights representing the Order's commitment to the quadricentennial, a day the *Connecticut Catholic* referred to as based upon "the discovery of America [as] a Catholic event . . . and the first act of Catholic worship."[57]

With Catholic Columbus Day parades in cities and towns across the country and with the international gathering to honor him in Chicago in 1893, this homage to the Order's patron appears to have been the dominant factor in the national expansion of the Knights. However, the appointment of Thomas H. Cummings as chief organizer also had a strong impact on this expansion. Though several bishops in New York had viewed the Order's ceremonials as a capitulation to masonry and other forbidden secret societies, they were eventually convinced of the benign character of the fraternal side of the Knights. The strength of Columbianism was its national status grounded in commitment to its civic ideals. John J. Delaney, first State Deputy of New York and a highly effective leader of ceremonial teams, who traveled to neighboring states to preside at the initiation rites of the first council, was Supreme Knight John Phelan's (1886–1897) representative during those critical years when the New York bishops questioned the propriety and orthodoxy of the Order's ceremonials. By this time, Edward Hearn had become Supreme Knight (1899); the movement for the establishment of the new degree had resulted in the formation of a committee of three members accountable to the Board of Directors and charged with designing changes in the ceremonials to include an additional degree. From March 15 to late 1899 material was collected, but there were no definite proposals for a new degree. Supreme Knight Hearn then appointed a committee of nine charged with developing the Fourth Degree.[58]

This appointment of the first committee occurred five weeks before the United States Congress declared war on Spain, allegedly because of its violent suppression of a Cuban insurrection and for destroying the battleship *Maine,* sent to Havana harbor to protect American lives. With over 250 Americans killed, the public was subjected to an unrelenting barrage of sensational journalism. Vehement expressions of American national pride and honor animated the demands for war with Spain; "Remember the Maine" became the war cry. By the time the committee of nine met to write the ceremonials for a degree on patriotism, the "splendid little war" of less than four months had ended.[59]

The impact of the war on the development of the Fourth Degree will be taken up later in this chapter. It is important to note here, however, the influence of the national contexts for understanding how the patriotic degree had been affected by the war. The institution of the first council in St. Louis that year marked the Fourth Degree's expansion west of the Mississippi. As early as 1892 concerns for a rise in membership areas remote from New Haven raised issues regarding insurance rates, but the problem was resolved when the Order officially approved associate—that is, noninsurance—membership in 1892. The fraternal appeal alone generated rapid expansion. Edward Hearn eventually placed the Order's insurance program on an actuarial basis, which also led to an increase of insurance members.[60]

After receiving the report from the committee of nine, Hearn appointed a blue ribbon committee to compose the final draft of the Fourth Degree ceremonial. Among those chosen to serve on the committee was John Delaney, along with the National Secretary, Daniel Colwell; Monsignor Joseph H. Conroy, vicar-general of Ogdensburg, New York, and later bishop of that diocese; Patrick McArdle of Chicago, and a National Director and a principal ceremonialist; and Charles A. Webber of Brooklyn, also a director. Rounding out the committee were two other New Yorkers, John Hogan of Syracuse and William H. Bennett of Brooklyn, and two Bostonians, William S. McNary and William J. Cashman. However, a subcommittee made up of Delaney, Conroy, and Webber actually composed the draft of the text for the Fourth Degree.

The rules governing the new degree were the following: membership for at least three years and evidence of distinctive service to the Order, the church, and the community. Practical Catholicity had been a qualification for membership in the Knights of Columbus, but to be a "Sir" Knight in the Fourth Degree a letter stipulating that the prospective member had received Holy Communion within two weeks was required. To obviate criticism that the degree was separatist and elitist, meetings of the Fourth Degree were to be held in the council chambers after the regular meeting of the Third Degree members. Then after programs and membership expanded, Sir Knights began to meet separately as the Fourth Degree, and separate districts were formed under the direction of the National (later Supreme) Board of Directors.

The first induction was scheduled to take place at the Astor Hotel in New York, but because eleven hundred Knights were selected among the many applicants it was held at the Lennox Lyceum, "a large frame building erected to display a mammoth painting of the Civil War."[61] The date for the first "exemplification" (as the initiation was designated) of the patriotic degree was quite fitting, February 22, 1900, the "feast day" or birthday of George Washington. The ceremonial of the Fourth Degree, as noted earlier in this chapter, underscored the significance of Catholic citizenship—"the proudest boast of all is . . . I am an American Catholic citizen"—as if it were a direct response to Josiah Strong's *Our Country: Its Progress and Its Crisis* with the inclusion of Catholics in the possessive "Our." Analogous to a litany of "Catholic civil religion," the ceremonial extolled the Order's American heritage. "Catholic America gives thanks for her discovery, her exploration, her very name. They baptized this continent, our rivers, our lakes, our mountains, our valleys and our hearthstones." After a lengthy treatment of Christopher Columbus, whose "prophetic name" translates in English to "Christ-bearer dove," symbolic of both the baptism and the Holy Spirit's graced presence in the "Confirmation" of the nation, the candidates for the degree were regaled with stories of Catholic explorers such as Amerigo Vespucci, Robert La Salle, and Pierre Marquette, as well as several other explorers and missionaries who brought Christianity to the land.[62]

Central to the ceremonial was the Catholic contribution to religious toleration, a principle related to the development of republicanism. Though recent historians view Lord Baltimore's commitment to religious toleration as motivated by the self-interest of minority Catholics to live peacefully with their Protestant neighbors and to be protected from the majority, the Order perceived this historical development as a major achievement and a source of American Catholic pride. In this vein, the ceremonial continues, "what he [Lord Baltimore] did in Maryland, the 'land of sanctuary,' Dongan [a Catholic governor] did in New York. The two oldest and grandest movements of religious toleration in the world are, therefore, to be credited to the sons of the Catholic Church." It is equally significant to note, wrote the authors of this initiation rite, "what our republic has done for the Church." Just as Archbishop John Ireland spoke eloquently on the dynamic, providential congeniality of Americanism and Catholicism, so the author of the ceremonial stated: "under our laws of toleration and freedom she [the Catholic Church] had engaged in peace and progress, a prosperity unequaled and beyond all expectation." Catholics, therefore, must be committed to

> the virtue and permanence of our republic. If it is to endure in the future as in the past, the Catholic church must be a potent and an indispensable agent. Her sons, by the morality of their lives, their loyalty to the Constitution and their conscientious performance of the duties of citizenship, and above all, by their steadfast adherence to Catholic principles, must strengthen the Church, stem the tide of irreligion, preserve the Reign of God in the land, or see the republic perish.[63]

The Knights, particularly those in the Fourth Degree, articulated this crucial role of Catholic men to "stem the tide of irreligion," or secularism, as integral to their patriotism.

There is a significant relationship between the Fourth Degree's ritualization of Catholic citizenship and patriotism and the intensity with which the APA, Josiah Strong, and others denied Catholic civic loyalty and vilified the Catholic Church. As mentioned earlier, they made the mythical "little red schoolhouse" into an icon of republicanism, and since many Catholics were separated into "Vatican-controlled" parochial schools, they were perceived by their critics to be beyond the pale of honest citizenship. The Spanish-American War, occurring during the early phases of the composition of the Fourth Degree ceremonial, was engendered by a shallow jingoism raised to a high pitch by the yellow journalism of the day. Once the war began Cardinal James Gibbons, joined by Archbishop John Ireland, who had in his own way worked for a peaceful solution, supported the nation's call to arms.[64] At the Maine State Convention in 1899 John F. Crowley noted that the Catholic people, "imbued with the teachings of our Holy Church, to be ready to sacrifice everything for our Faith and Country" had joined the fight for the "Country's cause." Crowley's interpretation of the K. of C.'s support of the war was symbolic of a noble "reply to the cheap agitators whose only principle is hatred of Catholics who, although professing ardent love for Americans and American institutions, fly to the woods when danger threatens the flag they profess to love so much." Hence, he portrayed the anti-

Catholic forces as almost intrinsically cowardly."[65] Though John Lancaster Spalding of Peoria, a friend of the Order, did oppose the war, he was the only bishop to take that stand.

The prophetic model of the church, dormant in Europe during this period, was evident in Cardinal Gibbons and other Americanist bishops, who broke from European tradition and adopted the modern spirit of American liberty. This process may be perceived as an expression of evangelical hope in the Catholic mission to America and the American mission to the universal church. Because this position was misunderstood as a capitulation to modernity by the Vatican, the "Americanism" of Archbishop John Ireland, Cardinal James Gibbons, and others was condemned in Pope Leo XIII's 1899 apostolic letter, *Testem Benevolentiae*. Thomas Cummings waxed eloquent on a Columbian theme that was congenial to Americanism, while the patriotic response of the Knights during the Spanish-American War reveals not an unreflective nationalism but rather a complex motivation, including the drive to assert the legitimacy of Catholicity in American life and to express gratitude for the enormous quantitative and qualitative growth of Catholic culture in American society. Had there been a generally excessive nationalism during the war that was prevalent in the foundation of the Fourth Degree, then one would expect the Knights to assume an uncritical stance toward the nation's postwar imperialism, such as President William McKinley's decision to take control of the Philippine Islands and "christianize" the people, who, of course, had been evangelized by Catholics in the sixteenth century. Instead, we find D. P. Toomey, the editor of the *Columbiad*, critical of the "bloody conquest and greed of gain" that had replaced the "old national ideals," particularly the "essentially Catholic concept to respect the natural rights" of humanity.[66]

Toomey noted that the seizure of Puerto Rico and the Philippines represented the Protestant tradition so dominant in the United States. "Protestant nations who have acquired dominion over weaker races have exterminated the latter, or the so-called inferior race has been held in vassalage and exploited in the commercial interests of the conquerer." To illustrate this he indicted Protestants "for their harsh treatment of Indians and Negroes."[67] Toomey's anti-Protestantism and anticolonialism may have derived from his Irish-American animus toward the British for their domination of Ireland. Like many Irish-Americans, Toomey easily assimilated into American society, and he enthusiastically accepted the new degree. "A man's membership in the fourth degree will of itself be ample evidence of the fact—as indeed his membership in the Order ought to be—that he is 'Catholic gentleman' in all that those two pregnant words mean."[68] Racism will be taken up in chapter 3, but it is appropriate to point out here that Toomey did not imply that Catholics, blacks, and Indians would be welcomed into the Third Degree, the membership pool for the Fourth Degree.

The ceremonials of the Fourth Degree, particularly their historical content, were derived from the research and writings of John Gilmary Shea, the first historian to establish a scholarly record of Catholic life in America. With a tendency to narrate the story according to institutional developments and to the lives of heroic bishops, religious, and laity, Shea asserted the Catholic contribution to American history, one of the prominent features of the Fourth Degree. According to a recent scholar, ritual is defined as "action wrapped in a realm of symbols. . . . Through ritual, beliefs about the universe come to be acquired, reinforced and eventually changed. . . . Ritual helps give meaning to our world in part by linking the past to the present and the present to the future."[69] Though the Fourth Degree ceremonials do not fit neatly into this definition, as rituals they did add an element of meaning and order to the Catholic experience in America. The candidate was awash in the Catholic currents in the mainstream of American life; indeed, there was a positive synthesis of American and Catholic: "Proudest boast of all time is ours to make 'I am an American Catholic citizen.'"

A 1901 official description of the Fourth Degree emblem reads "it is a red Isabella cross, a white dove and blue hemisphere, our national colors. It signifies: a dove, 'Columbia,' flying with the Cross of Faith to the western hemisphere; also the Holy Ghost, dove of peace, conveying Christianity to the New World."[70] The watch charm is a miniature emblem on the front side, while on the back is the escutcheon of the constitution, which was also worn on the red, white, and blue baldric. In accord with Christian knighthood, the sword's handle was in the shape of a cross. The uniform was the formal wear of the period: top hat, black Prince Albert cutaway coat, white shirt and black tie. The first uniformed corps to act as honor guard occurred in Brooklyn in 1902, but the corps was dressed in the three uniforms of the armed services: Marines, Army, and Navy. The following year, the Supreme Board of Directors stipulated that the original formal wear was the only uniform allowed in the color guard with one exception, the New York first regiment uniform that originated in the Civil War.

2

Growth, Reform, and the Bogus Oath

I

THIS CHAPTER ONCE AGAIN CHARTS the rivalry between the Fourth Degree and those driven to delegitimize Catholics. As the Order expanded throughout the nation, so did the Fourth Degree achieve national stature, expressed particularly by its dominant presence at the unveiling of the Columbus Memorial in Washington, D.C. Concurrently there developed a major anti-Catholic offensive illustrated by the remarkable growth of *The Menace*, a rabid anti-Catholic newspaper. While Josiah Strong's book referred to Catholics as the embodiment of the national crisis, Wilbur Franklin Phelps referred to Catholicism's presence as a menace to the nation's progress. Josiah Strong was a middle-class exponent of a "Christian" republicanism that was threatened by immigrant Catholics loyal to the "despot" in the Vatican. Phelps's *Menace* was apocalyptical and inflammatory, aimed at exciting its readers to perceive the uniformed Fourth Degree as a Vatican elite corps, and the Knights of Columbus in general as the war department of the papacy determined to extirpate Protestants, Masons, and other upstanding citizens of the republic. In this offensive, Phelps drew upon the now infamous Fourth Degree bogus oath, as proof of how far the Knights of Columbus were willing to go. In response to this and other forms of nativism and anti-Catholicism, the Order established its Commission on Religious Prejudices (1914–1917), which was terminated with the United States' entrance into World War I. After the war the Fourth Degree bogus oath resurfaced and once again energized the Order's antidefamation character.

The Fourth Degree was founded as the Knights were crossing the Mississippi and moving westward. Third Degree teams traveled by rail from St. Louis to Kansas City to Denver, and on to Salt Lake City, terminating in San Francisco in a little over a year. John Reddin, the first State Deputy of Colorado, who later became the first Supreme Master of the Fourth Degree (1910), was the head of the Third Degree team that instituted San Francisco Council No. 615 on January 19, 1902. The principal leader in promoting the national expansion of the Order was James J. Gorman of Fall River, Massachusetts, who was hired as a national organizer by the Board of Directors under Supreme Knight Edward Hearn.[1] The dominant figure among the California Knights was Joseph Scott, first State Deputy and first Master of the Fourth Degree in California. Scott was close to the bishops and archbishops of Los Angeles, as well as to Pope Pius X's secretary of state, Cardinal Merry del Val, his teacher at Ushaw College in England and a vigilant opponent of modernism. In 1904, the editor of *Columbiad* noted that Scott was then corresponding with Merry del Val "on terms of affectionate intimacy." He also described him as a "hard-working lawyer in active practice and . . . is recognized as a trenchant, fluent speaker . . . , universally recognized by all sections of religious belief."[2]

In an article for *Columbiad,* "The Mission of the Order in the Land of the Missions," Scott enumerated the Franciscan Friars' missionary advance among the Indians of Mexico and California, their introduction of the Bible in native languages, and the foundation of mission churches and schools. He also noted the harsh treatment of the Indians by the Puritans of New England," dispatching them to Happy Hunting Grounds." Scott considered the cause of the rise of Protestants in southern California to be their need to escape from Catholic immigrants in New England.[3] "The Order's expansion came just in time: to my mind it seems a bounden duty on the part of the men responsible for expelling the Puritans from their native hearths into this land of the Mission Fathers to give the Faith in this southwest country as an antidote against the poison in Puritan doctrine."[4] Scott concluded that the "Knights of Columbus have enormous work to do" in helping Catholics "cope with the steadily increasing bigoted and prejudiced Easterners" bent on a "crusade to evangelize the poor children, and to teach them the bible from an 'English' version."[5] He had witnessed the rise of the American Protective Association in California and associated this anti-Catholic movement with the traditional animus of Puritanism. The Catholic response to the advance of nativism that motivated the creation of the Fourth Degree permeated Joseph Scott's interpretation of the antidefamation role of the Order.

The Knights' expansion to the Pacific extended to Washington in the Northwest and to Arizona and Texas in the Southwest. By 1905 the Order was in every state, in four of the nine provinces of Canada, in Mexico, and in the Philippines. Though the original councils in each of the latter countries were founded by Americans, within a few years Mexicans and Filipinos dominated these councils. For example, Manila Council was founded by many American members who had become active in the cathedral parish of Archbishop Jeremiah J. Harty, the first American ordinary of the diocese. Though they formed the membership of Manila Council 1000, by 1920 Filipinos dominated the council, encouraged by priests concerned about the attraction of the Masons.[6]

As mentioned earlier, one of McKinley's justifications for American imperialism in the Pacific was to christianize the Philippine Islands. From the point of view of D. P. Toomey, editor of the *Columbiad*, there was considerable doubt that the United States government would deal justly with Filipinos, just as Protestants had had a poor record in dealing with blacks in the United States; he perceived Protestants as exploiting those people under the "protection" of America in the Caribbean and in the Pacific.[7] Manila Council symbolized a defense of Catholics in a battle against "delegitimacy," as opposed to the United States and Canada, where the struggle was for legitimacy. The need for the Order to take a stand against the deligitimacy of Catholicity in the Philippines and the promotion of Catholic interests there was clearly stated in a letter of July 8, 1908, by James P. Monaghan, S.J., who had returned to the States from the Philippines. He reported on Archbishop Harty's call for the Knights to take a lead in "contradicting the proselytizing efforts of Protestantism."[8] Monaghan cited the influence of "Protestant Mission Societies" in Washington, D.C. Eventually the Order became the singular Catholic Action organization in the parishes, and the Fourth Degree flourished in the Philippines as well. But these developments occurred only after World War II.

The progress of the Fourth Degree required an organizational reform. The initial structure was quite simple: Fourth Degree members met in council assemblies. To adapt to growth in membership and in the number of assemblies, it was necessary to bring several assemblies into districts and assign a Master to each district. The authority of District Masters was to manage membership and to arrange for the annual exemplifications, which included a large banquet on either Columbus Day or Washington's Birthday; only one day was set aside for the ceremony initiating Third Degree members into their patriotic degree.[9] Victor Dowling, a judge of the Supreme Court of New York, was a "charter" member of the Fourth Degree in New York City on February 22, 1900, and the first Master of the district in Manhattan and Brooklyn. One of the most popular speakers on the Catholic circuit, he was a self-taught expert on the significance of Columbus. At the 1909 exemplification, the Master of the second district of New York, William J. McGinley, who later became Supreme Secretary, directed the class of over 120 through the ceremonials extolling the themes of Catholicity's contribution to American life and thought. The entire sixth floor of the Hotel Astor was reserved for the exemplification and the subsequent banquet.

The New York Assembly of the Fourth Degree sponsored a series of lectures in 1909 on "Catholic American patriotism." The project aimed "to tender receptions to distinguished Catholic Americans eminent in literature, and to express to these selected guests the appreciation of Catholic Americans for services rendered to Catholic progress and education and to social advancement by the work of these distinguished Catholic men." The first guest of honor for February of 1909 was a Knight who taught physics at the Christian Brothers' Manhattan College, a Professor Potamian. Though his address was on "the Magnetic Discoveries of Columbus" the news article in the *Columbiad* did not include a hint of the contents of the speech. It did note that "it was a topic novel to the Knights of Columbus and therefore, of unusual interest."[10] The reporter referred to the physicist as their fraternal Brother Potamian, a Knight who represented patriotism and Columbianism which the Sir Knights of the Fourth Degree tended to articulate as twin virtues inherent in their Catholic citizenship.

The 1907 exemplification of the Fourth Degree in Augusta, Georgia, was a particularly festive event in the public Catholicism of this southern town. It drew upon four southern states—Georgia, North and South Carolina, and Florida—for its class of one hundred candidates. Still a missionary area with few priests, there were only two parishes in Augusta, which was located in the diocese of Savannah, covering the entire state of Georgia with a Catholic population of only 23,000; this may be contrasted to the Archdiocese of Boston with 750,000 Catholics in 1907. Anti-Catholicism was endemic in much of Georgia. Thomas Watson, a rabid anti-Catholic as well as an anti-Semite, articulated his views in his own journal, *Watson's Magazine*. As will be noted later, he perceived the Knights of Columbus as a sort of "fifth column" in the advance of papal imperialism.

The tone and content of the article in the *Columbiad* on the Augusta exemplification were congenial to the theme, "Catholic Gentlemen in Fraternity," coined by Thomas H. Cummings. At the banquet following the exemplification, with Supreme Knight Edward Hearn in attendance, "the speeches were of a high order of excellence and were most liberally applauded. The Supreme Knight was listened to with exceptional interest. He spoke of Knighthood as a factor in good citizenship and he spoke of patriotism which is inseparable from principles held and advocated by the Order. . . . The exercise closed with the singing of America." Apparently not only Catholics were invited to the "regular Georgia barbecue" and the subsequent "grand reception ball" in honor of the Supreme Knight. An editorial in the *Augusta Herald* stated: "The gathering of the Knights of Columbus . . . has been one of the most enjoyable assemblies ever held in the city."[11]

The Order in New Orleans drew upon a rich history of southern lay activism. On Sunday October 14, 1906, at New Orleans Council No. 714, more than one hundred men were initiated into the three degrees, while later that day nearly 150 Knights from Louisiana and neighboring states passed through the Fourth Degree. The day started with mass celebrated by Archbishop James H. Blenk at St. Joseph's Church, which was decorated for the event, while "incandescent lights in the center over the sanctuary blazed the letters 'K of C.'" In his sermon, Archbishop Blenk said that "he was greatly edified to see the largest Church in New Orleans packed to the very doors with men from every walk of life and every occupation . . . practical Catholic men, banded together in this great and grand organization of the Knights of Columbus for the sake of Holy Church." Later at the banquet in his honor, the archbishop called upon the Knights to aid the "Church's battle against infidelity and atheism." Patrick McArdle, one of the original committee members responsible for the foundation of the Fourth Degree, "pledged to the Archbishop the support of the Catholic Knights of the North in case he would find it necessary to call on them to co-operate with Knights in the South."[12]

A characteristic expression of the themes of the Fourth Degree was voiced by Charles Jeannier, chairman of the assembly.

> As citizens of the grandest government upon which the sun has always smiled, as members of an eternal church, holding within herself a mighty uplifting power, and carrying upon her immaculate brow the divine promise of everlasting life, as a Knight of an Order destined by the grace of God to wield an

> influence for good which the most sanguine, even in the favorable light of the present, cannot approximate, we pledge to our revered leader not only our wholesome allegiance but our untiring zeal in the promotion of Truth, of Justice, and of Charity, upon which our Order is grounded and whose expanding propagation and practice must and will advance the welfare of the State, the happiness of its citizens, the prosperity of the church, and in ennobling humanity will glorify God.[13]

This is gilded-age rhetoric in its most embellished form, but it does reveal the positive anthropology and incarnational spirituality with its conclusion—"ennobling humanity giving glory to God."

As noted in the previous chapter, no American episcopal leader was more in accord with an active Catholic citizenship than Archbishop John Ireland. At a Knights' gathering in Minneapolis in June 1907, he spoke extemporaneously for a half hour as he responded to the toast "the Catholic layman." He opened with the conventional metaphor of the Catholic laymen as "the soldier of the Holy Church"; but then he added that "the Knights of Columbus . . . bring these soldiers into one body under the banner of Catholicity." He drew upon his sermon at the first Lay Catholic Congress of the United States that included the laity and the hierarchy, honoring the centennial of the appointment of John Carroll as the first bishop of Baltimore: "The layman must give his strength, his time and his energies to advance the cause and promote the honor of the Church."[14] In his 1889 sermon he said: "Laymen are not anointed in Confirmation to the end that they merely save their own souls and pay their pew rent. They must think, work, organize, read, speak, act, as circumstances demand, ever anxious to serve the Church and do good to their fellow men. . . . In America, in the present age, lay action is particularly needed for the Church. Laymen have in this age a special vocation."[15] In the 1907 Minneapolis address he elaborated on the civic responsibilities of the Knights and of all laymen: "Be good citizens. Mingle in all movements that make for the advancement of civic, state and national development." Implicitly criticizing Catholic separatism, he said, "one of the most unfortunate things for the Catholic Church in America has been the tendency of its members to hold aloof from non-sectarian movements for the general good. Take an active interest in the general affairs. Do not give the impression that Catholics are a separate body—that we seek to isolate ourselves. We have done this too much and too long." To be active in the political, social, and economic spheres of American life entails "working for better citizenship." He urged the Knights not "to wait for your bishop and priest to take the initiative, do things yourself, as you have done but do them in greater measures." Archbishop Ireland concluded with a reference to the Knights of Columbus as "the elite of the Catholic laymen," who should be models for citizen activism and leadership in the "good works of the private soldiers of the Holy Church."[16]

Since the members of the Fourth Degree were so explicitly committed to civic activism, they clearly represented ideals of Archbishop John Ireland. As noted earlier, Ireland was identified with the unique mission-to-America theme that is distinctive because of the singular character of the nation.

> The church's mission to the world is the same as it has been during nineteen hundred years; but the world has changed and is changing. With the new Order has come new needs, new hopes, new aspirations. To conquer the world for Christ, the church herself must now be adapting in a manner of life and its method of action to the conditions of the new Order, thus proving herself, while ancient, to be ever new, as truth from heaven is and will be.[17]

In a speech entitled "Father Hecker The Citizen," published in the *Columbiad,* W. Bourke Cochran, a charter member of the Fourth Degree and a judge of the New York Supreme Court, said that Hecker's worldview lay in his understanding that "the democratic movement throughout Europe . . . was atheistic and . . . called Republican . . . [but] was in no sense an imitation of real American sentiment which prevailed in this land of ours." Hecker viewed the Americans as "essentially religious people even though we did not have a state religion. Nay, we were a religious people because we did not have a state religion." Hecker's own positive religious aspirations found Catholicism clearly congenial to his Americanism; in contrast he considered Protestantism to be based on a pessimistic view of humanity incompatible with American freedom. This is a curious reversal of the Protestant exclusivist notion of republicanism voiced by Josiah Strong on the Catholic immigrants' presumed loyalty to a foreign monarch. Hecker's citizenship, according to Cochran, was based on the understanding of the providential character of American republicanism: "From the hour that the gospel was preached, the dawn of republicanism was inevitable. True, the process was slow. But Father Hecker realized, when seeing it here in its splendor and in its success that there is danger of its decay unless republicanism is founded in religious faith and the moral law." Cochran concluded: "If, therefore, this country becomes Catholic, as Father Hecker prayed, and hoped and labored that it should become, and as we believe it will be, then indeed will we be sure that this republican system of ours will be permanent." Because republicanism had allowed Catholic institutions to thrive and because Catholicism preached the incarnational presence in humanity, the Catholic Church and American republicanism dwell in a positive mutuality. As Cochran put it, republicanism will be "protected by honest men and women whose hearts and souls will be wrapped up in . . . preserving . . . their church's teaching [then] their church's progress will be insured throughout the length and breadth of the country and [as America's mission to the world] Republicanism spread over the whole face of the civilized world."[18] This is the articulation of Catholic republican virtue, so vital to the progress of the United States.

The largest gathering to foster the American mission movement was held in Chicago November 16–18, 1908. At this Missionary Congress, over seventy-five bishops and many heads of religious orders were present along with Archbishop Diomede Falconio, the apostolic delegate to the United States, who presided at the opening pontifical high mass. The Fourth Degree played a prominent role at the congress. Not only did it provide an impressive honor guard and escort for the dignitaries but also the Sir Knights of the northern Illinois jurisdiction hosted a banquet for notable visitors and in honor of the Chief Justice of Canada, Sir Charles Fitzpatrick. With over eight hundred dinner guests, the banquet was one of the most prestigious events sponsored by the Fourth Degree. According to an article in the *Columbiad,* "The banquet followed a magnificent exemplification under the direction of Master William F. Ryan. . . ."[19] The congress was called to achieve four objectives: since Pope Pius X had removed the missionary status of the United States in 1908 and elevated it to "full share in the efforts of the Church universal," the congress "marked this change . . . by striking a note of unselfishness clearly and forcefully." Another objective was "to crystallize the missionary sentiment growing among the clergy and laity," sentiment committed to "preserving and extending the Church of Christ." There was also a commitment to bring specialists in missionary activity to study ways to improve U.S. Catholic efforts. The fourth objective was "to pledge to the Holy Father America's loyal support and active cooperation in the mighty task of restoring all things in Christ."[20]

As the founder (1905) and director of the Catholic Church Extension Society, Father Francis Clement Kelley (1870–1948) was the organizer of the 1909 congress. The Extension Society, sponsored by Chicago's Archbishop James E. Quigley, was founded to fund the construction of churches in small rural parishes. The historian of the U.S. missionary movement, Angelyn Dries, O.S.F., notes that Kelley, who "was hoping to unify mission efforts springing up around the country," initiated the first National Catholic Mission Congress.[21] In his introductory remarks at the banquet,

Jerome J. Crowley, Expositor of the Constitution, an officer of the Fourth Degree team of the northern Illinois jurisdiction, proudly informed the audience: "The work of the Catholic Extension Society has claimed the interest of the K of C; some of its councils have already subscribed life membership. . . . James Maher, State Deputy of Illinois and the principal presider at the Fourth Degree ceremonials that morning, spoke about the mission of the Order: "Our progress and our power for good must be dependent upon how much the individual membership of our Order is brought to a higher life where religion and education have their dwelling place." Maher was concerned that the "badge of Knighthood be something more than a mere symbol." Representing the muscular Christianity of the day, the Illinois State Deputy urged the Sir Knights, indeed the entire Order, to strive "for the advancement of manly qualities and religious zeal" with loyalty and obedience and guidance to the Church.[22] The State Chaplain of the Order in Illinois, Bishop Peter J. Muldoon, ordinary of the Rockford diocese, opened with "a few words . . . to waft a message from this assemblage to the Holy Father . . . that there is no body of men in the United States in whose hearts are deeper in sentiments of loyalty, affection, and obedience to authority than the Knights of Columbus." With special reference to the predominance of the Fourth Degree, Bishop Muldoon stated: "I have said on other occasions that you stand for what is best in Catholic manhood, and that which is best in my Catholic heart is obedience to constituted authority, and hence, Sir Knights, tonight, . . . we solicit . . . the Vicar of Jesus Christ and tell him in our tenderest sentiments that we love him because he speaks as one having authority."[23]

Among the other dignitaries who lauded the Order, no Knight present was more historically significant than the last living incorporator and long-time Supreme Secretary, Daniel Colwell. Reflecting on the significance of the occasion, Colwell said: "In all these years, I have never attended a function that I considered as great in its importance to the Order as this Fourth Degree given this afternoon . . . followed by this splendid banquet in honor of the distinguished members of the Catholic Church Extension Society." It was the twenty-first Fourth Degree Colwell had witnessed, and though "partial to the east" he said that "the Knights of the East have got to take off their hats to Chicago." Colwell had been in the first class of the Fourth Degree at the Lyceum in February 22, 1900. Though he did not reflect on that experience, he did expound on the Fourth Degree's role in raising $50,000 for the endowment of a Chair of American History at the Catholic University of America and on the commitment to raise $500,000 "for that great seat of learning in the city of Washington. . . ." As an easterner conscious of "the old families [i.e., Yankee descendants of the Puritans] to contend with," Colwell referred to "Hustlers of the West," those Knights of Illinois who were "building up what in the future years will be the successful families." He concluded with urging East and West to pull together . . . [to] convince the world that we are not only Catholic in name, but Catholic in aim, purpose, and determination."[24]

Several other Knights spoke at the banquet. Dr. J. K. Barrett of Winnipeg, Manitoba, told of joining the Order during a visit to Los Angeles where Bishop John Conaty introduced him to the Knights and to Joseph Scott. Upon his return, he organized a council in Winnipeg and subsequently traveled three thousand miles establishing Canadian councils from the Atlantic to the Pacific.[25] James Kennedy, State Deputy of Connecticut, a friend of Daniel Colwell, was also a member of the first Fourth Degree class. He was followed by Patrick J. Haltigan, head of the Order in the District of Columbia and a Fourth Degree Knight, who foresaw a time when there would be one million members in the Order; "then we can truly say that the Knights of Columbus, as the great exemplars of Catholic manhood in this nation, will stand in all their strength, in all their beauty for the advancement of all our people and the glory and honor of God."[26] The rhetorical display of Catholic masculinity did not originate with the Fourth Degree, but it was augmented by the uniformed honor guard with swords drawn, as prelates, priests, and people of civic and ecclesiastical status passed through the honor guard of formally attired Sir Knights.

II

The growth of the Order, well beyond two hundred thousand members in 1909, was reflected in the popularity of the uniformed degree. The national growth of the Fourth Degree required some form of centralized authority, while the growing sophistication of the membership called for a reform of the ceremonials as well. In 1909, John H. Reddin of Denver, a Knight of national repute as the leader of the degree team instituting councils throughout the West, revised the ceremonials for the Fourth Degree. Under the mandate of the National Board of Directors on which he served, John Reddin created a national structure for each of the six provinces. In 1910, Reddin was appointed the first Supreme Master of the degree, a title that derived from the new national structure; the six provinces, named for explorers of the region are: Champlain Province in Ottawa, Ontario; Cabot Province in

Boston; Calvert Province in New York; Marquette Province in Milwaukee: De Soto Province in New Orleans, and La Salle Province in Seattle. Prior to the reorganization of the Fourth Degree, assemblies were organized into districts, but each assembly was self-governing with only a minimum of central direction from the Board of Directors. Besides the appointment of a Supreme Master, there were Vice Supreme Masters for each of the seven provinces (an eighth was created for the Order's growth in the Canal Zone, Mexico, Puerto Rico, and Newfoundland). Provinces were divided into districts with a National Board of Directors appointing a Master for each district. The local assembly was headed up by a Faithful Navigator, comparable to a Grand Knight for each Third Degree council. The Fourth Degree Masters of Districts and Vice Supreme Masters of provinces were appointed rather than elected (as were the officers in the Third Degree), a distinction that John Reddin frequently traced to the decision to remove politics from the patriotic degree committed to selfless patriotism. At the biennial Supreme Assemblies, Masters and Vice Supreme Masters were entitled to submit motions for consideration.[27] The National Board was the final authority on the Fourth Degree: "it approves all acts of the General Assembly. Officers of the Fourth Degree do not have any authority in the Third-Degree nor carry any rank or precedence outside the Fourth Degree." Reddin expected "comity and harmony"[28] to characterize relations between the Fourth Degree assemblies and Third Degree councils. Reddin, the principal author of the ceremonial, described its characteristics:

> The ceremonial is based upon an exalted concept of American Patriotism, and teaches an enduring appreciation of our American institutions, reverence for the Constitution of the United States and the founders and preservers of the Republic, as well as an appreciation of the part our Catholic ancestors and progenitors have played in the discovery, exploration, evangelization and making of America. In countries foreign to the United States the ceremonial is based on similar concepts applicable to those countries.[29]

Published in 1931, Reddin's pamphlet on the Fourth Degree has the benefits of hindsight, particularly the experience of the "tribal twenties" and the opening years of the Great Depression. Catholic patriotism, which blended national sentiment with pride in the American Catholic heritage, was a distinctively public form of Catholicism. The commitment to the Republic derived from the original defense of Catholic loyalty, which was reiterated over the decades and, in 1931, was expressed in the aftermath of the Al Smith campaign of 1928.

In the *Columbiad's* article on the clarification of the degree's structure,

John Reddin was portrayed as "a leading member of the bar in Denver and a man of ripe judgment and experience, a true Catholic citizen and a stalwart Knight."[30] The seven Vice Supreme Masters were also prominent in professions and business; in Ontario and Seattle were the Gorman brothers: Michael J. in Ontario was an attorney, while T. J. of Seattle had his own canneries in Puget Sound and in Alaska. J. Gorman of Boston was a city assessor; George W. Young, a banker in New Orleans; W. J. Boyd of New York and August Rabhan did not have their occupations listed, but all were apparently of the upper middle class. Most had achieved success as leaders in the exemplification of the degree. The titles of the officers who led the charge of the Fourth Degree are congenial to the themes of Catholic patriotism and citizenship: Expositor of the Constitution, Historian, Sentinel, and Defender of the Faith. "Defender of the Faith" conveys the spirit of the origins of Fourth Degree and its development in opposition to the pervasive ideology of Josiah Strong, who had attacked Catholicism as inimical to republicanism.

But the uniformed degree, by providing honor guards for ecclesiastical dignitaries and participating in religious processions and civic parades, also gave the publishers of the anti-Catholic press a very visible target for their campaigns against what they perceived as the advance guard of papal imperialism. The rise of the Order's uniformed degree occurred at the same time as the new waves of immigrants from southern and eastern Europe many of whom were Catholics and Jews. This resulted in a nativist xenophobia mixed with anti-Catholicism and anti-Semitism, generating a kind of parallel antidefamation effort between the Knights of Columbus and the B'nai B'rith. The oldest Jewish fraternal society, B'nai B'rith was founded in 1843; one of its objectives was "alleviating the wants of the victims of persecution."[31] However, it did not establish its Anti-Defamation League (ADL) until 1913.[32] A year later the Knights established its Commission on Religious Prejudices, which was not intended to be permanent, while the ADL is still a vital arm in the struggle against anti-Semitism. However, the Knights of Columbus and the B'nai B'rith shared common characteristics: an insurance program to protect widows and orphans; dedication to the principles of unity, charity, and patriotism; assimilation of immigrants of a shared religious tradition; and defense of political legitimacy for people subjected to nativism.[33] Thus, the two societies have a tradition of cooperation.

The Knights' devotion to Columbus won popular appeal through the activities of the Fourth Degree. As mentioned earlier, the two days designated for the annual exemplification were Columbus Day and Washington's

Birthday. The Colorado legislature approved the first state holiday for Columbus Day, and soon several more states followed suit; so that by 1912 there were thirty states in the ranks. The Knights were vigorous in their promotion of Columbus Day, with parades in many towns featuring the Fourth Degree in full regalia. Through the lobbying efforts of the Order, Congress passed a bill to subsidize a Columbus Memorial in 1908.[34] But the Order's role on the commission to oversee the development of the monument became widely known, and this fed the fires of more anti-Catholic hostility. Even before the monument's unveiling, the unofficial alliance of nativist and anti-Catholic groups attacked the Fourth Degree Knights, principally because they were perceived as a uniformed and militant corps of fanatics aimed at destroying all that was presumably essential to American republicanism and decency.

Possibly no scholar can rival John Higham in analyzing nativism, anti-Catholicism, anti-Semitism, and the "Yellow Peril," as movements grounded in common ideologies. The first decade of the twentieth century was driven by two opposing forces: progressivism, which tended toward a cosmopolitan worldview, and nativism, which moved toward a racist, exclusivist perspective. The progressives fought against political corruption by advocating reforms to support direct democracy and to rid the nation of political bosses. There were state commissions on immigration and housing. In contrast to the anti-Catholic nativists such as Josiah Strong, there were Protestants who were committed to the social gospel and who avoided nativism and promoted assimilation.[35] Notions about the supremacy of Anglo-Saxon peoples prevailed among social scientists and intellectuals, as well as among patrician politicians such as Henry Cabot Lodge of Boston. These notions gained momentum and ultimately became a "scientifically" based view validating immigrant restrictionism.[36]

The gradual decline of the Progressive movement, symbolized by President Taft's disenchantment with reformers whom he came to regard as "exciting class conflict,"[37] was followed by a long period of polarization. Frustrated with the slow pace of reform, the political left turned to socialism. In the West, the International Workers of the World (IWW or Wobblies) gained popular support among miners and other industrial workers. On the political right were antiradical groups alienated by the alleged militancy of unions. The left vented its "religious xenophobia"[38] in the form of a virulent anti-Catholicism that was initiated around 1910. Though this new movement revived the stereotypical attacks upon "the moral iniquities of the confessional and convents" and the inherent despotism of the papacy, its principal sources of support were from those groups who experienced the frustration of rising expectations for liberal reform and who therefore displaced their antimonopolistic sentiment upon the growth of the presumed monster of monopolistic power, the pope's Roman Catholic conspiracy. The thesis of John Higham is that "[i]t is hard to explain the re-birth of anti-Catholic ferment except as an outlet for expectations which progressivism raised and then failed to fulfill."[39] Two frustrated radicals, armed with their own periodicals, attacked Catholicism in terms that clearly illustrate Higham's thesis. Since the Knights of the Fourth Degree were obviously perceived as representatives of the advance of papal power in America, members of the uniformed degree were particularly subject to wrath from the left. "There is a foreign foe at our gates," said the southern radical Tom Watson, in *Watson's Magazine*, "and that foe is confidently expecting the spies within to unlock the portals. Those domestic traitors are the Trusts, the Roman Catholic priesthood . . . [and] the Knights of Columbus."[40] Wilbur Franklin Phelps, editor of *The Menace*, published in Aurora, Missouri, was also a strongly disillusioned advocate of reform.

This weekly newspaper was entirely devoted to exposing the "Romanist" threat to labor unions, social reform, true patriotism, and democracy. Next to the paper's title was a caricature of the pope in the form of a skull and crossbones wearing the triple crown with "Temporal Power" above the crown and "Public Menace" below the crossbones.[41] On a 1913 letterhead is this statement: "The Roman Catholic Political Machine: The Deadliest Menace to American Liberties and Evangelization."[42] Several other anti-Catholic periodicals, similar to *Watson's Magazine* and *The Menace,* were published in small towns by reform-minded editors who drew upon the traditional Protestant cant even though the vast majority of Protestant newspapers were cosmopolitan in tone and content and eschewed religious intolerance. As Higham points out, the new wave of anti-Catholic hysteria "found its most valiant champions among hicks and hillbillies. They at least had not abandoned the old time religion."[43] The portrayal of the Knights of Columbus in *The Menace*—particularly the members of the Fourth Degree, as a military unit allegedly in the service of papal imperialism—was so distorted that its readers must have been shocked at seeing public parades, honor guards, and drill teams made up of Knights of the Fourth Degree.

The soon-to-be-infamous bogus oath of the Fourth Degree, which was interjected into the election campaign of 1912, may have had its origins in the Guardians of Liberty, founded in 1911 by retired officers of the armed services. General Nelson Miles, former chief of staff of the United States

Army, gave the Guardians the mask of respectability. In an article entitled "The Forces Are Assimilating," *The Menace* reported the formation of the Guardians as dedicated to the "preservation of all that is clear to the hearts of the sons and daughters, the Revolutionary forefathers, the protection of the Constitution of the United States, the separation of Church and State and the uplifting of American ideals"[44]—that is, all that is in sympathy with the anti-Catholic paranoia of *The Menace*. The spurious oath appears to have been adapted from two other false documents: the Jesuit oath of the seventeenth century and the priests' oath recently published.[45] I cite the entire text of the bogus oath, grammatical errors and all:

> I, ________ __________, now in the presence of Almighty God, the blessed Virgin Mary, the Blessed St. John the Baptist, the Holy Apostles, St. Peter and St. Paul, and all the saints, sacred host of Heaven, and to you, my Ghostly Father, the superior general of the Society of Jesus, founded by St. Ignatius Loyola, in the pontification of Paul the III, and continued to the present, do by the womb of the Virgin, the matrix of God, and the rod of Jesus Christ, declare and swear that His Holiness, the Pope, is Christ's vice-regent and is the true and only head of the Catholic or Universal Church throughout the earth, and that by virtue of the keys of binding and loosing given his Holiness by my Savior, Jesus Christ, he hath power to depose heretical kings, princes, States, Commonwealths, and Governments, and they may be safely destroyed. Therefore, to the utmost of my power I will defend this doctrine and His Holiness' right and custom against all usurpers of the heretical or Protestant authority whatever, especially the Lutheran Church of Germany, Holland, Denmark, Sweden, and Norway, and the now pretended authority and Churches of England and Scotland, and the branches of same now established in Ireland and on the Continent of America and elsewhere, and all adherents in regard that they may be usurped and heretical opposing the sacred Mother Church of Rome.
>
> I do now denounce and disown any allegiance as due to any heretical king, prince, or State, named Protestant or Liberals, or obedience to any of their laws, magistrates, or officers.
>
> I do further declare that the doctrine of the Churches of England and Scotland, of the Calvinists, Huguenots, and others of the name of Protestants or Masons, to be damnable, and they themselves to be damned who will not forsake the same.
>
> I do further declare that I will help, assist, and advise all or any of His Holiness' agents, in any place where I should be, Switzerland, Germany, Holland, Ireland, or America, or in any other kingdom or territory I shall come to, and do my utmost to extirpate the heretical Protestant or Masonic doctrines and to destroy all their pretended powers, legal or otherwise.

I do further promise and declare that, notwithstanding that I am dispensed with to assume any religion, heretical for the propagation of the Mother Church's interest to keep secret and private all her agents' counsels from time to time, as they instruct me, and not divulge, directly or indirectly, by word, writing, or circumstances whatever, but to execute all that should be proposed, given in charge, or discovered unto me by you, my Ghostly Father, or any of this sacred order.

I do further promise and declare that I will have no opinion or will of my own or any mental reservation whatsoever, even as a corpse or cadaver (perinfe ac cadaver), but will unhesitatingly obey each and every command that I may receive from my superiors in the militia of the Pope and of Jesus Christ.

That I will go to any part of the world whithersoever I may be sent, to the frozen regions of the North, to the jungles of India, to the centers of civilization of Europe, or to the wild haunts of the barbarous savages of America without murmuring or repining, and will be submissive in all things whatsoever is communicated to me.

I do further promise and declare that I will, when opportunity presents, make and wage relentless war, secretly and openly, against all heretics, Protestants, and Masons, as I am directed to do, to extirpate them from the face of the whole earth; and that I will spare neither age nor sex, or condition, and that I will hang, burn, waste, boil, flay, strangle, and bury alive these infamous heretics, rip up the stomachs and wombs of their women, and crush their infants' heads against the walls in order to annihilate their execrable race. That when the same cannot be done openly, I will secretly use the poisonous cup, the strangulation cord, the steel of the poniard, or the leaden bullet, regardless of the honor, rank, dignity, or authority of the persons, whatever may be their condition in life, either public or private, as I at any time may be directed to do so by any agents of the Pope or superior of the Brotherhood of the Holy Father of the Society of Jesus.

In confirmation of which I hereby dedicate my life, soul, and all corporal powers, and with the dagger which I now receive, I will subscribe my name written in my blood in testimony thereof; and should I prove false or weaken in my determination, may my brethren and fellow soldiers of the militia of the Pope cut off my hands and feet and my throat from ear to ear, my belly opened and sulfur burned therein with all the punishment that can be inflicted upon me on earth and my soul shall be tortured by demons in eternal hell forever.

That I will in voting always vote for a K. Of C. in preference to a Protestant, especially a Mason, and that I will leave my party so to do; that if two Catholics are on the ticket I will satisfy myself which is the better supporter of Mother Church and vote accordingly.

That I will not deal with or employ a Protestant if in my power to deal with or employ a Catholic. That I will place Catholic girls in Protestant families that a weekly report may be made of the inner movements of the heretics.

> That I will provide myself with arms and ammunition that I may be in readiness when the word is passed, or I am commanded to defend the Church either as an individual or with the militia of the Pope.
>
> All of which, I, __________ ________, do swear by the blessed Trinity and blessed sacrament which I am now to receive to perform and on part to keep this, my oath.
>
> In testimony hereof, take this most holy and blessed Sacrament of the Eucharist and witness the same further with my name written with the point of this dagger dipped in my own blood and seal in the face of this holy sacrament.[46]

This violent imagery and excessive departure from the truth is in a sense verification of P. T. Barnum's dictum to the effect that the larger the lie the greater its credibility. One of the strongest indictments in this document is the denunciation of the Sir Knights of the Fourth Degree as given to blood lusts and rampages of terror against all "heretics, Protestants, and Masons." To place it in the contexts of general anti-Catholic bogus oaths, the quotation is similar to the priests' oath circulating a few years before the appearance of this so-called Fourth Degree oath,[47] which gained wide circulation in 1912 when Eugene C. Bonniwell, a Fourth Degree Knight of Pennsylvania, claimed that his defeat in the congressional election was due to his opponent's citation of the oath to brand him as a traitor in league with the pope. Since Bonniwell took his case to Congress, the oath was published in the *Congressional Record* of February 15, 1913. In July 1912, before the Bonniwell case, *The Menace* published a brief article entitled "The Knights of Columbus Oath," which was curiously cautious:

> From all parts of the country *The Menace* has received copies of what purports to be the oath taken by those who enter the sacred organization known as the Knights of Columbus. We have been requested time and again to publish this oath, but for the benefit of those who have made this request . . . The Menace publishes only what it is convinced to be authentic matter, and, we have not as yet been able to authenticate this obligation we do not care to give it space in The Menace. The bait is rather enticing, but we are not disposed to walk into a deadfall with our eyes open.[48]

The issue of October 12, 1912, featured *The Menace's* article on the Knights' Columbianism, a blast at the Order's leadership for appropriating Columbus as their patron, a claim that "certainly takes the blue ribbon over all the gigantic frauds ever attempted by the minions of the devil on God's footstool." According to N. M. Phillips, the author of this article, "Columbus took possession in the name of the Spanish sovereign but not in the name of the 'dago' on the Tiber or any other church power." The Knights' claim to Columbus's name was a "pretext to make a show of reason for their inordinate efforts to rule and dominate the American people." It was considered a truism that the Knights of Columbus "was planned in the higher courts of the Catholic church and was dictated by its dupes." The reform goals of *The Menace* were evident in Phillips's reference to the devil's presence "in the slums of humanity," but he then associates the devil with the pope; "the man of sin, the apostate . . . who has stood out as a great wart on the face of humanity," while the Knights of Columbus are the "war department of the papacy."[49]

The Aurora, Missouri, anti-Catholic publication tapped a rich vein of sentiment in rural America; within two years its circulation reached nearly five hundred thousand, which at fifty cents for an annual subscription generated income that reversed the unemployment rate in Aurora. As noted earlier, *The Menace* mocked the plans for the unveiling of the Columbus Memorial and criticized the patriotism of the Knights and the sincerity of their respect for Columbus.[50] In the celebrations at the unveiling of the monument (June 8, 1912) the Knights, particularly the Fourth Degree, were thrust onto the national scene. The leadership of the Order had been a significant lobbyist in favor of legislation for the erection of the Columbus Monument. A commission had been established composed of the Secretaries of State and War, the chairmen of the House and Senate Committees on the Library of Congress, and Supreme Knight Edward Hearn, who stayed on the commission even after he chose not to be a candidate for office in 1909. Among the speakers at the unveiling ceremony was Victor J. Dowling, who, as mentioned earlier, was a prominent New York Supreme Court judge and a charter member of the Fourth Degree. His address on Columbus was a rhapsody on the themes of Catholicity and the foundation story of America. "Here was no Alexander, sighing for new worlds to conquer, but here was the apostolic spirit for one who sighed for quicker ways to make known . . . the sweetness of Faith and the light of Hope. Here was a man, who, like Napoleon, believed in his star; but the star of Columbus was the star of Bethlehem."[51]

Immediately after President William Howard Taft's address, the parade began, and as one reporter noticed, "the Knights of Columbus—the men who made possible this great demonstration . . . [numbered] nineteen to twenty thousand of them in a line—perhaps more and from first to last they made a showing of which not only they themselves may be proud, but which must have been a source of pride and pleasure as well to every Catholic who viewed them."[52] Hearn noted that the "patriotic display" was "a spectacle of twenty thousand men representing the flower and chivalry of Catholic manhood."[53] A note of irony: General Nelson Miles, Chief Guardian of the Guardians of Liberty,[54] was on the reviewing stand as the twenty thousand Knights led by the Fourth Degree in top hats and formal wear passed in review. *The Menace* then published a piece of revisionist history on the discovery of America that concluded with the usual attack on the Knights of Columbus:

> The attempt of the Knights of Columbus to rob the Norsemen of the glory of discovery of America, is on a par with many other claims of the Roman church—false in history and based only upon the legends and superstitions. The Columbus monument in Washington, D.C., had better be removed and placed in some K. of C. backyard—away from public view—off from national ground. It does not represent American ideals or American achievements. It is papish—sectarian and Jesuitical. Remove the stone of stumbling and rock of offense.[55]

The bogus oath had been published in the 1913 *Congressional Record,* but as mentioned earlier the oath had entered the public forum during the election of 1912. The pastor of the First Methodist Church in Seattle included portions of the oath in his sermon. The Seattle Knights submitted the official Fourth Degree pledge to three Protestants who had stature in the community. They concluded that the oath was "a blasphemous and horrible travesty." In contrast, the Fourth Degree pledge was of the "highest type of American citizenship."[56] The pledge was certainly a clear illustration of Catholic patriotism, American citizenship, and practical Catholicity.

> I swear to support the Constitution of the United States. I pledge myself, as a Catholic citizen and Knight of Columbus, to enlighten myself fully upon my duties as a citizen and to conscientiously perform such duties entirely in the interest of my country and regardless of all personal consequences. I pledge myself to do all in my power to preserve the integrity and purity of the ballot, and to promote reverence and respect for law and order. I promise to practice my religion openly and consistently, but without ostentation, and to so conduct myself in public affairs, and in the exercise of public virtue, as to reflect nothing but credit upon our Holy Church, to the end that she may flourish and our country prosper to the greater honor and glory of God.[57]

In late 1914, one California Thirty-third Degree Mason and two Thirty-second Degree Masons "were furnished a complete copy of all the work, ceremonies and pledges used by the Order . . . and found that [they] were intended to teach and inculcate principles that lie at the foundation of every free state." This report was presented on the floor of Congress and placed in the *Congressional Record* by Congressman William Kettner, a Thirty-third Degree Mason who was "privileged to present this report." The three Masons concluded their assessment with an attack on the authenticity of the oath itself. "We find that neither the alleged oath nor any oath or pledge bearing the remotest resemblance thereto in matter, manner, spirit or purpose is used or forms a part of the ceremonies of any degree of the Knights of Columbus. The alleged oath is scurrilous, wicked and libelous, and must be the invention of an impious and venomous mind."[58]

Despite the fact that the bogus oath was obviously a reference to the Fourth Degree, *The Menace* and others of that stripe tended to consider the oath as simply the Knights of Columbus oath. In response, Supreme Knight James Flaherty, a lawyer from Philadelphia, and the Supreme Advocate, Joseph C. Pelletier, with the approval of the other Supreme officers, pursued a legal suit against the printers who published the bogus oath related to the Bonniwell defeat in the congressional election. The plaintiff in the case was not the injured Bonniwell but rather Charles B. Dowds, a member of Brownson Council No. 933 of Philadelphia. He charged that Charles Megonegal, a printer, and Clarence H. Stage, a barber, did "willfully and maliciously . . . [expose] the Knights of Columbus as a body and Charles B. Dowds, James Flaherty Supreme Knight, and Philip A. Hart, Master of the Fourth Degree [all of Philadelphia] to public hatred, contempt, and ridicule, to their great damage, disgrace, scandal, and infamy." In their defense Megonegal and Stage contended that they purchased numerous copies of the alleged oath from *The Menace* before they printed these copies. Megonegal pleaded guilty and Stage asserted the plea of *nolo contendere* to charges of criminal libel; with the consent of the plaintiffs, all jail sentences were suspended.[59] *The Menace* responded with attacks on the Order for its revival of the Inquisition, the "couple of poor men of Philadelphia," that is, Charles Megonegal and Clarence Stage, who were subjected to the Knights of Columbus legal "serpent," the criminal libel case against the printers. *The Menace* denied that it circulated the oath: "*The Menace* kept its columns clear of the evident bate [*sic*] and refused to aid the politicians [in the 1912 election] or on the one hand to walk into the Jesuit trap on the other." Though the Knights were "supposed to be good and practical Catholics they have gone with spasms on what they say is an absurd and unbelievable fraud." James Flaherty, "one of the chief inquisitors," led the "Columbuses" in "rejoicing and being glad to put some one in jail, burn someone and break somebody's business—get even with the heretics." *The Menace* rejected the pledge presented to the group of Seattle Protestants as simply part of the conspiracy to place Megonegal and Stage in jail: "the heads of the Order must have been queering the ritual. A nice frame up surely!"[60]

Three days before the latter article was published, the editors of *The Menace* Publishing Company in a letter to Leroy N. King, the attorney for Megonegal and Stage, admitted that "they are not in possession now of the ritual and the secret work of the Knights of Columbus, but we believe we are in a fair way to get it, and the statement in a recent issue of *The Menace*, which led you to believe we have it in our possession was *somewhat of a bluff* on our part was based upon the fact that we know that it can be had." As mentioned earlier, *The Menace* stated that it could not prove the veracity of the "oath" and therefore did not print it and in fact waited until it was published elsewhere before featuring it. In this letter to Leroy King, the editors actually referred to the "alleged oath" and went on to tell him that this oath "which your clients were arrested for distributing, was circulated in practically every state during the late campaign and the demand for this document was something great, and we had received copies of them from so many sources we simply printed them and handled them as we would any other job of printing, to supply the demand, and while we have no apologies to make for so doing, we do not have any evidence that the oath is the one which is taken by members of the Knights of Columbus." Because of these facts the editors were "sure that it would be foolish for you to undertake to base your defense on the authenticity of this document." The letter closed with a remark on the Knights' claim not to be "an oath-bound Order, which of course is subterfuge and untrue." As if the Fourth Degree were on trial, the editors suggested that the leaders provide the court with the actual oath, "to clear the matter up in the minds of the people." On the letterhead of their official stationery, running across the top of the page above *The Menace* is: "The Roman Catholic Political Machine: The Deadliest Menace to American Liberties and Civilization."[61]

In the issue following the letter to King, *The Menace* reported on the publication of the oath with widespread coverage and lengthy quotations from the text in the *Congressional Record*. Though there was a libel suit against *The Menace* for interjecting the oath into a political race in Missouri, this did not prevent the paper from printing the entire oath on the front page of September 12, 1914.[62]

The bogus oath was sent to President Woodrow Wilson by W. J. Smith, Clerk of the Western Presbytery [*sic*] Church. He prefaced it with a request that since the oath had been published in the *Congressional Record*, there was a need for the president to clarify the authenticity of the oath. Smith and his colleagues seem to have been convinced that indeed it was an actual oath or they would not have bothered to send it to the White House.[63] Wilson received another copy of the oath with a cover letter from A. A. Kaisse, Vice President of the Bank of Dayton in Dayton, New Mexico. Dated November 4, 1913, Kaisse's letter referred to the oath as achieving national circulation and "purported to be the oath taken by the Knights of Columbus." With a sense of balance he asked the president to "investigate this, if it is true then those taking this oath should be deported from this country as undesirable citizens. If it is untrue, it is an outrage and should be exposed as an infamous lie." Kaisse closed the letter with the "hope your secretary will let this letter go to you, as an ex school teacher I am proud of your splendid administration."[64] Perhaps Kaisse was referring to Joseph Tumulty, President Wilson's secretary, who was a Catholic. *The Menace* took particular satisfaction in attacking him as a significant participant in a papal conspiracy even before Wilson's inauguration.[65] He was identified by the newspaper as a Knight of Columbus, even though he did not enter the Order until 1915.[66]

On both local and national levels the Knights of Columbus sought to refute the attacks of *The Menace.* An editorial in the *Catholic Columbiad*, out of Columbus, Ohio, perceived the anti-Catholic newspaper to be "simply the tool of socialism." Clearly in support of John Higham's thesis on the socialist identity of monopoly capitalism with Roman Catholic power, the editorial considered *The Menace's* animus to be derived from the church's exposure of the "treasonable, revolutionary, tyrannical, free-love and impracticable atheistic doctrines of Socialism."[67]

Many articles decrying socialism's inherent anti-Catholicism were written not only as antidotes to socialism but also as clarifications of Leo XIII's encyclical *Rerum Novarum,* which legitimated associations of labor—that is, trade unions—and the role of the state in the mitigation of social and economic evils. For example, Father Andrew P. Doyle, a Paulist missionary to non-Catholics, described *Rerum Novarum* as "the *Magna Carta* of social reform," and he urged the Knights to read Father John A. Ryan's work on "The Living Wage," which was inspired by Pope Leo's encyclical.[68] In Ryan's article in *Columbiad* he advocated "The Legal Minimum Wage."[69] Mary B. O'Sullivan, another social reformer active in trade unionism, also appeared in *Columbiad* writing on "The Child Labor Question," with particular emphasis on the demoralizing effects of laissez-faire capitalism on employers of children.[70] To further the cause of social reform and to remedy the evils of "blatant wealth" juxtaposed to the giant figures of poverty," Father Doyle suggested "the creation of clubs for social studies . . . . Moreover, the fascinating charms of these studies in social reform captivate the hearts of those who give themselves to it." The Knights' Councils should sponsor these clubs as well as lecture series on economics, trade unionism, and other topics. Doyle concluded with another challenge to the Knights:

> . . . socialism has the call these days. The two camps are swiftly forming on either side of the valley of Terebinth, and the giant Goliath of social injustice daily taunts the armies of the living God. We need our Davids who will come forth with a thorough knowledge of social matters to grapple with the scoffer, and it is in the ranks of the Knights of Columbus that the champions of the faith can and must be found.[71]

Doyle's indebtedness to *Rerum Novarum,* which also included Pope Leo's attack on socialism and industrial violence, was matched by Catholic labor leaders, as well as by the vast majority of bishops. Because trade unions were headed by Irish-Americans, the American Federation of Labor (AFL) was permeated by Catholic social thought during its formative years. The emphasis on class cooperation rather than conflict set the AFL on a track opposed to the development of socialism.[72] Members of the German-American Catholic Central Bureau were conservative social reformers opposed to the individualistic market ethic but also committed to *Rerum Novarum* and to educating the rank and file of the AFL in Catholic social teaching, as well as helping to organize Catholic workingman's societies in opposition to socialism.[73] There were few Catholics socialists; Father Thomas J. Hagerty was the only well-known priest socialist in the early twentieth century.[74]

Socialism made significant national progress in 1912 when Eugene V. Debs became the Socialist Party's candidate for the presidency. This was also the year when the bogus oath was injected into the political campaign. Anti-Catholic lecturers of the left were gaining some popularity. Indeed it is important to recall the leftward direction of anti-Catholic periodicals such as *The Menace*, which, according to John Higham, "wore a progressive air . . . [stating] that the Catholic Church was combining with big business to break the labor unions; it showed a vague guarded sympathy with the Socialists . . . ."[75] The links between socialism and anti-Catholicism were evident among Marxists, the Socialist Party, and the readers and supporters of *The Menace.*

To combat socialism the Order began an ambitious education campaign. The Supreme Master, John H. Reddin, became an impassioned advocate of the free lecture movement. Reddin believed that the promotion of American citizenship through the medium of public lectures was a duty of each assembly; Masters of the Fourth Degree should promote lecturers to enlighten the public about Catholicism. Because of the general enthusiasm for public lectures, and because society needed a balanced view of Catholicism, Reddin became an effective advocate: "Why should we remain idle when we have but to imitate the Chautauquas, summer schools, and lecture bureaus throughout the country? Success for us means a broader knowledge, a more intelligent and militant Catholicism, and a better and finer citizenship. This is the work of the Fourth Degree."[76] Supreme Knight James Flaherty acknowledged Reddin's "inspiration" behind the idea of a free lecture bureau. "Indeed, the spirit has gone forth; that spirit has awakened other inspirations that will only be answered when such an ideal lecture bureau is working wherever our Order is established."[77]

At the 1913 Supreme Council convention, a lecture program was approved. Despite Reddin's appeal for lecturers to emerge from the ranks, the most prominent free lecturers were appointed from the outside. The lack of financial resources and the "sporadic" interests of the Masters prompted Reddin to ask the Supreme Board of Directors to take responsibility for financing the project. Reddin later recalled that with the "unanimous vote at the Boston Convention in 1913, . . . the Supreme Board . . . ever since has kept in the field such men as Peter W. Collins . . . and others. Millions of fair minded citizens who have heard these men have acquired a better understanding of the Church and a realization of the dangers to be guarded against if this Republic and our Christian Civilization is to be preserved."[78]

The Order's educational campaign featured primarily David Goldstein and Peter W. Collins, both experts on the dangers of socialism. Goldstein recalled that it was "in the spring of 1914 I was called by the Knights of Columbus to take a leading part in the Educational Campaign of the Order." He also wrote about John Reddin, "through whose initiative this educational campaign was started."[79] Though the sponsorship was not limited to the Sir Knights of the Fourth Degree, the campaign was Reddin's priority and was identified, therefore, as a Fourth Degree project. Yet he continued to promote the lecture bureau and vigorously urged local assemblies also to initiate them.

David Goldstein was born in 1870 into a Jewish working-class family that had moved from London to New York and then to Boston. As a young man he became active in the cigar-makers union, and in his twenties, as a zealous member of the Socialist Labor Party, he ran for mayor of Boston.

He engaged in the socialist cause for over a decade but became disillusioned because party politics tended to "infringe upon the rights of the minority."[80] The major reason for his resignation from the Socialist Party was based on a critique of the Marxist notion of the withering away of the State. In his letter of resignation, Goldstein also included his disagreement with the socialism's attack on "the present marriage system, [and] at a party convention" he unsuccessfully challenged the Socialist Party to disqualify from the platform those speakers "who attack theological doctrines or advocate violence, [and] 'free love.'"[81]

After breaking with the Socialist Party, he became active in the American Federation of Labor (AFL) of Samuel Gompers. He frequently lectured with Mrs. Martha Moore Avery, also disillusioned with socialism. Indeed, they traveled the same road: they had belonged to a study group on Marx in 1896; seven years later they left the socialist movement; Goldstein soon converted to Catholicism in May of 1905, followed by Avery the next year. In 1910 Goldstein and Avery joined with four priests of the Archdiocese of Boston in presenting lectures on Catholic social thought.[82] This was a particularly significant topic for the two former socialists, because *Rerum Novarum* had been influential in their conversion to Catholicism. The two were also co-authors of *Socialism: The Nation of Faithless Children* (1903) based on their repudiation of the Marxist attacks on marriage.[83] Goldstein was commissioned to lecture on the evils of socialism by the Central Bureau, the German-American Catholic Society headquartered in St. Louis, Missouri. Later sponsored by the Knights of Columbus, Goldstein was a member of Mt. Pleasant Council in Boston, and secretary of the Boston School of Political Economy. Though a vigorous antisocialist Goldstein was a dedicated trade unionist.[84]

Both David Goldstein and Peter Collins were pro-AFL members of the Militia of Christ for Social Service, an antisocialist organization founded by Father Peter Dietz on November 21, 1910, at the national convention of the AFL in Toronto. Influenced by *Rerum Novarum,* the Militia of Christ "was founded by a band of Catholic Trade Union leaders [as] a religious, patriotic and unionist fraternity" dedicated to "collective bargaining, conciliation, and arbitration of industrial disputes."[85] The socialist periodical *The Masses* critically noted: "The American Federation of Labor [which had repudiated the Socialist Party] is getting more and more into the hand of the Militia of Christ."[86] As executive director, Dietz was advised by fellow officers and directors who included all the major Catholic trade unionists, such as Peter Collins and John P. Mitchell, former president of the United Mine

Workers. When he was commissioned to lecture for the Knights of Columbus, Collins was former international secretary of the International Brotherhood of Electrical Workers and had been editor of *The Electrical Worker* for eight years. However, according to Philip S. Foner, a historian of the U.S. labor movement, "Collins was part of a machine that ran that Brotherhood of Electrical Workers in the most corrupt and undemocratic fashion, making deals with employers at the expense of the workers, and that he was forced to resign as the Secretary of the union by the rank and file."[87]

Understanding that the Order had implicit trust in its lecturers, John Reddin urged the Fourth Degree members to take advantage of this "opportunity [to promote the lecturers] that may not be as readily grasped again. . . . All around you are men, good men, who do not understand why Catholics oppose Socialism and their lack of knowledge often begets suspicion and distrust, whereas proper understanding of our attitude would undoubtedly win support for the Catholic point of view."[88] To promote Catholic truth and to place the church in the foreground of social movements compatible with the free flow of ideas was and is one of the paramount purposes of the patriotic degree. Because of the identity of socialism and anti-Catholicism clearly embodied in *The Menace*, the Sir Knights were indirectly responding to the bogus oath in their promotion of the lectures by Goldstein and Collins.[89]

In an article in *Columbiad* in May 1913, Peter W. Collins cited several socialists who had vented their frustration at the leadership of the trade unions being out of touch with the rank-and-file worker. Collins replied by remarking on the many socialist leaders who denied the existence of God, a denial that tended to separate them from the religious views of their workers. Collins charged that the socialists and the Industrial workers were "organized to destroy the Trades Unions."[90]

On the lecture circuit between March and July 1914, David Goldstein addressed sixty-eight audiences at free public meetings, which, according to a report in *Columbiad*, numbered over "100,000 persons [who] heard Bro. Goldstein's' defense of Christian principles against the Socialist assault on God, on home, and on country." A newspaper report of his lecture in Victoria, British Columbia, stated, "Mr. Goldstein answered numerous questions during the evening, quoting from books by eminent Socialist writers as authority for his answers. His conception that Socialism was atheism called forth applause from the Socialists."[91]

In his *Autobiography,* Goldstein recalled his address in Denver, John Reddin's home city: "the anti-Catholic spirit was intense," he wrote. Shortly before his arrival, Otis L. Spurgeon, "an anti-Romanist agitator connected with *The Menace*" had been kidnapped, beaten, and abandoned in a desolate place outside Denver, presumably because he had been retailing pornographic stories of priests and sisters. "This incident added considerable interest to my coming," wrote Goldstein. At the close of his address to a gathering of three thousand, one-third of whom were socialists, Goldstein took questions from the audience. When asked about the treatment of Spurgeon, Goldstein expressed his disapproval but said that such violence could not be attributed to members of the Order. "I believe Rev. Spurgeon ought to have been arrested and put in jail. But remember this—the Order of the Knights of Columbus is a law abiding and liberty loving body of American citizens and it, therefore, repudiates the action of men who assaulted Spurgeon."[92]

The year 1914 was, according to John Higham, "The summit of Prewar Nativism."[93] This is verified by 1.5 million subscribers to *The Menace*. The economic recession of 1913 and the depression the next year engendered a rise in xenophobia among many Anglo-Americans who were envious of jobs going to Catholic immigrants from southern and eastern Europe. Job insecurity in the mining areas of southern Illinois prompted a group of nativist miners to seize an Italian from the local jail and to hang him simply on the grounds that he was suspected of conspiring to assassinate a mine superintendent. Lynch mobs had been most flagrantly violent against African-Americans before, during, and after this year of the rise of anti-Catholic and anti-Semitic nativism. An instance of the latter was the hysteria that accompanied the murder charges against Leo Frank, a Jewish employer, whose employee Mary Phagan was found murdered in the factory managed by Frank. "Most aroused were the working-class, who saw in Frank a symbol of northern capitalist exploiting southern womanhood," wrote John Higham.[94] Without any strong evidence, the trial nevertheless rapidly concluded with a conviction. At the eleventh hour the governor commuted the death penalty, but it was not long before Tom Watson, the impassioned anti-Catholic and anti-Semitic nativist, stirred up hatred against the "parasitic race."[95] Frank was taken from prison by "the Knights of Mary Phagan," a lynch mob, and brought some 175 miles from the prison to the hometown of Mary Phagan, where they "butchered [him] almost in their own back yards."[96] The Tom Watsons, Otis Spurgeons, and the editors of *The Menace* had indeed reached the summit of their nativist hysteria in 1914.

The Supreme Council of that year reflected concern about this upsurge of anti-Catholicism. James Flaherty's report focused on the Goldstein lecture series: "our latest effort for God and Country . . . has been an unprecedented success and must certainly bring to full share of glory to the Order as it will bring its benefit to the country."[97] The State Deputy of Kentucky, Patrick Henry Callahan, submitted a resolution on the Good of the Order for the establishment of a Commission on Religious Prejudices which was passed the next day after some caucusing.[98] P. H. Callahan was appointed commission chairman and was in communication with John Reddin. Callahan was indebted to Dr. Washington Gladden for his inspiring article in *Harpers,* "Anti-Papal Panic," a conciliatory article that led him to propose the commission. Gladden, who was later considered one of "the Fathers of the American Social Gospel" for his blending of scripture and progressive reforms, had severely criticized the resurgence of anti-Catholicism and urged Protestants and Catholics to be committed to mutual understandings.[99] P. H. Callahan was the owner of the Louisville Varnish and a social reformer who worked with Father John A. Ryan to establish a profit-sharing scheme for his company, the Ryan-Callahan Plan.[100] Flaherty appointed five other commissioners: Joseph Scott, president of the Los Angeles Board of Education; Albert G. Bagley, State Deputy of British Columbia and president of the Vancouver Board of Trade; Thomas Lawler, State Deputy of Michigan and former state Attorney General; Joseph C. Pelletier, Supreme Advocate, 1907–1922, and District Attorney for Suffolk County, Massachusetts; Benedict Elder, lawyer, journalist, and a close friend of Callahan, who was the chairman's administrative assistant.

At its first meeting in January 1915, the commission decided that its goals would be: (1) to investigate the sources of religious prejudice; (2) to conduct an education campaign by informing and correcting editors and journalists who allowed religious prejudice to appear in their newspapers and "by seeking the cooperation of all fair minded citizens showing that the Catholic, as a citizen, is the equal of any other"; (3) to support the Department of Justice in its criminal libel suits against "bigoted publications" and to urge the Postmaster General to ban such publications.[101] The Canadian government had banned *The Menace* from its mail service in 1914, but the U.S. Postmaster did not proscribe this newspaper since he assumed that the Justice Department would prosecute it. Though not specifically a Fourth Degree project, the commission and P. H. Callahan worked in tandem with the Fourth Degree and John Reddin. It was Callahan's activist style of patriotism and his historical sense of citizenship that were responsible for the commission's strategy. Running along the side of the commission's stationery were quotations from George Washington's letter "To the Roman Catholics of the United States," from Cardinal William O'Connell of Boston, and from Leo XIII, each of whom extolled the virtues of patriotism, loyalty, and religious toleration. In a letter to President Woodrow Wilson in June 1916, Callahan wrote that the commission is "opposed to all manner of discord; we frown on religious prejudice and stand for religious liberty. . . . The fundamental idea governing this commission is to create sympathetic relations among citizens of all creeds, who will stand as a body for the betterment of public morals, the furtherance of social justice and the very best in citizenship."[102]

P. H. Callahan and Reddin agreed on the Fourth Degree's sponsorship of the lecture tours of Joseph Scott in 1916. The latter was well known for his skills as a sophisticated and persuasive speaker. The *Columbiad* published several of his addresses, which stressed the themes of "Catholic loyalty and love of America, and the hope and trust that all would respect religious liberty." Callahan reported on one lecture: "I think we can not be too emphatic in applauding the cooperation of the non-Catholic citizens in the cordiality of their response to the invitation of local committees to attend these [Scott] lectures."[103] There were accounts of tolerance in the 1916 report on the Commission on Religious Prejudices, as well as reports on activities of local committees related to abuses of toleration. A local Knight in Mississippi said that he had "often seen people going to church with the Bible in one hand and *The Menace* in the other. . . . *The Menace* was read from the pulpit in lieu of a sermon. . . ." He had heard of a school teacher reading "extracts from *The Menace* and such a paper to the Bible classes." Callahan reported a decrease in the circulation of the anti-Catholic press and considered *The Menace* and such papers as anti-Protestant as well as anti-Catholic because they masqueraded as Christian but were actually in the publication business solely for profit. He then cited instances of local prohibition of "professional" anti-Catholic speakers by non-Catholic proprietors of halls, such as the "Masonic Association in Trenton, New Jersey [that] closed their doors upon learning the kind of speech that was to be made." With an emphasis on civility, the commissioners' report urged the membership to evaluate textbooks used in public school, especially those in history "that are so decidedly biased and unfair, particularly to Catholics. . . . We urge our members to attend to this important matter and urge in a courteous, kindly way to assure that the K of C does not contradict the principle of tolerance."[104]

On August 11, 1916, in a letter to John Reddin, P. H. Callahan praised the Fourth Degree's sponsorship of the Scott tour and urged him to hold a mass meeting on Washington's Birthday on February 22, 1917, "similar to the one recently held in Davenport [Iowa, where the Supreme Council met and when the previous Commission Report was distributed]."[105] In anticipation of the 1917 gathering he suggested "an orchestra, some [patriotic] songs, and a non-Catholic presiding, however . . . a prominent Catholic, either Scott or myself," should speak for "about seventy-five minutes." The program "should be under the auspices of the Fourth Degree, and the Commission should not be mentioned." Callahan added that the commission "should pay all the expenses of those selected to do the speaking and for the rent of a hall, or rather, a theater, as in the past." Callahan expected the mass meeting to "certainly make copy for newspapers and magazines for quite a while to come."[106]

Callahan, who appears as a micro-manager, included a list of instructions for Reddin to follow: "we are going to prepare an address here for submission to the speakers, for it is necessary that they 'sell our goods' and not be distracted by something else. The seventy-five-minute addresses, sponsored by the Fourth Degree, should be broken down into five fifteen-minute topics: "George Washington," "The Founding and the Institutions of Our Country," "Catholic Allegiances," "Sympathetic Relationships Between Citizens of All Religions," "The Betterment of Public Morals," and the "Furtherance of Civic, Social, and Industrial Justice and Righteousness." Since the commission's *raison d'être* was to foster toleration among citizens of all religious denominations, Callahan sent Reddin a list of topics "to Leave Out."[107]

> Religious Prejudice, with the exception of touching upon . . .
> allegiance. The "fake oath" and any reference in any way to it.
> "*The Menace*," the polluting of the mail.
> All personal messages and monologues.
> The faults of your neighbor.
> "Knocking" is not good salesmanship;
> The past glories of the Church, because she is not dead.[108]

The final list of twenty-four speakers assigned them to cities from Jacksonville to Boston, from New Orleans to St. Paul, from Los Angeles to Seattle. The speakers included four senators, four governors, four judges, three members of the Commission on Religious Prejudices (including Callahan), and various dignitaries such as Charles J. Bonaparte, Catholic Secretary of the Navy in the Theodore Roosevelt administration.[109] With such detailed plans, including prepared copies of speeches, this celebration of Catholic patriotism and American citizenship was very significant, particularly as the United States entered the war less than two months later, in March 1917.[110]

The war prompted the Commission on Religious Prejudices to decide to terminate its work in June of 1917, the end of the fraternal year. However, in his final report, Callahan noted the distinction between individual and social prejudice and took credit for the Commission's contribution to the decline of the anti-Catholic movement, as indicated by the drop in anti-Catholic newspapers from sixty to two or three. He attributed its success to its well-thought-out strategy of removing the discourse of public religion from the heated arena of passion and bitter invective to the dignified realm of "sane, calm, open discussion." The report of 1917 concluded "that the war will kill bigotry. The personal preferences and dislikes of religion will continue to be expressed, this is nothing but part of intellectual discussion. But the jealousies, enmities, bitterness and hate, wholesale inventions and studied falsehood, agitated feelings of anxiety, fear and suspicion born of dark thoughts and rumors, will be reduced to quiescence."[111]

SUPREME MASTERS OF THE FOURTH DEGREE*

John A. Reddin
1920–1940

Timothy P. Galvin
1941–1945

William J. Mulligan
1945–1965

Virgil C. Dechant
1966–1967

*Unless otherwise designated, all illustrations are courtesy of the Archives and the Department of Photo Archives of the Knights of Columbus.

Frank C. McGillen
1967–1970

Daniel L. McCormack
1970–1983

Alfred N. Nicolas
1983–1987

Hilary F. Schmittzehe
1987–1991

Darrell W. Beck
1991–1996

Charles H. Foos
1996–2000

Nestor Barber
2000–

February 22, 1900, New York, Lenox Lyceum. Leadership of the First Grand Exemplification of the Fourth Degree. 1,100 Knights experienced the lessons of Catholic historical memory and the significance of American patriotism and citizenship.

LECTURERS ON PATRIOTISM AND ANTISOCIALISM, 1910–1930

Joseph Scott, First State Deputy of California, member Commission on Religious Prejudices, and a frequent speaker on the virtues of patriotism and the links between anti-Catholicism and socialism.

Peter W. Collins, General Secretary of the Brotherhood of Electrical Workers, AFL, and an ardent opponent of radicalism and anti-Catholicism.

David Goldstein, convert to Catholicism in 1905; once active in Socialist Labor Party, he joined the AFL, well known as lecturer on Catholicity, patriotism, and antisocialism.

The Ku Klux Klan
or
The Knights of Columbus Klan
BY ARTHUR H. BELL

A patriotic and literary friend of the Protestant cause has written this new pamphlet. It is without question the greatest defense of our Protestant fraternal orders and the greatest unmasking of the Papal church that has been written in this country in half a century. As a defense of the K. K. K. and as an exposure of the K. of C., it is an education and an inspiration.

To know the whole truth about the Pope's Knights of Mob and Murder, his Militia of Christ, his pliant tools who have bound themselves together in secret, unholy compact to destroy our free American Public School system, our constitution and its guarantees, to prevent as far as laws within their power the circulation and use of the Holy Bible, read carefully every line in this soul stirring pamphlet.

To know the whole truth of the K. K. K., a great fraternity, whose members have bound themselves to shield the sanctity of home and the chastity of womanhood and to conserve, protect and maintain the distinctive institutions, rights, privileges, principles, traditions and ideals of pure Americanism, read this pamphlet.

Send your orders by return mail for the strongest and most fearless defense of Protestant Christianity and our free American institutions that has been written for half a century. Help us put this pamphlet in the hands of every Mason, Odd Fellow, Knight of Pythias, Klansman and fraternalist of every Protestant American organization just as rapidly as possible. Price 10c; three for 25c; seven for 50c; fifteen for $1.00; 100 for $5.00.

Address The Rail Splitter Milan Ill.

In the tribal twenties, KKK propaganda projected the Klan as 100-percent American and Christian, dedicated to exposing the Knights of Columbus as the War Department of the Vatican. Article in *The Rail Splitter.*

THE COILS ARE TIGHTENING

This cartoon calls all "patriots" to defend the public school, the "icon" of republican virtue, in opposition to parochial schools, symbolic of "Catholic disloyalty" to American democracy and supportive of "papal imperialism." Copy is from *Roman Oaths and Papal Curses,* Rail Splitter Press, Milan, Illinois.

This cartoon, which depicts the light of liberty threatened by the darkness of "popery," was a warning against Catholics who feigned patriotism to advance "papal power." Cartoon by Wm. Lloyd Clark, Rail Splitter Press.

The *Menace,* which distributed the Fourth Degree bogus oath, is represented as the defender of American liberty against two Fourth Degree Knights in formal garb, frustrated in their effort to undermine the spirit of American democracy. From *Menace Cartoons: Fun and Facts,* compiled by Bruce Malcolm Phelps, Aurora, Missouri. The Menace Publishing Company, 1941.

A postcard, published by William Lloyd Clark, Milan, Illinois, depicts Pope Pius X allied with Ireland against American liberty, the public schools, and the life of the American Republic.

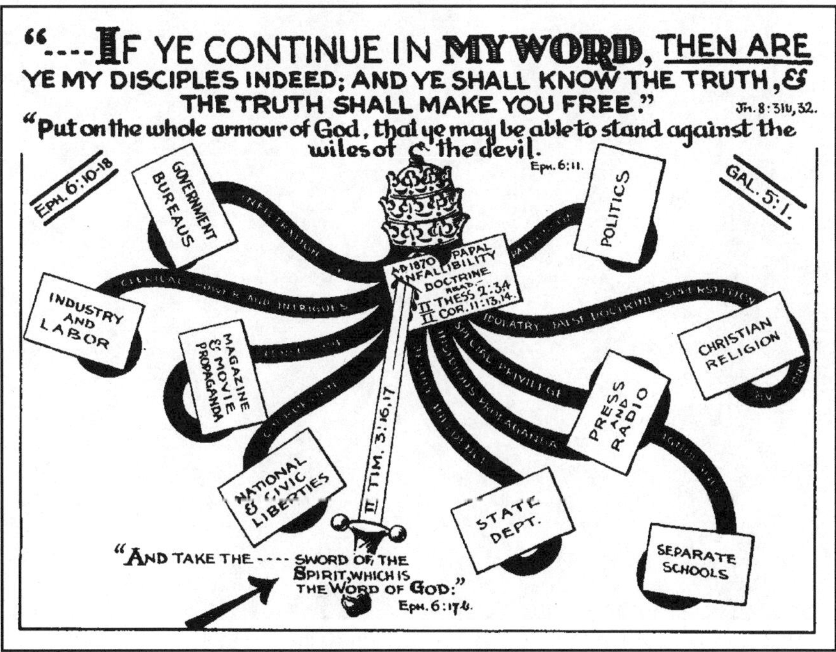

From the periodical *The Converted Catholic,* April 1947. Courtesy, The Archives of the University of Notre Dame.

October 1940. Columbus Day parade, Cleveland, Ohio.

April 27, 1947. The Color Corps of Archbishop Ryan Assembly drills following a Fourth Degree Exemplification at the Benjamin Franklin Hotel in Philadelphia, Pennsylvania.

April 1957. Banquet following Exemplification of the Fourth Degree. Philadelphia, Pennsylvania.

March 31, 1957. Cardinal Francis Spellman approaches the reviewing stand at the dedication of the statue of Knights of Columbus founder Fr. Michael J. McGivney, located in Waterbury, Connecticut. Credit: Life Magazine/Walter Sanders (this photo did not appear in the 5/57 issue).

May 30, 1954. Senator John F. Kennedy, member of Bunker Hill Council #62, takes part in the Exemplification of the Fourth Degree for 235 candidates. The class was named for James L. Connelly, Bishop of Fall River, Massachusetts, also a candidate. At left is Bishop Connelly, Master John W. McDevitt, later Supreme Knight, and Senator Kennedy.

October 11, 1961. Supreme Knight Luke E. Hart presents President John F. Kennedy with a framed copy of the Pledge of Allegiance containing the words "Under God," which the Knights were instrumental in having added to the text during the Eisenhower administration.

August 17, 1971. A Fourth Degree honor guard flanks Cardinal Terence Cooke, Archbishop of New York, as he prepares for the opening Mass at the annual Supreme Council meeting.

November 3, 1984. An honor guard of Fourth Degree Knights of Columbus salutes as Supreme Knight Virgil Dechant visits the monument of patriot Manuel Colayco, erected by Paway City Council 4267 in Metro Manila, Philippines. The ceremony took place during an eleven-day tour of the Philippines.

Fall 1992. Auxiliary Bishop Robert Clune of Toronto, during dedication ceremonies at the Father Michael J. McGivney High School in Markham, Ontario, outside Toronto.

Baltimore, October 7, 1995. Fourth Degree Knights provided an honor guard for the pope during his visit to Baltimore following his visit and Mass in New York City and surrounding areas. Shown with the pope is Vice Supreme Master Francis J. Loughney (center) of Calvert Province and Edgar D. Haynes, Master of the Maryland District.

April 2000. Supreme Master Charles Foos and Supreme Secretary Carl Anderson place a wreath at the Tomb of the Unknown in Arlington National Cemetery.

April 2000. Over 1,000 Fourth Degree Knights formed the honor guard at the pilgrimage Mass held at the Basilica of the National Shrine of the Immaculate Conception, which was part of the celebration of the one hundredth anniversary of the Fourth Degree.

Fourth Degree Patriot Award. Presented to the three assemblies that sponsored the top patriotic programs. The award illustrates the central role of the Fourth Degree emblem as a symbol of Catholic patriotism. The triad emblem of the Fourth Degree features the dove, the cross, and the globe. The dove—classic symbol of the Holy Spirit and peace—is shown hovering over the orb of the earth (globe). Both are mounted on a variation of the Crusader's cross. In Italian Christopher Columbus translates as Christ-bearing dove.

3

War and the Tribal Twenties

I

During World War I the Knights of Columbus, as well as Protestant and Jewish welfare groups—the Young Men's Christian Association, the Salvation Army, the Jewish Welfare Committee—were committed to serving the social and religious needs of soldiers and sailors both at home and abroad. Though there was some tension between the Young Men's Christian Association and the Knights of Columbus, there was general amity among the denominations in the war effort. However, there continued to be right-wing Protestant groups who perceived the Catholic presence in the war as more evidence of the advance of the "tyrant on the Tiber" into American life. The early postwar period entailed a revival of anti-Catholicism, aggravated by economic depression and increased immigration. The Knights of Columbus antidefamation program was energized by the resurgence of bigotry and in the process the Order became a principal opponent of the immigrant restrictions and historical revisionism.[1]

Prohibition, mandated by the Eighteenth Amendment, precipitated a head-on collision between mounting lawlessness, symbolized by gangster bootleggers and speakeasies, and a new drive for social conformity. "Riding the wave of 100 percent Americanism 'the Drys' identified their crusade to regulate behavior with the preservation of the American way of life."[2] In opposition were "the Wets," stereotyped as organized gangsters by nativists and other guardians of prohibition. Some of the educated class embraced the racialism of those eugenicists and social scientists who, in the words of Higham, "spread [their doctrines] downward from patrician circles . . . [and] it blended with the cruder form of Anglo-Saxon nativism that was pushing upward from the grass roots of the South and West."[3] In a new garb of nativism was the white robe of the Ku Klux Klan allied with nativist Protestant preachers; both groups were armed with the Fourth Degree bogus oath.

The Fourth Degree, as well as the entire Order, marshaled its forces against these new forms of anti-Catholicism. Once again, the patriotism of the degree was in conflict with opposing forms of historical memories. However, the membership never descended to the violent rhetoric of its detractors, nor did it manifest any air of victimization. Instead, it proffered the Catholic "foundation stories," those historical memories and symbols that underscored the patriotism vital to self-government in a republic. During the war, the nativists had masqueraded as vigilant patriots determined to root out such hyphenated immigrants as German-Americans and Italian-Americans, along with others whose loyalties were suspect. As one historian of nativism remarked, "What is clear is that the war unleashed much more aggressive demands for cultural conformity, aimed indiscriminately at individuals and groups that were in the eyes of the Americanizers in any way 'foreign.'"[4]

II

"He kept us out of war" was the 1916 campaign slogan of Woodrow Wilson's victory in November. Less than six months later, on April 2, 1917, the president spoke before Congress seeking a declaration of war against Germany. Allied propaganda, the generally pro-British attitude of business interests, the revival of German submarine warfare—particularly the sinking of the passenger ship *Lusitania*—and increasing anti-German public sentiment led the nation to the brink of war; the accumulation of other alleged national humiliations pushed the nation beyond the brink. The declaration of war was supported by leaders of Protestant, Catholic, and Jewish groups. The National Council of Churches affirmed: "The war for righteousness will be won. Let the Church do her part." One Protestant leader in the nation's capital referred to the war as "a crusade. The greatest in history—the holiest. It is in the profoundest and truest sense a Holy War."[5] Cardinal James Gibbons's response to Wilson's war message underscored the responsibility of "every American citizen to do his duty, and uphold the hands of the President and the Legislative department in the solemn obligation that confronted us. . . . It behooves all of us, therefore, to pray that the Lord of Hosts may inspire the national legislature and Executives to frame such laws in the present crisis as will redound to the glory of our country, to righteousness of conduct and to the permanent place of the nations of the world."[6]

Gibbons wrote a letter to Wilson on behalf of the archbishops (who were to meet ten days later) assuring him that "he could count on the Catholic citizens for their loyalty and support in the war effort."[7] Catholic support—if not the theology—of the war effort was so overwhelming that of 3,989 conscientious objectors registered only four were Catholics.[8] Wilson responded to Gibbons a week later: "The very remarkable resolution [of the archbishops] warms my heart and makes me proud indeed that men of such large influence should act in so large a sense of patriotism and so admirable spirit of devotion to our common country."[9] The day before Gibbons's letter on behalf of the archbishops, Supreme Knight James Flaherty wrote to President Wilson pledging the "devotion of 400,000 members of the Order in this country to our Republic and the Congress of this nation in their determination to protect its honor and its ideals of humanity and right."[10] In a letter dated May 23, Flaherty told Wilson of the proposal "to establish centers for the large body of men who will be concentrated in mobilization camps. These will be for the recreation and spirituality not only of members of the Order or Catholics, but for all others, regardless of creed."[11] Eventually the Order was recognized both by governmental agencies and the archbishops to establish Catholic social and recreation centers throughout the various theaters of war.

The precedent for this work was the social-center programs for Army units stationed along the Mexican border as a deterrent to further raids by Pancho Villa in 1916. The YMCA had been involved in such work for years with 212 recreation centers and 376 secretaries in the border camps. Though the K. of C. centers along the border were intended to provide social service for Catholics and others "regardless of creed or color," they were also used as makeshift chapels for Sunday masses. Quite modest and staffed by volunteers, the K. of C. centers were amateur endeavors in contrast to the organized YMCA efforts.[12] However, during World War I the K. of C. Huts program was more professional and included chaplains to work in tandem with the secretaries.

P. H. Callahan, well known in the Democratic Party and chairman of the

Order's Commission on Religious Prejudices, was the obvious choice to head the War Activities Committee. This committee reported to the administrative committee of the National Catholic War Council chaired by Bishop Peter J. Muldoon of Rockford, Illinois, a Fourth Degree Knight and chaplain of the Illinois State Council of the Knights of Columbus. Muldoon was committed to the Order's relative independence in administering the Huts program because the government had recognized the Order as "standing for the Catholics of this country." He concluded with a pastoral commission for the Knights' war efforts:

> [You] are the most important body of Catholic laymen that has ever existed in this country. . . . The Catholic Church is looking to you to make a record, you Grand Knights of the Gospel of Jesus. . . . The Knights of Columbus are doing a sacred work, a truly priestly work . . . you are one in Christ and in his prayer. You have behind you a united Catholic people. Therefore, go forth for Jesus Christ and for the Glory of the Church.[13]

In his 1918 report to the Supreme Assembly, John Reddin told the Fourth Degree members that following Flaherty's first letter to Wilson he had informed the president of the "principle of patriotism underlying this degree and that every Fourth Degree Knight of Columbus in the United States did at the time of his initiation swear allegiance to our constitution and flag and that this loyal body of American citizens was at his command ready to serve our country in any capacity he might appoint, ready to make any sacrifice that might be called for in defense of our common country so that human liberty and American ideals may endure." Reddin surmised that most of the K. of C. secretaries in the Huts program were members of the Fourth Degree and were "imbued with the most unselfish motives and with the high principles inculcated by this degree."[14]

Two special meetings of the Supreme Assembly resulted in several programs associated with the War Activities Committee: a series of choral concerts for the entertainment of soldiers and sailors; a two-thousand-dollar grant to the Canadian Huts program; five thousand dollars appropriated principally for athletic projects for the troops; a complete set of the *Catholic Encyclopedia* (K. of C. edition) sent to each of the thirty-nine army and navy installations in the United States. With only about fifteen thousand Fourth Degree members, Reddin's programs took the form of subsidies rather than the direct-action involvement of the Third Degree.[15] The Order's war work entailed several problems and was criticized by a group of Catholic leaders from New York who wished to participate in managing the Catholic effort. The YMCA challenged the Order's policy of providing all food and other materials free; a solution was achieved by mutual agreement that each group administer its own program. The Masons were opposed to the government's putative partiality for one particular fraternal order; the government defended its position as being the choice of a Catholic organization rather than of a fraternal society.[16]

By the time of the armistice in November 1918, the K. of C. had raised fourteen million dollars and was a participant in a forty-million dollar campaign; in all, two thousand K. of C. secretaries served in the Huts program, while the balance of its funds went to its postwar reconstruction programs, including a law school (later incorporated into The Catholic University of America), a correspondence school, and an employment bureau. The Knights of Columbus members represented 20 percent of the eleven thousand civilian volunteers.[17]

In December 1918, Father John F. Noll, founder and editor of *Our Sunday Visitor*, wrote a form letter to all the archbishops in the country. In his letter to Archbishop George Mundelein, Noll suggested that since there was a rise of anti-Catholicism among the Masons and the "Rationalistic and Socialistic forces behind the whole anti-Catholic movement," the Knights of Columbus "should internationalize" in order to be in the vanguard of a Catholic defense of civilization and "become stronger than international Masonry. The Knights of Columbus should launch this movement now before the troops are demobilized and the Catholic civilian personnel had the opportunity to act." Though there is no evidence that Archbishop Mundelein responded to this letter and though the Knights did not internationalize, Noll was prescient in his concluding proposal in the form of a question. "Does it not seem that the organization known as the National Catholic War Council . . . should now become a National Catholic Advisory Council for the unification of thought and action in this country?"[18]

The war encouraged the principles of the modern organization of industry and the centralization of several spheres of public and private interests that had been developing at the turn of the century. In the words of historian Elizabeth McKeown,

> America's declaration of war transformed both the country and the Catholic Church. Two and a half million men were mobilized, millions of women provided social and industrial war work and the suddenly enlarged federal government imposed controls on labor, transportation, and industry. Crisis driven adrenaline produced a feverish quality in public life and American Catholics joined up.[19]

Eventually the bishops under the leadership of Cardinal Gibbons, and based on the effective administrative organization of the war council, approved the establishment of the National Catholic Welfare Council in 1919 (after 1922, "Conference"), the predecessor of the present-day National Conference of Catholic Bishops and the United States Catholic Conference. Bishop Muldoon and Father John J. Burke, C.S.P., had been strong advocates of a permanent national organization. This "transdiocesan source of identity and leadership" was necessary to provide unified education and public policy for the local church as well as to function as a lobbyist for Catholic welfare. Without an official Catholic presence in the nation's capital, stated John Burke, "our opponents and the opponents of our church" would have a clear field to affect "religious and moral interests."[20] Cardinal Gibbons noted that without the NCWC Catholic lay groups could individually influence public policy and play a vital role but without the direction of the hierarchy. Eventually, an administrative board of seven bishops became the voice of the hierarchy and directed the staff, with leadership lodged in a general secretary who was John J. Burke from 1919 until his death in 1936. Though the K. of C. was very supportive of many programs of the bishops, the permanent establishment of the NCWC prevented the Order from playing a dominant role among the laity in World War II as it had in World War I. Then it was a society of organized Catholics able to respond to any crisis. Since 1919 the paramount institution capable of organizing many groups of Catholics, particularly in World War II, was the NCWC. However, the Order and the NCWC together defended the church against its enemies in the tribal conflicts of the decade. For this struggle against the renewed forces of nativism and anti-Catholicism, the Order had a total membership of nearly eight hundred thousand by 1923. This was largely the result of the four hundred thousand Catholic veterans who joined because of the appeal of the Knights' hospitality and their postwar education programs.[21]

At the Peace Convention of the Supreme Council, held in Buffalo in the summer of 1919, the Order celebrated its ties with France by voting to offer to the town of Metz an equestrian statue of Lafayette. It was in Metz that the French general had decided to join the American War for Independence; Marshal Ferdinand Foch had attended the Jesuit college in the city; and General John J. Pershing was of Alsatian heritage. Supreme Master John Reddin, one of the 235 Knights on the tour to Metz and Rome, recorded the patriotic character of this journey in his diary. The unveiling of the statue was preceded by a solemn high mass at the cathedral with thousands present for the occasion. Inscribed on the pedestal of the Lafayette statue were several tributes: General Pershing's celebrated proclamation, "Lafayette, we are here . . ."; Woodrow Wilson's war address to Congress; Marshal Foch's remark that through his nation's military "genius" "Prussianism" had been defeated.[22]

Fifteen days later, the K. of C. pilgrims were honored with a private audience by Pope Benedict XV. Dressed in formal wear closely resembling the official garb of the Fourth Degree, the Knights represented American Catholic devotion to the Holy See. Supreme Knight James Flaherty declared, "All the blessings of modern civilization we owe to the Church, which has the secret of peace for turmoil and unrest."[23] The principal outcome of the visit was the establishment of K. of C. recreation centers in Rome at the Pope's request to combat Protestant proselytization "through the pleasure of sports."[24] In 1870 Italy's seizure of Rome, the last outpost of the temporal power of the papacy, and subsequent constitutional guarantees of religious toleration led several Protestant denominations to establish churches in Rome. One church's cornerstone stated that it was dedicated "on the 10th of September, 1895, the twenty-fifth anniversary of the downfall of Papal power."[25]

Edward Hearn, who had been the K. of C. representative in Paris during and after the war, became the head of the K. of C. recreation centers until 1931, when the engineer-architect Enrico Galeazzi became director. Hearn remarked that the "Methodists were allied with an anti-clerical element" and were as "savage in their attacks upon the Pope and the Church as ever was Tom Watson."[26] The Knights' presence in Rome has expanded over the years to include funding television links with communication satellites, supporting the charities of the pope, helping restore the facade and other areas of St. Peter's Basilica. These and many other programs were illustrative of the Knights' continuing devotion to the Holy See. Since most of the leaders of the Order were also members of the Fourth Degree, this pilgrimage symbolized the Catholic dimension of their patriotic loyalty and the American dimension of their Catholic loyalty.

Shortly before the journey to Metz and Rome, a Knight from New Jersey sent a recently circulated copy of the "bogus oath" to Joseph Tumulty, which "had been widely distributed to many of the summer colony and is causing some little excitement." He appears to have been unaware of the group that had distributed the "oath," but it was an abbreviated copy of that printed in the *Congressional Record* of February 15, 1913 (the Bonniwell case). The distributors, H. S. Burmell's Universal News Depot, experienced a significant increase in readership in 1920 when the Supreme Master of the Fourth Degree was depicted as the leader of "the papist militia" because of his audience with the pope in 1920.[27]

The bogus oath and other expressions of anti–K. of C. animus will be discussed later in this chapter. But a more subtle form of nativism, masked by science, was popularized by the proponents of 100-percent Americanism and opponents of immigrants, whose loyalty was suspect. On the other hand, progressive reformers such as Jane Addams and other cosmopolitan groups sponsored settlement houses dedicated to helping immigrants assimilate by affirming their European heritage. When the war came, the nationalist Americanizers engaged in a crusade against immigrants. John Higham captured the spirit of those who "opened a frontal assault on the foreign influence in American life. They were about to stampede immigrants into citizenship, into adoption of the English language and into unquestioning reverence for existing American institutions."[28]

The tempo of Americanization movements accelerated during and after the war, and anti-German propaganda reached such a peak that innocent German-Americans were imprisoned on the flimsiest sign of "disloyalty," such as not flying the American flag. The American Protective Association, which had about 350,000 members, formed a vigilante group assisting the U.S. Justice Department in its campaign against treason. The department imprisoned nearly 6,500 Germans during the war. In 1917 Dr. Karl Muck was interned even though he was the conductor of the Boston Symphony Orchestra; he was only one of the many German artists, musicians, and teachers who were arrested. It was said that Muck refused to play the national anthem, and he and his orchestra were barred from appearing in Baltimore, the home of the "Star-Spangled Banner."[29] After the armistice he and his wife were deported to Germany. Theodore Roosevelt was a major proponent of deporting those who were not "100 percent" American. Cecilia Elizabeth O'Leary describes the effect of these internments and deportations. "By the war's end, the German-American community lay in shambles; German language presses . . . had suffered irreversible losses. . . . Americanizers had effectively eradicated German American culture, forcing the disappearance of German-Americans as a publicly identifiable group."[30] The forces of wartime anti-Germanism were linked with the campaign against socialists and Communists and followed the model of the suppression of Eugene Debs's IWW. This spirit permeated the Justice Department led by A. Mitchell Palmer, who without regard for the First Amendment's free-speech clause, prosecuted "traitors" with the threat of jail and deportation.

The exclusivist language of patriotism drew upon the militant ideology of anti-Catholicism, anti-Semitism, and racism fostered by the KKK. The immigrant restrictionists employed the language of science and eugenics in their rationale for excluding those "races" presumed to be not assimilable by the dominant "Anglo-Saxons." The precipitous rise in immigration after the war (430,000 by June of 1920) led to the passage of an emergency restriction law, commonly called the "three-percent measure," in June of 1920. The act limited the number of immigrants to 3 percent of those living in the country in 1910. The 1924 law reduced the percentage to 2 percent of those immigrants living in America and pushed the year back to 1890.[31]

After the passage of the 1920 law, the Fourth Degree of the Knights of Columbus established its Historical Commission. Supreme Master John H. Reddin, influenced by Edward F. McSweeney, achieved a consensus for the commission. At the Supreme Council Assembly meeting in 1921, Edward McSweeney (b. 1864), became chairman of the commission. A native of Marlboro, Massachusetts, he was a leader in Catholic temperance and literary societies and had been the town auditor for three years. As a result of successful fund-raising and other political efforts, Massachusetts Democrat Grover Cleveland sought his help as a publicist in his campaign of 1892. Because of Cleveland's victory McSweeney was appointed to the office of Assistant Immigration Commissioner in New York, a position he held until he was replaced by an appointee of Theodore Roosevelt. He returned to Massachusetts politics and became editor of the *Boston Traveler*. But it was as a dedicated leader of the Friends of Irish Freedom (FOIF) that he became most renowned for his opposition to the campaign to form a British-American alliance based on a common "Anglo-Saxonism."[32]

Immediately prior to the Easter Rebellion (1916), the FOIF became the dominant voice of Irish-American nationalism; Lawrence McCaffrey has written that it was the "public face of the small, secret Clan Na Gael" committed to "physical force republicanism."[33] The large FOIF membership—270,000 at its peak—mustered popular support for the Easter week casualities and later for the Irish Republican Army (IRA). During the 1919–1921 Anglo-Irish War, the FOIF supplied ammunition to the IRA. In the struggle between Michael Collins, who accepted a non-Ulster settlement, and Eamon de Valera, who refused to compromise, the FOIF, under Judge Daniel Cohalen, sided with Collins. Edward F. McSweeney was a close confidant of Cohalen, and he was on the FOIF speakers' circuit. When McSweeney died, a eulogy by Cohalen was published in the *Journal of the Irish Historical Society*.[34]

McSweeney led the assault on the English Coalition, headquartered in Boston, for its support of Ulster's separation from an independent Ireland. What was called "Anglo-Saxonism" was a powerful force in immigration restrictions of the eastern and southern European people, that is, the "weaker races." In a letter to the national secretary of the Friends of Irish Freedom, McSweeney described the "progress of the British Propaganda movement." After the war "the army of foreign propagandists were working unchecked. The elementary [school] text-books had already been poisoned [by pro-British historians]." He noted that the first check on their influence came from the Supreme Advocate of the Knights of Columbus, Joseph Pelletier, in his criticism of a pamphlet published by the YMCA and the United States government extolling the war activities of the YMCA and "glorifying the valor and success of England's arms." Moreover, the pamphlet did not refer to the war work of the K. of C. or the Salvation Army. Pelletier initiated the "first protest" to this pamphlet and urged the Secretary of War, Newton Baker, to stop "further issues of this kind."[35]

McSweeney considered two of his own pamphlets, *America First* and *De-Americanizing Young America,* as "going directly to the problem." Both were published by the Friends of Irish Freedom. One of these pamphlets, with a wordplay on the attack against those with divided loyalties, was entitled *The Super-Hyphenate: The Anglo-Saxon American.* Each of these pamphlets was a broadside against the Anglo-Saxonists and the historical revisionists who were deemphasizing the American Revolution as a war against British imperialism by maintaining that it was merely a family quarrel among Anglo-Saxons. True American patriotism for McSweeney was represented by the multiethnic character of the Revolution and the cosmopolitan Americanism responsible for such foundational documents as the Declaration of Independence, the Constitution, and the Bill of Rights, and embodied in the War of 1812. Hence, the pamphlet *America First,* promoted the primacy of the United States and protested against forging any entangling bonds with England. *De-Americanizing Young America* followed the same path of exposing historical inaccuracy by criticizing the new historians who debunked patriotism and the idealism of republicanism and extolled an economic interpretation of American history that disparaged the courage of the founding fathers.

To substantiate the dominance of the British point of view in high school textbooks, McSweeney quoted George Haven Putnam, the executive secretary of the Society to Promote American-British Union and also president of the American Book Sellers of North America:

> The influence of the British elements in our population has proved sufficiently strong to enable the English Americans to bring under control and weld into a nation . . . the great medley of racial factors that make up the population of the continent . . . text books are now being prepared which will represent a just historical account of the events of 1775–83, 1812–1815, and 1861–65.[36]

According to McSweeney, the ultimate sources of these "sinister influences" were the Anglo-Saxon revisionists of the mid-1890s who founded the Rhodes Scholarships and the Carnegie Foundation. Both promoted such propaganda endeavors as the Anglo-Saxon myth which "engendered" immigrant restrictionism.[37] It was to oppose these endeavors that the Fourth Degree Historical Commission was founded. Edward McSweeney told the financial secretary of the Friends of Irish Freedom that the Fourth Degree Historical Commission gave the movement against Anglo-Saxonism "real-standing." He noted that other patriotic societies, such as the Sons of the American Revolution and the American Legion were allies in the worthy cause of American opposition to Great Britain and its imperialist policy.[38] George Haven Putnam, the publicist of American-British Unity, not only denigrated the multiculturalism of McSweeney and his allies; he was also a promoter of the anti-Semitic document "The Protocols of the Elders of Zion." Originating with the czarist secret police at the beginning of the twentieth century, the "Protocols" revealed "a conspiratorial plan for establishing Jewish world dictatorship. Purportedly drawn up by the leaders of world Jewry, the plan involved financial monopoly, chaos, war, and revolution."[39] The "Protocols" were used to explain the Bolshevik revolution of October 1917. The bogus document surfaced in the United States in 1918, but it was George Haven Putnam who, in *The Cause of World Unrest,* published for American readers a polemical piece based on the "Protocols." Henry Ford, who became obsessed with Jewish financial conspiracies, published the "Protocols" in his periodical, the *Dearborn Independent.*[40] By the time the anti-Semitic document had been incorporated into such nativist rhetoric, McSweeney was prompted to establish the Historical Commission. It was not coincidental that later the commission published *The Contribution of the Jews in the Making of America.*

The dominance of McSweeney in the foundation and development of the Historical Commission is so evident that it is obvious his publications were highly respected by Reddin and Flaherty. His chairmanship of the commission provided McSweeney with an international forum to broadcast his impassioned views on the dangers of immigrant restrictionism and on the significance of the contributions of non-British peoples to the making of America. In his resolution at the Supreme Assembly of the Fourth Degree, John Reddin stated that the purpose of the Commission "was to combat propaganda . . . inundating our country [attempting to undermine] the spirit of American nationalism and solidarity by obscuring and falsifying the records of the national history," particularly in textbooks aimed at "erasing from the students' minds" the real significance of the documents and movements leading to independence in 1776. The commission was charged "to investigate the facts of history, to correct historical errors and omissions, to amplify and preserve our national history, to exalt and perpetuate American ideals, and to combat anti-American propaganda by means of pamphlets, each to be complete and authoritative in itself, and by other means and methods as shall be approved by the Supreme Assembly."[41]

In a letter to Judge Daniel Cohalen, president of the Friends of Irish Freedom, Edward McSweeney reported on the enthusiastic response to the Historical Commission at the 1921 Supreme Council meeting in San Francisco. "The Convention was a huge success as far as my matter was concerned." He was pleased that the meeting was in San Francisco far from the controversies over the cause for a free Ireland, as well as over opposition to the League of Nations because of its exclusion of the Irish Republic. There was "probably a proper skepticism" about his chairmanship of the commission, particularly "accentuated by the almost open distrust of the Canadian delegates with some pro-British sympathetics who in some way, all had accurate knowledge of my connection with the Irish movement." With the support of Archbishop Edward J. Hanna and through his own rhetorical powers, McSweeney convinced the delegates: "those who had been distant, became cordial. Even the Canadians accepted and congratulated [me]."[42] Some weeks later, McSweeney told Cohalen about the prospects of the commission:

> . . . as you can imagine I am reasonably busy getting the "agenda" ready. It is not as if we are meeting all of one mind. Some of the members of the Commission are the "academic" type, wait a few years and see what happens to that type, and you can see that is not possible. Others are afraid that we must not do anything that will indicate a bias against England, and . . . I am convinced every man on the Commission is all right, if he is handled right; it is my job to see that the program is so comprehensive that it will go across.[43]

The members of the commission were well-known Catholic professors and independent scholars: Admiral William S. Benson, former Chief of Naval Operations, president of the National Council of Catholic Men, incorporated into the NCWC, and a convert to Catholicism; Charles H. McCarthy, Ph.D., occupant of the K. of C. chair in American History at the Catholic University of America; George Hermann Derry, Ph.D., professor of political economy at Union College, Schenectady, New York, and a prominent Catholic lecturer; and Maurice Francis Egan, former U.S. ambassador to Denmark and co-author of *The History of the Knights of Columbus in Peace and War,* an authorized two-volume history of the Order published in 1920. Additional appointments were made later that year: Henry Jones Ford, Ph.D., a convert to Catholicism and a professor of political science at Princeton; Harris Taylor, Ph.D., an authority on American and English constitutional law and former ambassador to Spain; and Joseph Dunn, Ph.D., occupant of the chair in Celtic languages and literature at Catholic University.[44]

A million-dollar subsidy from the Supreme Council was the basis for the name change from "Fourth Degree" to "Knights of Columbus" Commission, an acknowledgment of the former's financial dependence on the Order's general funds. McSweeney designed an ambitious and comprehensive program for awarding cash grants in six categories: allocation for publication of books and pamphlets "for the best studies, based as far as practicable on original research in the fields of American History," with the authors receiving a $2,500 award; $1000 to a school administrator or teacher for the best curriculum in history; for the best proposal from anyone in the general public interested in social sciences and biography; for students who have access to documents in the Western Hemisphere; for students with access to documents overseas; and for students in colleges in the United States. In a press release after the first meeting of the commission, its purpose was amplified. "The Knights of Columbus do not intend to rewrite American history. What the organization has in mind is to produce authoritative chapters on phases and personalities in America that have been insufficiently treated and even obscured and totally neglected in certain textbooks." The release included John Reddin's cautious statement that the commission was not to cause controversy but to promote "scholarly research" according to the "documentary evidence."[45]

The two historians awarded $3,000 each were Samuel Flagg Bemis for his book *Jay's Treaty: A Study in Commerce and Diplomacy,* and Alan

Nevins for his book *The American States During and after the Revolution.* Published by Macmillan as the first volume in the Knights of Columbus Historical Series, Bemis's book interpreted Jay's treaty not as a capitulation to British interests but, because it kept the United States out of the war with revolutionary France, as a document that allowed the young American republic "to develop in population and resources and above all a consciousness of nationality that eventually led to a more effective resistance to the British in 1812 than was possible in 1794.[46] *The American States During and After the Revolution* (like Bemis's book, submitted with a pseudonym to assure objectivity among the judges) was also representative of the Historical Commission's goals. Nevins provided a detailed summary of the exceptional character of the American Revolution as not simply a war for independence. An editor of the *New York Post* when he wrote the book, Nevins eventually entered academia, where his works were well received by specialists as well as by general readers.

Other sponsored works were in varying degrees related to McSweeney's interests as well as those of the commission. *The Monroe Doctrine* by Thomas A. Mahoney (McSweeney's son-in-law and Joseph Pelletier's Assistant District Attorney in Suffolk County) placed the doctrine in the context of the American Revolution and the diplomacy of the young republic. Mengchien Bau's *The Open Door in Relation to China* was, according to McSweeney, like Admiral Benson's book, *The Merchant Marine,* another K. of C. work, representative of the commission's interest in the principles of open trade and commerce and their relationship to America's growing economic power in world markets. Even more significant than the economic and diplomatic studies was the publication directly aimed at demythologizing the Anglo-Saxon connections that allegedly brought England and the United States into a cultural alliance. The pamphlet *Charters of Liberty* traced the origins and development of liberty to the early Christian era rather than to the heritage of the Magna Carta.[47] Its author, the former Episcopal bishop of Delaware and a convert to Catholicism, Frederick Kinsman, went back to the early church fathers as the sources of faith and culture. Edward McSweeney was so enamored of Charles Edward Russell's *Origins of the Propaganda Movement* that he had it printed "for the use of the delegates to the Knights of Columbus August, 1922, Supreme Council Convention in Atlantic City."[48]

In a letter to the members of the Supreme Board of Directors, McSweeney reflected on the origins of the commission:

> when in June, 1921, the Fourth Degree of the Knights of Columbus dedicated specifically to the furtherance of patriotism, came to realize that there was a

> deliberately conceived and skillfully executed plan underway to weaken the spirit of American nationality and undermine the solidarity of the American people . . . , the Historical Commission was appointed.[49]

The commission had approached Herbert Bolton, the noted Catholic historian and chair of the history department at the University of California at Berkeley, who was willing to serve but "could not get the consent from the President of the University." One of his publications was on Spanish and French influences in the United States, a study in accord with the goals of the Fourth Degree and with Edward McSweeney's perspective on American history. McSweeney was strongly opposed to the Anglo-American interpretation in history textbooks. The *New York Times,* he wrote, "accepted as gospel the work of the Sulgrave Institute on the Monroe Doctrine and Magna Carta organization, and the various inspired propaganda societies of like nature." Frustrated because "the university world was practically a closed door to the idea that there was any propaganda, especially in the school books,"[50] McSweeney's strategy was to gain a hearing in the press. The *New York American* published a series of articles by Grant Miller entitled "Treason to American Tradition," which reflected McSweeney's view on the de-Americanizing character of school history books. He had this series printed and three thousand copies distributed as a publication of the Historical Commission.[51] In light of the encounter with "the closed door" of academia, the commission's prestigious publication of books by Bemis and Nevins substantiated its commitment to counter the "propagandists" on several fronts.

Several Fourth Degree Vice Supreme Masters on the provincial level announced the establishment of the commission. The *Post* of Leavenworth, Kansas, reported that Thomas P. Flynn, Vice-Supreme Master of the Marquette Province, composed of ten states in the Midwest, endorsed the commission: "A type of propaganda seems to be inundating our country, the apparent object of which is to undermine the spirit of Americanism and solidarity." Flynn may have been citing the press release of October 1921 and other sources published by the commission or by Supreme Master John Reddin. For example, Flynn noted that "propaganda has been spread in this country that our war with England in 1812 was unjust." Speaking at a banquet after the initiation of seventy members into the Leavenworth Assembly, Flynn concluded that "something must be done to repudiate this propaganda and we are looking for the Knights to do their duty in this manner."[52]

In his August 1922 report to the Supreme Council convention in Atlantic City, McSweeney concentrated on those economic historians who viewed the idealism and patriotism of the founding fathers as a mask for cupidity and greed. In line with the Anglo-Saxonists such historians ignored the glaring truth that during the period of industrialization it was the Catholic Church that provided the "spiritual impulse and moral urge" to a nation in the grip of industrial strife. He said, "It was the despised aliens who had been the custodians of the spiritual forces without which the nation could not have endured." Motivated by religion rather than greed these people reacted to the crisis with "a strong patriotic sentiment" that was in all American people "only waiting to respond."[53]

The textbook that was replete with the Anglo-Saxon myth was David Saville Muzzey's *American History,* a work that was finally discarded in the 1960s because of the protest voices of blacks, white ethnics, Native Americans, and women, all of whom were alienated by its obvious biases. McSweeney assembled a list of suggested topics for graduate students interested in entering the Commission's American History competition, a list that appears as an agenda for dissent in the 1960s and beyond: The American Indians, Past and Present, Contribution of Alien Races; and Democracy vs. Caste in the United States.[54] McSweeney's vision for the commission was that it should focus public attention on the diversity of peoples who formed the multivalent character of the American nation. This vision was most evident in the commission's Racial Contribution Series, the publication of three books on those American groups most negatively affected by the proponents of 100-percent Americanism: Germans, Jews, and blacks. John Higham described the climate of exclusivism. "Ethnic hatred reached an all time high in the riots, hysteria and proscriptions that accompanied and immediately followed the First World War. This 100% Americanism [was] an indiscriminate rejection of all deviant groups."[55]

In the autumn of 1922 McSweeney designed a unique series of books that would include several other ethnic and racial groups, but the commission decided to publish only the following three: *The Gift of the Black Folk: The Negroes in the Making of America,* by W. E. Burghardt DuBois, Ph.D. (Harv.) (as he was described on the front of the book itself); *The Jews in the Making of America* by George Cohen; and *The Germans in the Making of America* by Frederick Franklin Schrader. In an article in *Columbia,* McSweeney elaborated on the need for this particular series:

> Immediately after the war, an army of propagandists proceeded to expound the theory that the bulk of the nation are "hyphenates" who are not, and never can be, true to the United States. This was accompanied by special drives on the Negroes and Jews, but particularly on Catholics of all racial

> derivation. More than a score of organizations with a wide diversity of methods but identity of aim, in which the false history textbooks were common to all, have been at work on this program steadily for five years. To assert that . . . a citizen of the United States is unworthy of the right of citizenship because of color, racial descent, or religious belief is abhorrent to the spirit of the Declaration of Independence and the Constitution of the United States, but this attempt is being made nevertheless, and openly supported by agencies and organizations that pretend to work under the cloak of "Americanization."
>
> This series is unlike any heretofore published, since it gives the actual history of racial contributions to the making of the United States, not from the isolated viewpoint of a single race, concerning other races, but from the viewpoint of each race concerning itself.[56]

Edward McSweeney's vision implicitly rejected the melting-pot image of assimilation. That image was derived from a play by Israeli Zangwill entitled *The Melting Pot* (1908), which "permanently attached a vivid symbol to the old assimilationist ideal of American Society." The moral lesson of Zangwill's melodrama was that "America was God's fiery crucible, consuming the dross and fusing all of its warring peoples into 'the coming superman.'"[57] In her autobiography, *The Promised Land,* Mary Antin wrote of the total transformation she experienced as she moved from czarist Russia to democratic America.[58] These assimilationist ideals were embraced by some middle-class Irish, but because of their antipathy to Anglo-Saxonism, the numbers were small. In opposition to the melting-pot concept, McSweeney advocated a cultural pluralism in which each group defines itself in the making of America. He linked ethnic survival to a culture war against the ideal of an Anglo-American alliance. His commitment to Irish liberation was joined to his love of America as a nation also founded on a war of liberation from the British. His vision of America as a polyglot people could be preserved only by celebrating "racial contributions" in the making of America. This was the cultural pluralism that DuBois articulated, as well as the American Jewish scholar Horace Kallen. The latter published in 1915 an article entitled "Democracy versus the Melting Pot," and later said that "Democracy involves not the elimination of differences but the perfection and conservation of differences."[59] Although Kallen was a Harvard Ph.D. and McSweeney was self-educated, each embraced cultural pluralism that had a significant impact on American democracy.

W. E. B. DuBois "fought against the kind of assimilation that breeds contempt for one's origins."[60] However, his was not the pluralism of Kallen but rather a dualism—black and white. Though he believed in a future when the two races converge into one, he urged strengthening racial consciousness among black Americans in order to develop a strong sense of identity. This would counteract "the sense of inadequacy and inferiority."[61] Cultural pluralism appealed to McSweeney because the Irish-Americans had already been assimilated into society on their own terms as Irish and as Americans, but in reaction to the advocacy of Anglo-Saxonist hegemony he asserted the legitimacy of others—black-Americans and German-Americans—not in the pejorative sense of "hyphenate" but as proud of their roles in the making of America.

McSweeney stated in the general introduction to the three books that the "Racial Contribution Series in the Knights of Columbus historical program is intended as a much needed and important contribution to national solidarity because these groups, like other minorities, have been subjected to the waves of intolerance and in the case of the black people to the chains of slavery followed by the bonds of perceived inequality." He was particularly critical of immigrant restrictionism, which, filtering down from Anglo-Saxonists to the grass roots, was manifested in race riots, in the deportation of pacifists and radicals, in anti-German phobia, and in anti-Semitism.[62]

McSweeney noted that in the climate of postwar nativism the groups treated in the series were considered hyphenates and mongrels. "These [immigrant] restriction laws are haphazard, unscientific, based on unworthy prejudices, and . . . disastrous in their economic consequence. . . . Such laws worked out in the hysteria of 'after war psychology' [appear to be] one of the instances so frequent in history, where Democracy must take time to work out its own mistakes." Hence all the "more reason that the priceless heritage of racial achievement be told by the descendants of various racial groups in the United States."[63]

W. E. B. DuBois edited *The Crisis*, a journal dedicated to raising the consciousness of African-Americans to confront the racial biases of the postwar era; he also was the first scholar to write a comprehensive history of the black people in the United States. The first sentence of his Foreword is in accord with McSweeney's purpose in publishing the series: "It is not uncommon for casual thinkers to assume that the United States of America is practically the continuation of English nationality." After referring to the French and Spanish influence and to that of the more recent European immigrants, he asserted that "it is high time that the course of our thinking should be changed." Rather than considering the blacks in American history as "an unmitigated error," it is important to understand their historical contribution: "The labors of black people brought prosperity, they fought in wars;

they have a place in literature and formed their own black American literature; Negro folk lore and music are among the choicest heritages of this land."[64] DuBois's conclusion is a presentiment of the later voice of Dr. Martin Luther King, Jr., and was perhaps the inspiration of the Boston-University-trained minister: "Finally, the Negro had played a peculiar spiritual role in America as a sort of living, breathing test of our ideals and an example of the faith and hope and tolerance of our religion."[65]

During and after the war, Dr. Thomas Wyatt Turner, a professor of biology at Howard University and the leader of the committee for the Advancement of Colored Catholics, which later became the National Federation of Colored Catholics, had criticized the Knights for not establishing black councils. This was part of his overall strategy of pressing for the desegregation of all Catholic institutions, including the Catholic University of America. He and others had also made a strong case for a black Catholic clergy.

These views were expressed in a meeting with the apostolic delegate, Archbishop Giovanni Bonzano.[66] Turner and John LaFarge, S.J., were allies in the 1920s, but they ultimately went separate ways. LaFarge founded the Catholic Interracial Council, aimed at converting whites to the cause of desegregation; Turner was intent on unifying black Catholics in the struggle against Jim Crow Catholicism, while also being committed to social justice and desegregation.[67]

There did exist at the time a black Catholic fraternal order, the Knights of St. Peter Claver founded in 1909 by several Josephite priests in the Diocese of Mobile. Modeled on the K. of C., this society "became a very important element in the religious life of black Catholics,"[68] wrote Cyprian Davis, O.S.B., the historian of the black Catholic experience. A ladies' auxiliary was founded in 1922 soon followed by a junior order; the Knights of St. Peter Claver eventually extended into the North and became a national organization.

Dr. Turner was sympathetic to DuBois's goals. Critical of the Catholic Church's "color separation and discrimination" in schools, universities, and seminaries," W. E. B. DuBois nevertheless respected the "great tradition of Catholicism" and considered the K. of C. series in which his book appeared as an "admirably conceived series of monographs for inter-racial understanding in the making of America." However, he was disappointed that despite the fact that "Catholicism has so much that is splendid in the past and fine in its present, it is the greater shame that 'nigger haters' clothed in its Episcopal robes should do to black Americans all the KKK ever asked."[69]

Active in the foundation of the NAACP and a professor at Atlanta University, DuBois became a highly respected Marxist interpreter of black history in America.

George Cohen's book on the Jewish contribution was a comprehensive treatment of Jewish life in America that included a chapter on the "Psychology of the Jew" and "the mysterious Jew."[70] This work implicitly answered the anti-Semitic "Protocols of the Elders of Zion." Frederick Franklin Schrader's book on the Germans was, like the other books, written in a style accessible to the general reader.[71] Though statistics on sales are not available, books in the Racial Contribution Series were distributed to bishops and universities and reached the shelves of many libraries throughout the country. Based on the importance of education to dispel prejudice and discrimination, the series was intended to include other works, such as a book on the Irish-Americans. In 1923 the commission was subjected to severe criticism by a group of dissident Knights who signed "the Reconstruction Program." The dissidents also attacked James Flaherty because he defended Supreme Advocate Joseph Pelletier, who had been convicted of extortion. Flaherty regarded the conviction as a clear case of anti-Catholic discrimination.

The Reconstruction Program was led by Patrick Henry Callahan and included William Mulligan, State Deputy of Connecticut, and Judge Joseph A. Moynihan of Michigan. One of their goals was simply to put an end to the commission. Though they never directly criticized the Fourth Degree or John Reddin, the latter's continuous support of McSweeney and the commission was obviously implicit in the attack. The Reconstruction Program stated: "[we] deplore the misdirected effort of the History Commission, which has failed to correct misconceptions of history, or to take any note of the propaganda in the guise of history published in the metropolitan dailies." It included a statement on such "remote and impractical topics as Jay's Treaty, the Monroe Doctrine, Trade and Foreign Policy."[72] Irate at the "campaign of personal vilification and slander" to the point of sowing discord on the commission, McSweeney resigned and was succeeded by Guillard Hunt, who proposed a more ambitious program.[73] Hunt died in 1924, and McSweeney returned merely to prepare for the commission's quiet termination in 1925.

In his report to the 1926 meeting of the Supreme Assembly of the Fourth Degree, John Reddin noted that the Historical Commission made a "real contribution and changed the current of propaganda, which for a generation sought to poison the minds of our children and thus future generations, against the ideals which animated the Fathers of our Republic." Since this was the first meeting after the commission's termination, it is significant that Reddin did not refer to any of the books nor to the Racial Contribution Series and the role of Edward McSweeney. He did note that the struggle against propaganda was "gratefully acknowledged by American educators, historians and statesmen."[74] The administration won the war with the dissidents on the program, but the conflict brought an end to the Historical Commission, clearly the most ambitious intellectual and social program sponsored and staffed by Fourth Degree Knights. The commission had challenged the membership to support historical scholarship and popular books on the contribution of several outsider groups—blacks, Jews, and Germans—who had been targets of the KKK armed with the bogus oath and "The Protocols of the Elders of Zion."

III

The Klan originated in the post–Civil War period as a vigilante group of night riders who through intimidation and violence sought to impose new anti-black codes that would have destroyed every plank in the platform of Reconstruction, particularly with regard to guaranteeing the freedmen the right to vote, to hold office, and to enjoy all liberties granted by the Bill of Rights of the Constitution. In short, the Klan sought to restore white supremacy and to establish a Jim Crow system based on the "natural inequality" of black people. Any violations of the system, or even the "appearance" of such, could result in Klan punishments ranging from beatings to lynchings. Even in the late 1950s and the 1960s, the Klan lashed out at the civil rights movement aimed at achieving for blacks their full rights as citizens. As one historian remarked, during this period of the second Reconstruction "reformers pressured the federal government to extend basic liberties to black Americans and . . . [the] Ku Klux Klans acted as shock troops of white supremacy."[75] Like the first Klan, that of the 1960s engaged in violence and intimidation of any persons associated with black protests and voter registration.

In the 1920s, the second Klan was intent on gaining political power in state and local government. This resuscitation of the Klan took place in 1915 at Stone Mountain, Georgia, soon to be the site of the memorial to the Confederacy. D. W. Griffith's *Birth of a Nation,* the first full-length motion picture, depicted the original Klan as made up of noble crusaders, restorers of law and order, as well as of Christian righteousness in a South that was suffering from the social breakdown and moral decay derived from Reconstruction laws. William Joseph Simmons, the founder of the new Klan, was a self-styled Methodist preacher, insurance salesman, and promoter of the Woodmen of the World, who had been active in the Masons and the Knights of Pythias. He and those attached to the Klan were enthralled by *Birth of a Nation.* Limited to Georgia and Alabama, the second Klan numbered only two thousand members and during World War I became active in "protecting" the nation from draft dodgers, enemy aliens, and union leaders; in short, all those who were "polluting" American life.[76]

The Klan's 100-percent Americanism was energized by the immigrant-restrictionist movement, which provided a stimulus to recruitment. Various groups were attracted to the Klan, particularly those aroused by stereotypes of greedy Jewish moneylenders, Bolshevik labor leaders, and Roman Catholic Vaticanists all conspiring to destroy authentic American values. The rural poor whites, subscribers to *The Menace* in 1914, would have found the Klan to be an honorable representation of Americanism vis-à-vis the "hyphenates" representing the "mongrelization" of the nation. In the larger cities the Klan found members among those alienated by southern and central European people "invading" sacrosanct and stable neighborhoods. In 1920, after they launched their membership campaign, based on a paid commission for members enrolled, there were one million Klansmen with a strong political organization and with considerable influence on the press. The Klansmen in some states, such as Indiana and Colorado, represented a cross-section of society rather than simply poor whites infected by the politics of paranoia. Though there were many Protestant ministers in opposition to the Klan, churches became the principal recruiting places. The new Klan carried on the violent vigilantism of the original Klan; in 1919 there were seventy lynchings for various violations of the Jim Crow codes of behavior. The latter "violations" were undoubtedly the result of many returning black veterans who had an expectation of justice after risking their lives "to make the world safe for democracy."[77]

As early as 1921, the *New York World* published a series of articles that exposed the Klan's violent programs and sought to undermine the Klan's reputation as a patriotic society. Headlines in its edition of September 14, 1921, featured a story about the Klan Kleagles—recruiters—using the bogus Fourth Degree oath as an effective tool in membership campaign.[78] Though anti-black and anti-Semitic biases were part of the collective animus, anti-Catholicism was the driving force in the Klan's triumphant march through the 1920s. In response to the *World*'s exposé eighteen other newspapers carried the series, and there was pressure for a congressional hearing on the Klan and its activities. But when Joseph Simmons testified to its patriotic fervor, a congressional advocate of the Klan called instead for the investigation of the K. of C. The *World* perceived the rise of the KKK in terms of its skill in exploiting "modern improvisations," that is, new styles of showmanship and salesmanship—as if the rise had not been caused by exploiting the strong veins of anti-Catholic, anti-Semitic, and anti-black sentiment. John B. Kennedy, the editor of *Columbia,* criticized the articles in the *World* for depicting the Klansmen as merely gullible and not motivated by deep-seated prejudices.[79] The noted sociologist John M. Mecklin verified Kennedy's assessment. "The Klan drew its inspiration from the ancient prejudice, classical hatreds, and ingrained social habits. The germ of the disease of the Klan, like germs in the human body, have long been present in the social organization and needed only the weakening of the social tissue to become malignant."[80]

So popular was the Klan during the 1920s that dozens of state legislatures fell into its hands. In Colorado, John Reddin's home state, the Invisible Empire gained the political ascendancy in 1924–1925; Governor Clarence Morley and several members of both houses of the legislature were Klansmen or sympathetic to them. Many legislators introduced anti-Catholic proposals such as the prohibition of altar wine, thereby making the celebration of mass illegal. Another bill would have transferred the care of unwed mothers from the Good Shepherd Sisters to a state charity facility. Though the Klan failed to pass such severe anti-Catholic legislation, there was some anti-K. of C. activity and at least one violent incident. Besides broadcasting excerpts from the bogus Fourth Degree oath, the Klan circulated rumors of a K. of C. conspiracy to provide arms to take over the city of Denver. As a result Catholic churches were subjected to cross burnings. Robert Goldberg, the historian of the Klan in Colorado, captured this extremism: "anti-Catholic Klansmen brought the ex-'nun' Mary Angel to Denver where she delivered sixty lectures," which, because their content was pornographic, elicited this comment from the *Denver Catholic Register:* "It was vomit not of the red-light district, but of hell's depths."[81] Goldberg noted that "both Jewish activists and Catholic priests were subjected to physical harassment and death threats; feelings ran so high that just the sight of a white collar set them off." One of the two acts of violence was against a Jewish rabbi, who was kidnapped and beaten with blackjacks and warned not to defend the "bootleggers," that is, Catholics, in court. Goldberg recounts another incident that occurred on October 27, 1923: "five Klansmen kidnapped Patrick Walker, member of the Knights of Columbus, drove him to a spot near Riverside Cemetery, and clubbed him with butts of their rifles."[82] This violent behavior not only represented bigotry but was an expression of the Klan's pledge "to shackle minorities."[83] Among the charges that the Knights of Columbus were in the vanguard of Vaticanism, none was more humorous than that related by Kathleen M. Blee, author of *Women and the Klan.* "According to the Klan, the Knights planted Catholic girls in Protestant homes as maids and child helpers who then filed weekly reports with the Vatican on the activities and conversations of Protestant families."[84]

In the reports of the Fourth Degree Provincial Assemblies there were occasional references to the period of Klan activities. In the report of the Provincial Assembly, Hennepin Province, which included Michigan, Indiana, Kentucky, West Virginia, and four assemblies in Ohio, the Master of West Virginia, M. J. Cullinan, observed that his state had a very small Catholic population "and that Catholics have suffered quite a lot of persecution during the past two years due to the activities of the Klan and in some of the smaller cities it even resulted in a boycott of the Catholic professional men and business people."[85] But with dissension in their own ranks the Klan experienced a precipitous decline emphasized by Wheeling's statistics: 75,000 population but only 300 Klansmen. To obstruct the flood of malicious propaganda throughout the area, Cullinan told the Fourth Degree leadership to urge Catholic youth to enter journalism. "In the city of Wheeling there are two Catholic reporters on each of the four daily papers and it is gratifying to note that we always get a square deal from these newspapers."[86] The Master of the Virginia Assemblies of the De Soto Province also reported on Klan activity as the reason for the decline in membership. It is likely that in this period of militant KKK activity the Third Degree members found satisfaction in their anti-defamation work that may have inhibited the desire to join the Fourth Degree.

The bogus Fourth Degree oath was published in anti-Catholic newspapers such as the *New Catholic Menace* and the *Rail-Splitter*. The oath was simply one of many references to the nefarious papists so visibly in the vanguard of Vaticanism. By way of an example, the headline of the July 1923 issue of the *Rail-Splitter* reads: "The Knights of Columbus Unmasked." One article was a caricature of the Order's Third Degree ceremonial; the other referred to the criminal behavior of those who follow "the teachings of the Fourth Degree Oath." A. H. Bell, the author of the piece, portrayed the KKK as decent law-abiding patriots, while members of the Order were a "gang of K of C hoodlums [who] beat up on Protestants for no other reason than they are meeting without the consent of their Pope. . . . It is quite common to read about some Protestant minister, who speaks Americanism, being insulted by some Roman Catholic thug who wears a K of C button upon the lapel of his coat."[87]

The editor, William Lloyd Clark of *The* [old] *Menace*, proudly stated that the September number of the *Rail-Splitter* would be dedicated to the "Ku Klux Klan . . . the great and constructive [force in society] . . . and poorly understood order [in contrast to] the criminal and seditious record of the Knights of Columbus." Clark's "forces of reaction—[were those in] the booze traffic, the red-light industry, the Roman Catholic Church and the Knights of Columbus, [who were] mounting a presidential campaign for Governor Al Smith." Following the pattern of anti-Catholic propagandists of the previous half-century, the *Rail-Splitter* criticized Catholics as representing the forces of reaction on the one hand, while on the other they were also perceived as fomenting revolution with their alliances with "Jews and Negroes . . . with the corrupt underworld forces [i.e., Italians] and line this gigantic aggregation of Rum, Romanism and Rebellion up at the ballot box to put a dupe of the Pope in the White House." To fire up his readers, the editor of the *Rail-Splitter* wrote in inflammatory, almost apocalyptical, rhetoric: "[The] Knights of Columbus . . . represents the concentrated cussedness of all the treasonable organizations and all the infernalism of the papal system centralized into one body whose slogans are: 'The Pope is King' and 'To Hell with Government.'"[88]

Luke E. Hart, Supreme Advocate, vigorously pursued libel cases against any publisher of the bogus oath. In a letter to the editor of the *Rail-Splitter,* he insisted that he "discontinue the publication and distribution of the oath or suffer the consequences of a legal suit."[89] Editor Clark published Hart's letter and explained that it was a response to a pamphlet extolling the Klan and condemning the K. of C., which was, said Clark, "the greatest defense of Klan craft and the greatest unmasking of the K of C ever written." He also blasted Hart's letter as "the most damnable piece of papal insolence ever written."[90] The State Deputy of Kansas, Clarence Malone, who was subjected to a burning cross planted in front of his home in Topeka, informed Hart of the widespread publication of the bogus oath in the *Rail-Splitter.*[91] Hart assured him that if it continued to publish the oath after Hart's warning then he would pursue a libel case against the publication to the limit of the law.[92] Though the journal did continue to misrepresent the

K. of C. in characteristically excessive rhetoric, it never again published the oath. However, Luke Hart did initiate several libel suits between 1923 and 1928.

IV

No Catholic institution has been so persistently the butt of nativist and anti-Catholic vilification as the parochial school. In the tradition of the Know-Nothings and the APA, the *New Menace* and the *Rail-Splitter* attacked the schools as centers of political disloyalty, separatism, and Vaticanism. The Klan's general strategy was to delegitimate Catholic schools. Though some Protestants spoke out against the Klan, the anti-parochial school animus ran so deeply that even many anti-Klan leaders viewed the parish school as divisive. In several regions of the nation, leaders of Scottish Rite Masons, the Klan, and other anti-Catholic societies coalesced in a short-lived movement to lobby for laws requiring all students to attend public schools. This movement also supported the Smith-Towner bill and other Congressional bills establishing a federal Department of Education, which Catholic leaders feared was a covert effort at undermining private education and diminishing the autonomy of Catholic schools.[93] The Knights of the Fourth Degree mounted their own campaign against the bills and were directly engaged in combating on the state level compulsory public education initiatives, referenda, and other such efforts.

Although there was an attempt to pass a compulsory public education measure in Nebraska in 1919, it was in Michigan—with its automobile industry in Detroit attracting blacks, Catholic and Jewish immigrants, and poor whites—that the movement took root to indirectly proscribe Catholic and other denominational schools. Detroit had a legacy of anti-Catholicism—it was the home of the APA in the 1890s. James A. Hamilton of the Public School Defense League led the campaign for a constitutional amendment requiring all students ages five to sixteen to attend public schools. Held in 1920, the referendum failed by a two-to-one margin, but Hamilton, supported by the Klan and some Masons, pursued the cause for three years.[94] According to the members of the Fourth Degree, Bishop Michael Gallagher of Detroit enlisted the Knights of Columbus in the battle to save the parochial schools. In his report to the Supreme Assembly held in Cleveland in 1926, John J. Donovan, Vice-Supreme Master of Hennepin Province, focused on Michigan and attributed the large increase in Fourth Degree members to the struggle for the schools: "when our fundamental rights as citizens have been challenged then the teaching of the church and the ideals of the Order are most cherished." He concluded with the remark, "the valiant championing of civic rights and civic justice [was evident] in that state where promotion of iniquitous legislation against the parochial schools . . . put Knighthood to the test."[95] Other Hennepin Masters presented reports that revealed the tensions of the times. Sir Knight Murray of Blue Grass Assembly in Lexington, Kentucky, said that much good was accomplished "by promoting Catholic literature bearing on toleration, patriotism, Catholic belief, etc. . . . [among] our fair-minded non-Catholic neighbors and friends." The assembly's other activities included conducting "a very quiet but effective campaign against the Klan. . . . The result was that "[t]hey were never allowed to hold a parade in Lexington [where their headquarters was located] and the use of city and county buildings was denied them, and in all elections when they had a full ticket they met an overwhelming defeat."[96]

Such reports of vigorous antidefamation activity on the part of the Fourth Degree were not typical. The minutes of the Supreme Assemblies did not include a report from each of the provinces, and some reports indicated apathy stemming in part from the vitality of the activities of the Third Degree councils.

There is no evidence of Fourth Degree opposition to the successful drive by an alliance of Klansmen and Masons in Oregon to pass an initiative on compulsory public school education. Archbishop Alexander Christie of Portland, where the Klan focused its political campaign, organized a Catholic effort against the initiative. Though supported by Lutherans, Episcopalians, Seventh-Day Adventists, Presbyterians, and Jews, Christie's campaign failed to defeat the initiative. Of course, the K. of C. was ready to support the appeal but the National Catholic Welfare Conference, representing the bishops, wished to pursue the case independent of the K. of C., indicating a dispute comparable to that of the K. of C. and the National Catholic War Council during World War I. However, Christie sought a grant from the Order, and $10,000 was sent immediately. The injured party was the Sisters of the Holy Names of Jesus and Mary, whose school in Portland would have been closed if the courts supported the initiative. The appeal on the state level failed in 1924.

The next year, the Oregon School Case reached the Supreme Court and on June 1, 1925, the decision was unanimous: the initiative was declared unconstitutional on the basis of the Fourteenth Amendment's guarantees for equal protection. The opinion cited the Oregon law as an unreasonable "interference with the liberty of parents and guardians to direct the upbringing and education of children under their control."[97] By this time the Ku Klux Klan in Oregon was experiencing a decline driven by factionalism, both internal and external. After being charged with corruption, the Klan rapidly lost its credibility.

It revived briefly during the Al Smith campaign. The smoldering coals of religious prejudices were ignited, and the three R's of anti-Catholic bias—Rum, Romanism, and Rebellion—were again invoked. The bogus oath was also circulated—Al Smith was a Fourth Degree Knight—and there were other charges such as that of the Catholic candidate's "allegiance to the autocrat on the Tiber, who hates democracy, public schools, Protestant personages, individual rights and everything that is essential to independence."[98]

The 1924 Democratic candidate for the presidency, William McAdoo of California, did not in any way oppose the Klan and its allies in the anti-Catholic camp, an act of omission that Al Smith considered a sin just as wrong as a "sin of commission." Al Smith's own words on the significance of religion in the campaign of 1928 reflect the themes of the Fourth Degree. He criticized the members of the Klan, "who had the effrontery to refer to themselves as 100 percent Americans." He proudly referred to the constitutional protections against a religious test for full citizenship, particularly "the right to hold office." He was critical of those who would seek election by appealing to the Catholic vote. In the same way he attacked those who appealed to anti-Catholic voters as a form of religious test "not only because I am a good Christian but because I am a product of America and American institutions. . . . The absolute separation of church and state is part of the fundamental basis of the constitution. I believe in that separation, and all that it implies. That belief must be a part of the fundamental faith of every true American."[99]

The competition with this form of patriotism engendered a vigorous response. Just as the nativists and anti-Catholic groups drew upon old organized efforts to protect Protestant-American hegemony, so the Fourth Degree Knights drew upon the Order's antidefamation character evident in its own Columbian motif to claim the rights that were theirs because they shared the faith of the "heroic navigator who baptized this nation." The Fourth Degree made even more explicit the symbolic meanings of the *Santa Maria* vis-à-vis the Puritan's *Mayflower.* As citizens in a climate of religious freedom, the Sir Knights originally wore the symbol of the constitution on their baldrics, and with their top hats and formal wear hundreds of Fourth Degree Knights paraded down Pennsylvania Avenue on the occasion of the 1912 dedication of the Columbus Memorial. In 1924, the Holy Name Society with American and papal flags flanking the members also marched down Pennsylvania Avenue in a display of Catholic solidarity, symbolic of the blending of faith and freedom. Almost as a counter-symbol to the Holy Name event, the Ku Klux Klan dressed in their traditional garb without masks also paraded down Pennsylvania Avenue, as though to represent a white wave struggling against the defilement of alien pollutants: Catholics, Jews, blacks, and immigrants.[100] The following year Catholics numbering in the tens of thousands marched down Michigan Avenue in Chicago at the first American Eucharistic Congress. Fourth Degree Knights from several assemblies throughout the Midwest and beyond formed an honor guard along the lines of the parade route. Eucharistic devotion separates Catholics from several other Christian denominations who hold the Bible and the preached word as symbols of the real presence of God. The parade was not only a sign of eucharistic devotion but also a revelation of American-Catholic power.

This chapter's focus on the Fourth Degree and the Order's response to anti-Catholicism evokes the thesis of Stanley Cohen cited by Lynn Dumenil: "the decline of the Ku Klux Klan in the mid-twenties was because the political power of immigrants and Catholics was becoming too well entrenched in urban America to be turned back by nativist movements."[101] Still beaming in the luster of their historical commitments in the war, and proud of their struggles against "Kluxers" in the streets, against immigrant restrictionists in the political sphere, and against Anglo-Saxonist propagandists in the schools, the Fourth Degree Knights marched with pride in their significant contributions to American citizenship and Catholic faith.

In his message on the silver jubilee of the Fourth Degree, John H. Reddin urged the membership "to honor the church's Holy Year by special prayers and pilgrimages to the Holy See," and to make it "a patriotic year as well." It was particularly significant to link loyalties to church, nation, and Fourth Degree because "of the organized effort now in full swing to embitter our fellow citizens and this society against our Holy Church." He proudly noted the nearly one hundred thousand members involved in the patriotic degree, the Sir Knights who "represent high types of citizenship and Catholicity," and who exemplify "loyalty to both Church and State, each in their rightful sphere" against those venting their hatred toward the church and the Order. Reddin exclaimed, "Let the people know that there can be no better, safer, saner citizen than the Catholic man or woman who lives up to the teachings and practices of the Catholic Church. Prejudice is dissolved by the spread of truth, and the heart of America being solved, the way is open for the Knight of Columbus to bring about religious concord and peace and that amity contemplated by the founder of our country."[102]

4

The Great Depression to Postwar Anti-Communism

From the 1930s to the 1950s

I

THE IMMEDIATE CAUSE OF THE Great Depression was the stock market crash of October 1929. The twenties, characterized by large concentrations of finance and capital, began with a postwar recession in the adaptation from a controlled wartime market to a free-market economy and ended with the most severe economic crisis in the history of the industrial nations of the West. Within three years, unemployment reached fifteen million, or 25 percent of the work force, and the gross national product experienced a 33 percent decline. The large concentrations of industrial power that fueled speculation in the stock market were operating at increasingly high rates of acceleration; as a result overproduction surpassed demand, and with the banks entangled in a downward dynamic the entire economy was affected. Herbert Hoover's response to the Depression stressed local and philanthropic programs for relieving economic and social distress, while Franklin D. Roosevelt's projects were based on the three R's of the New Deal: relief, recovery, and reform. Catholics, African Americans, and most recent immigrants were drawn to the Democratic Party, but Supreme Knight Martin Carmody and Supreme Advocate Luke E. Hart were Republicans who supported Hoover's general economic and social policies. Joseph Scott, the first Fourth Degree Vice Supreme Master in California, gave one of the nominating speeches for Hoover in 1928.[1]

The Knights were a major voluntary and philanthropic society, with laws prohibiting involvement in partisan politics, but the Knights' leadership nevertheless tended toward the individualism of Hoover's public policy. Later the conflict between the Order's antidefamation policy and FDR's Good Neighbor policy, particularly as it related to Mexico, further isolated the Knights from the Democratic administration during the mid-1930s.[2]

When Hoover announced the establishment of a commission on unemployment, Carmody wired the president offering the services of 26,000 councils. The president congratulated the Order for its "fine spirit of cooperation" and later appointed Carmody to the administration's organization on Unemployment Relief.[3] Since local councils had functioned as employment agencies at the end of World War I, they were ready to act during the great economic crisis. In 1931, the Order's 1,056 employment committees placed 43,128 unemployed into jobs.[4] In a radio broadcast during the 1932 Supreme Convention, Carmody expressed the Order's commitment to voluntary services and its opposition to governmental projects and to the dole as demeaning and patronizing.[5] Though there was little pro–New Deal sentiment expressed publicly, local leadership was generally supportive of the New Deal. Monsignor John A. Ryan, head of the Social Action Department of the National Catholic Welfare Conference, was the most vigorous champion of the principal policies of the New Deal.[6] (It was Father Charles Coughlin who first referred to him as "the Right Reverend New Dealer.") As the author of the Bishops' Program on Social Reconstruction of 1919, Ryan advocated reforms that were realized in the New Deal. Three American Cardinals, William H. O'Connell of Boston, Patrick Hayes of New York, and George Mundelein of Chicago, greeted FDR's election as a providential sign of the nation's recovery.

The Catholic press was also enthusiastic about Roosevelt and his New Deal. Even the conservative editor of the *Catholic World,* James Gillis, C.S.P., treated him positively. Father Charles Coughlin, the Detroit radio priest, who later developed into a radical anti-Semite and a proponent of the "Protocols of the Elders of Zion," also lined up in support of the new president. Gillis and Coughlin later became severe critics of the New Deal, but most Catholic leaders remained in FDR's camp. When Roosevelt quoted from the 1931 social encyclical *Quadragesimo Anno* (*On the Reconstruction of the Social Order*), during the election campaign, "many Catholics were favorably impressed." He referred to it as "one of the greatest documents of modern times." Because the encyclical was opposed to both socialism and laissez-faire capitalism and because it defended state intervention in the market during times of high unemployment, Roosevelt said that it was "just as radical as I am." He quoted from the encyclical: "It is patent in our days that not alone is wealth accumulated, but immense power and despotic economic dominations are concentrated in the hands of a few, and that those few are frequently not the owners but only the trustees and directors of invested funds which they administer at their pleasure. . . . The accumulation of power, the characteristic note of modern times, is the result of limitless free competition, which permits the survival of those only who are the strongest, which often means those who fight most relentlessly, who pay least heed to the dictates of conscience."[7] Three years prior to the election of FDR and a year before the publication of the pope's social encyclical, the Fourth Degree had affirmed the general direction of the Order by energetically supporting Pius XI's call for Catholic Action.

In his 1922 encyclical, *Ubi Arcano Dei Consilio,* Pius XI first extolled lay Catholic Action. Later specified as the laity's participation in the apostolic mission of the bishops, Catholic Action was a principal base for many Fourth Degree programs. Though Carmody provided copies of this encyclical to the delegates at the 1930 convention, John Reddin quoted from a 1929 encyclical, *Mens Nostra,* in his 1931 pamphlet on the Fourth Degree. By way of an introduction, Reddin noted how the Fourth Degree assemblies are free from "cares, problems and business affairs"; assembly meetings "are usually devoted to matters of educational, religious and social betterment of the members." He urged the membership at the local and general assemblies to become "active and aggressive units of the Knights of Columbus in promoting Catholic Action." He then quoted from the encyclical of Pius XI: "with all our power we desire to promote action; and we cease not and will never cease to commend it; because the cooperation of the laity with the Apostolic Hierarchy is exceedingly useful, not to say necessary." The alignment of the lay "Apostolate in support of the hierarchical Apostolate," said Reddin, "makes Catholic laymen and Catholic lay organizations the shock troops in the everlasting war against error and irreligion." After noting that Catholic Action entailed more than simply attending Mass, receiving Holy Communion, paying pew rents, and obeying the Ten Commandments, he observed: "it is the translation of belief into action. It is Catholicism in motion. It means engaging in activities which vitalize Catholic teaching and principles for our fellow man, our country, and our humanity. . . ."[8] Every Fourth Degree assembly committed to Catholic Action would "redound to the glory of the Church as well as the good of the Country." Reddin then paraphrased the ceremonial statement "Proudest of all is the boast, I am a Catholic American citizen" by stating, "It is a trite but true saying that the better the Catholic the better the citizen."[9] Reddin's "trite statement" was an echo of a 1928 editorial in the progressive Catholic weekly *Commonweal.* The editor asserted the harmony of Catholicism and Americanism as "two conceptions of man which see eye to eye; hence the better Catholic the better American."[10] In a section on "The Bogus Fourth Degree Oath," Reddin noted the parallel between the bogus Jesuit oath and the one purported to be sworn by each Fourth Degree candidate. After presenting testimonials on the actual Fourth Degree pledge, Reddin traced the circuitous route of the bogus oath to Germany, where General Erich Ludendorf of World War I fame published it in his journal, *Ludendorf's Volkswarte* in late 1930.[11] By this time, he had become a member of Adolph Hitler's National Socialist Party.[12] It was not until January of that year that the Order was alerted to Ludendorf's circulation of the oath. Soon copies of the Order's *Criminal Libels* were translated with the intention of distributing them throughout Germany. In the meantime, Martin Carmody explained it in an official letter to a priest in Germany, "giving him authority to publish and circulate it so that the truth may be known."[13]

In *Mens Nostra,* Pius XI stressed the lay-retreat movement as "the soul of Catholic Action."[14] The Fourth Degree assemblies in New York were close to the origins of the movement in 1910–1911. At the 1910 Eucharistic Congress in Montreal, Father Terrance Shealy, S.J., first proposed the initiative for a lay retreat movement, and also dubbed the twentieth century the "layman's century."[15] With an emphasis on a blend of spiritual renewal and social reform, Shealy was in the tradition of *Rerum Novarum* (1891) of Pope Leo XIII. An opponent of both laissez-faire capitalism, with its individualistic ethic, and a proponent of governmental intervention to harness greed and protect the common good, he was a vigorous antisocialist and an ardent defender of private property. Though he assigned the state specific economic and social functions, Shealy said that these could become instruments of socialism if there is no conversion of the heart; "unless men are educated to the discipline of self control from within, state control from without cannot save us."[16] To build a Christian character requires a retreat aimed at a conversion of the heart, "an instruction, meditation and prayer" based on the principles of the Ignatian *Spiritual Exercises.* And to encourage commitment to social reform was the principal aim of the retreat movement. On Shealy's list of organizations aligned with the movement was the Knights of Columbus. And he indicated his familiarity with the Fourth Degree ceremonial when he stated: "'I am an American citizen' is a proud boast . . . and in this certainty we may have a justifiable pride—that we are citizens of a land whose mercy and justice have ever made her a haven for the oppressed."[17]

John Reddin's description of his own retreat experience was generalized into the third person: "Every man who has attended these exercises, away from the cares of business, family and the world usually comes out refreshed with a clarity of mind, a militant faith and a spiritual rejuvenation and a joy beyond what he acquires in the performance of his ordinary religious duties. It is there he regains his poise, there he gets a sure philosophy of life—objective principles, ideals, character—without which there is no full living."[18] In his book *Living Stones,* Joseph P. Chinnici, O.F.M., thoroughly explores the historical significance of Shealy and the retreat movement; he notes Pius XI's "model of the retreat-society relationship in terms of the upper chamber where the apostles hid themselves before the day of Pentecost. . . . Having thus rejuvenated themselves [on retreat] . . . the laity then reentered society and attempted to reconstruct it by participating in such instruments of Catholic Action as Catholic Evidence Guilds."[19]

In his 1931 pamphlet on the Fourth Degree, John Reddin informed his readers of this commitment to Catholic Evidence Guilds promoted by the Fort Pitt General Assembly, and other assemblies. He referred to David Goldstein, "well-known member of the Order and convert to the Catholic Faith," who was training lay people for Catholic Evidence work with the encouragement of Cardinal William H. O'Connell of Boston. Reddin said that the purpose of the Catholic Evidence Guild (CEG) in England is "to make known the truth of the Catholic Church from the street corners and public parks and places. The primary object is to do away with prejudice and to promote a friendly feeling on the part of non-Catholics toward Catholics."[20]

Debra Campbell describes the origins of the CEG in 1918. Vernon Redwood, a New Zealand layman, received permission from Cardinal Francis Bourne of Westminster to allow Catholics to "speak on behalf of their faith at Speakers' Corner in Hyde Park in an effort to counteract socialistic beliefs and blasphemies being expounded there." A year later there were 150 people enrolled in the Westminster Guild. In the early 1920s Frank Sheed and Masie Ward, a husband and wife "team" who met on Speakers' Corner, were prominent lay leaders. According to Campbell, "It was Sheed and Ward who established and refined a rigorous uniform method of theological and practical training to which all the prospective outdoor speakers subjected themselves, a method made accessible to Catholics far and wide in a series of editions of the *Catholic Evidence Training Outlines* and published by Sheed and Ward."[21] Soon a network of the CEG extended to the United States, with guilds opening in New York, Baltimore, Washington, D.C., Oklahoma City, Detroit, Philadelphia, and Buffalo between 1928 and 1935. Reddin eventually proposed the establishment of the CEG throughout the Fourth Degree assemblies, but in 1931 suggested it for "future thoughtful consideration." He was explicit in his anticipation that "the time may come . . . when the intelligent Catholic laymen composing the Fourth Degree may be called upon by the hierarchy to undertake in their respective communities work similar to that carried on in England by so-called Catholic Evidence Guilds."[22] Local Fourth Degree assemblies promoted and distributed Catholic literature—the *Catholic Encyclopedia* and the *Catholic Dictionary*—in public and non-Catholic college libraries.

The local program that gained national momentum was the "reverent observance of Good Friday," between the hours of 12:00 noon and 3:00 P.M. St. Francis General Assembly of San Francisco was the most vigorous proponent of the observance throughout the Bay Area. John Reddin urged assemblies to form committees aimed at obtaining the approval of their bishops or local pastors, and forming allies among Protestants and their pastors who would then seek proclamations from the mayor and the governor requesting businesses to close so that employees could attend "their respective places of worship." Reddin's directives for the committees included distributing "Closed" signs for businesses and contacting officials of public transportation to have them adopt the observance policy; buses and street cars were to stop for one or two minutes around 3:00 P.M. He concluded with remarks on the success of movement for the observance: "The results of such united efforts will be found amazing. . . . All Christian Churches, Protestant as well as Catholic, are filled to overflowing during these holy hours. This has been the experience of cities and towns in this country and Canada."[23] The Indianapolis Third Degree councils sponsored the Stations of the Cross in the central plaza of the city. With a Fourth Degree Honor Guard for the stations, this form of evangelical, public Catholicism was characteristic of Reddin's leadership.

Third Degree councils observed an annual Communion day as well as a day for memorial services in the council chambers for deceased members. These councils also celebrated an annual Communion Sunday, but Fourth Degree assemblies had no special day of their own. Hence, Reddin suggested that they "appropriate Mother's Day for that purpose and sanctify it by receiving Holy Communion in a body." The second Sunday of May, "the month of Mary the greatest of Mothers," could be so designated; the traditional son's gift of a flower would be the "sign of temporal pleasure," symbolic of the "Inward Flower, Christ in the Holy Eucharist." In contrast to the American observance of Mother's Day, the American Catholic celebration "certainly tends to the preservation of our Christian Civilization in America." Because the "perpetuity of the Republic" was now threatened by new forms of paganism propagated by the advocates of birth control,[24] a Catholic Mothers' Day would be countercultural. Reddin cited an editorial in the April 25, 1931 issue of *America* that reported on the Lambeth Conference's approval of artificial birth control in 1930, with the Federal Council of Churches in the United States following suit. Thus, the Catholic Church "is the sole defender of the family." The editorial in *America* lamented the fact that the enemies of the church point to her protests against these developments as proof that Catholics "are out of harmony with the temper of the day, and unfit for citizenship."[25]

Reddin articulated a distinctive public Catholicism when he urged the Fourth Degree members to evangelize America through Catholic Evidence Guilds, the Good Friday observances, and a Catholic Mothers' Day. In the promotion of patriotism the leadership of the Fourth Degree did not always invoke Catholicity, but rather proffered programs for students in public and parochial schools as simply practices of good citizenship. This idea was central to Reddin's Annual Fourth Degree Prize Essay Contests, approved by the Supreme Assembly in 1924. By imbuing high school students with "the ideals that brought the United States into existence and with the principles upon which it is erected," the contest "will have accomplished a work which guarantees the perpetuity of the Republic."[26] Hundreds of boys and girls in the last two years of high school participated in these contests with the three top essays receiving a district prize of $75, $50, and $25, and with the national prize essays receiving $500, $300, and $200. Though the money for prizes was drawn from membership dues, there is evidence of local apathy and resentment which appear to have been related to allocating funds that could have been used for patriotic programs of more immediate practical value. However, the essay contests seem to have achieved wider support, and in the second century of the Degree's history they are still popular in most districts.

John Reddin's 1931 fifty-page description of the Fourth Degree programs, both active and prospective, was issued amid the Great Depression, but did not include any references to the crisis. It was published before Pope Pius XI's social encyclical *Quadragesimo Anno: On the Reconstruction of the Social Order.* The subtitle is significant because the pope advocated an alternative to capitalism and to socialism, by way of a corporatist society in which representatives of labor, industry, and state would formulate social policy to fulfill human needs. Represented by authoritarian Austria and fascist regimes in Italy and Portugal, corporatism appears to have been in violation of the principle of "social justice," a term also included in the encyclical.[27] John A. Ryan Americanized the encyclical's "Reconstruction" principles under the title "economic democracy," based on union and employer groups forming industrial councils to determine general economic policy.[28] The state's role would be limited to an initiative and consultive function. The NCWC adopted Ryan's plan as the core of its social teaching. Though over 60 percent of Catholics voted for FDR in the 1936 election, the leaders of the Knights, including those of the Fourth Degree, became disillusioned with the president during the Mexican crisis of 1933–1936.[29]

II

This crisis of the 1930s was another act in the drama of church–state conflicts that began in nineteenth-century Mexico, but became more intense in the revolutionary period of 1900–1917, a period that concluded with a new constitution. This document included severe anticlerical and anti-Catholic measures, such as control of church property and prohibition of religious orders and of public displays of religion. In the early 1920s during the leftist military dictatorship (presidency) of Alvaro Obregon (1920–1924), anti-Catholic violence intensified. However, it was during the presidency of Plutarcho Eliás Calles that the government closed Catholic schools, expelled two hundred priests and prohibited all public religious ceremonies. During this period many Mexicans joined the Catholic League in opposition to Calles, and some were active among the Christeros, a militant guerrilla movement. Mexican Knights, including many Fourth Degree members, were active in the league and supported the Christeros. The exiled bishops, priests, sisters, and members of the Catholic League in the United States were protected by Bishop Francis C. Kelley of Oklahoma City and several other members of the hierarchy including Archbishop Michael Curley of Baltimore.[30] The conflict reached a *modus vivendi* in 1929 through the diplomacy of the Paulist General Secretary of the NCWC, John J. Burke, who represented the church in the negotiation between the U.S. Ambassador to Mexico, Dwight Morrow, and President Calles. Included in the agreement was the Mexican government's recognition of the legitimacy of the church's identity. During and after this period, the Knights condemned the "Bolshevist government" in Mexico and pressured the Coolidge and

Hoover administrations to condemn the revolution and Calles. Since the 1929 settlement was only a truce, it was not long before Calles renewed his anticlerical campaign by seeking to remove students from the church's religious education program. Also in 1934, Calles stated his intention "to capture the minds" of the young people, "because they do belong and should belong to the Revolution."[31] His successor, Lazaro Cardenas, convened a commission that called for a constitutional amendment closing Catholic schools and prohibiting religious instruction. The U.S. Ambassador Josephus Daniels naively responded positively to Calles's statement on education for the revolution, saying it was analogous to Thomas Jefferson's link between education and the American Revolution.[32] Daniels had campaigned for Al Smith and was an ardent anti-KKK Democrat from North Carolina. It seems he should have been more sensitive to Catholic opinion.

There was an enormous Catholic reaction to these events that culminated with the demand for FDR to condemn the religious persecution in Mexico. But President Roosevelt, committed to his Good Neighbor policy toward Latin America, was reluctant to appear as an interventionist. Senator William E. Borah of Idaho, the ranking Republican member of the Senate Foreign Relations Committee, called for an investigation.[33] The Knights included support for the Borah Resolution as part of their national campaign. The Friends of Catholic Mexico, with Robert R. Hull as chairman and Dorothy Day of the Catholic Worker as first vice president, expressed their gratitude to the Knights for their strong pro-Borah position.[34] An ecumenical group, composed of Henry Sloan Coffin, president of Union Theological Seminary, Bernard F. Richards, director of the Jewish Information Bureau, and Michael Williams, editor of *Commonweal,* formed the core leadership of the American Committee on Religious Rights and Minorities, who visited Mexico and whose report was quoted in *Columbia*.[35] Throughout 1935 the Order, along with leaders of the Mexican and American hierarchy, pressured FDR for a pro-Borah statement. Finally FDR agreed to meet with Luke E. Hart and Martin Carmody. The NCWC and John J. Burke were supportive of the meeting but did not want a Senate investigation of the religious situation of Mexico because it would tend to interfere with a diplomatic solution. FDR did indicate general support for religious liberty and later in San Diego, twenty miles from Mexico, stated: "We regard it is as axiomatic that each person shall enjoy the free exercise of his religion according to the dictates of his conscience."[36] Hart, Carmody, and others believed that FDR had given them assurance of a strong condemnation of Mexico's violation of the principles of religious freedom. Hence, they wrote a severe letter of protest to FDR, who responded negatively to any policy that represented a tacit intervention in Mexican affairs. Archbishop John T. McNicholas of Cincinnati stated in a public letter that the Knights did not represent the Catholics of his see in this dispute with the president. When FDR received the Laetare Medal from the University of Notre Dame, his friend Cardinal George Mundelein was on hand. As a sign that he endorsed McNicholas's views, he stated that no group had the authority to speak for the Catholics of the United States. Ultimately John J. Burke worked out a moderate diplomatic solution; in 1937 Archbishop Leopoldo Ruiz y Flores, the apostolic delegate to Mexico, was back in Mexico City, satisfied that priests were freely engaging in their pastoral ministry.[37] In a mural in Mexico City dominating the central *Plaza de Revolución*, one enemy force is portrayed in the Fourth Degree uniform of the Knights of Columbus.

III

On the local level no Knight was more vigorous in his pursuit of a Mexican solution than Thomas F. Mahony of Longmont, Colorado. A businessman from western Pennsylvania who moved to Colorado in the 1920s, he became active in Longmont Council and was state treasurer of the Colorado State Council. In the early 1920s Mahony became concerned with the harsh living conditions and low wages of the Mexican migrant workers in the sugar-beet industry. To mobilize the Colorado Knights and to publicize the deplorable situation of both Mexican and "Spanish-American" workers, he successfully proposed in 1923 the establishment of the Mexican Welfare Committee of the State Council of the Knights of Columbus. There were thirty thousand beet-field workers, 65 percent of whom were Spanish-speaking and included women and children. Mahony described the conditions: "under this system of family contract labor, the industries using it are able to escape responsibility and blame for the evasions and violations of Colorado's rather loosely enforced child labor and compulsory school attendance laws by claiming the children are employed by the parent and the parent needs the help of the children."[38] The growers' agents recruited workers and their families in the winter and early spring among the Catholic parishes in southern Colorado and in the southwestern states along the border; the average family's annual wage was between $600 and $650, a figure close to the subsistence wage of one person, that is, far below family subsistence level. The workers often had to wait for their wages until after the banks and mortgage companies had been paid. Poor housing, lack of sanitation, and the long hours imposed upon the children meant an "appallingly high death rate among women and children," reported Mahony. He quoted Leo XIII's *Rerum Novarum*: "It is shameful and inhuman to treat men like chattels to make money by and to look upon them as so much muscle and human power."[39] By 1931 Mahony's social-justice crusade had become well known. At the annual convention of the National Council of Catholic Women held in Denver, Mahony made an impassioned plea for Catholic social activism: "We Catholic men and women as individuals and organizations must cry out without ceasing—in protest against the bad social and economic conditions forced upon these our Spanish and Mexican poor, to the end that charity and justice for them shall prevail."[40]

John Reddin, Supreme Master from Denver, became Mahony's spokesman on the Supreme Board of Directors for funding the Mexican Welfare Work through grants which ranged from $500 to $1,000. Though this was not a Fourth Degree program, the Reddin connection was vital, while the money from the Mexican fund was certainly justified. For example, in his 1928 annual report—copies of which were sent to leading members of the hierarchy, friends at the NCWC such as John J. Burke, C.S.P, and John A. Ryan—Mahony noted the impact of the "Radicals of the Old Mexico Communist or Red Socialist Group" among the sugar-beet workers. "They have frequent closed meetings . . . schools for teaching of communism and other radical doctrines. Their propaganda is directed along anti-Catholic, anti-Religious, anti-organized government, and on Mexican-political lines. It is to some extent a sort of 'Help Calles movement.'" To compete with these anti-Catholic, pro-socialist developments, Mahony's committee distributed six thousand copies of the booklet *Red Mexico* in Spanish and twenty-five hundred copies of the monthly *El Propagandista Catolica*. The latter were sent free to any Colorado pastor with Spanish-speaking parishioners. The committee also distributed more than eight thousand holy cards, twenty-five hundred medals and fifteen hundred rosaries among priests and catechists involved in the religious education of Mexican children. Mahony noted: "To some it may seem strange to fight red socialism or communist propaganda, but methods of distribution have been worked out and results checked by the committee and found practical and effective."[41]

Without permanent residence in parishes, the workers were not easily accessible to the Spanish-speaking pastors. Mahony's group attempted to fill this void and influence families by encouraging women to become leaders in their communities. To foster effective interest in citizenship classes among the Spanish-speaking workers, Mahony's group adopted the NCWC's Civic Catechism, which was part of its "Americanization plan" but with none of the patronizing "offensive methods of the uplifter . . . we emphasize rights as well as duties, for as far as certain types of public officials are concerned, the Mexicans' rights are generally disregarded." Referred to as "The Book," the Civics Catechism in a Spanish edition formed the basis of discussion among the workers during free time. "At one meeting talks will be outlined for them on rights, at another on duties warning them of bootleggers, then on good health, education, the courts and so forth." In all their social and religious work the Mexican Welfare Committee "relied upon and cooperated with Catholic women in Denver" and several other places. Under the direction of the Diocesan Council of Catholic Women and the Catholic Daughters of America, many programs of religious education reached Mexican families throughout the state. Though he never mentioned the term Catholic Action, the energetic religious and social-justice activism of the Mexican Welfare Committee is a clear illustration of the term.[42]

As mentioned earlier, Mahony developed an extensive national network for his Mexican welfare work. He addressed the Catholic Conference on Industrial Problems and sent a copy of his address to John A. Ryan, who replied that "he was able to use part of [the paper] in discussing child labor in one of [his] lectures at the summer school" at Marygrove College in Detroit.[43] With one editorial in *America* on the significance of the Mexican Welfare Committee and Mahony's role in the campaign for social justice, leaders of the Order were proud of the efforts in Colorado that received such national attention. Mahony continued in this vital area of social activism until the 1950s.

IV

The Fourth Degree's patriotic defense of Catholic historical memory entailed conflicts with representatives of anti-Catholicism ranging from the American Protective Association to disillusioned Progressives and populists on the left who vilified the church as the *Menace* and condemned the Fourth Degree as the symbol of the militant advance of "monopolistic" Roman Catholicism. This religious paranoia had assumed various forms, but its most persistent identity, according to the Knights, was socialism and, after 1917, Bolshevism. There was a consensus among the Knights that socialists were involved in a world conflict not only with capitalism but with Catholicism as well. In the United States, socialists advocated a moral code in opposition to traditional religious and social values. *Rerum Novarum* was also antisocialist. During his thirty years as Supreme Master, John H. Reddin fostered many antisocialist programs: the lectures of David Goldstein and Peter Collins, the Historical Commission, the Mexican campaign, and the promotion of papal encyclicals. The antireligious and anti-Catholic propaganda must be countered by the Catholic truth campaigns articulated in the language of Catholic Action, and by a social-justice-based anti-Communism and anti-fascism. In these campaigns there were frequent references to the foundational principles of the American Republic. For example in the Order's pursuit of religious liberty in Mexico, the leaders invoked the principles of the Declaration of Independence and the First Amendment to the Constitution and blended them with the language of Catholic Action. The positive character of patriotism and antisocialism is illustrated by a letter from Thomas F. Mahony to John Reddin reporting on a visit by David Goldstein: "The Reds from Old Mexico have been . . . working along anti-religious and political-Mexican lines." Mahony also noted that before Goldstein arrived there was "little effective opposition . . . to these agitators." Mahony reported that there were sixty-five leaders in attendance at Goldstein's lectures and that he "was hearing very good reports of the meeting."[44]

On both the local and national levels there was a militant antisocialism and anti-Communism because these radical movements were perceived as inherently anti-Catholic, and because religion was considered integral to American patriotism. In the mid-1930s Communist parties in Europe and in the United States responded to the advance of Italian Fascism and German Nazism by advocating united-front strategies against ideologies embodied in Mussolini and Hitler. The Spanish Civil War was viewed by most American Catholics as a religious war, almost a war of liberation, because the forces of General Francisco Franco were seen as restoring the church in opposition to the anticlericalism of the left-wing parties dominating the Republic. When Italy and Germany armed the forces of Franco, and the Soviet Union armed those of the republic, some American Catholics, such as George Shuster, editor of *Commonweal*, refused to support Franco and urged Catholics to remain neutral on the grounds that both sides were equally anti-Christian. But this remained a minority position among American Catholics. The Order strongly opposed the anti-Catholic, antidemocratic and pro-Bolshevist character of the republic and viewed Franco as the defender of Christian civilization. Indeed, the Order distributed twenty thousand copies of the pastoral letter of the Spanish bishops appealing to Catholics of all nations to support Franco.[45] The American Communist

Party's united-front strategy, which included seeking volunteers to join the republican forces against the pro-Fascist army of General Franco, served to convince the leaders of the Order that there was indeed a threat of Communism in the United States.

During this period the Knights joined the anti-Communist crusade with local rallies in several sections of the country. Supreme Knight Carmody, with the support of the Fourth Degree, identified Communism with "atheism and irreligion . . . the bedrocks of the curse of man." Communists make "bewitching promises . . . [and] beguiling trickeries" that must be exposed. In defense of the family, Carmody warned that "[b]irth control, divorce, lax parents and lawlessness . . . are but stepping stones to the communist citadel of the Kremlin." He also called for the promotion of truth and justice "against the social injustices" which form the "seed of communistic growth."[46]

Pope Pius XI's encyclical *Divini Redemptoris,* "On Atheistic Communism" (March 19, 1937), gave impetus to the crusade that was unanimously adopted at the Supreme Council meeting the following August. After discussing how the theory and practice of Communism are diametrically opposed to the teachings of the church, the pope called upon the faithful to detach themselves from worldly goods, to practice Christian charity, and to be committed to social justice and Catholic Action. Nearly one million copies of the encyclical were published and distributed by the Knights.[47] Shortly after the 1937 convention the Board of Directors approved Carmody's proposal to hire George Hermann Derry as spokesman. Derry was a member of the Fourth Degree Historical Commission who had recently resigned as president of Marygrove College in Detroit. His program, dependent on approval of the hierarchy, included public lectures sponsored by a local council and a presentation on anti-Communist leadership to meetings of the diocesan clergy. As much an anti-Fascist as he was an anti-Communist, Derry was also committed to social justice as the positive feature of the national movement. A new crusade, the Knights of Columbus Crusade for Social Justice, was inaugurated in 1938 and perceived as an outgrowth of the original anti-Communist crusade: "It will not be sufficient that these destructive forces [of Communism] be merely exposed. . . . The public must be aroused to realize that only by the application of Christian principles, in private and public affairs will there be eliminated, so far as humanly possible, the distress and suffering upon which these forces [of Communism] thrive."[48]

Derry was joined by the noted Catholic Action lecturer from Australia Paul McGuire, in a tour to inform local councils, study clubs, and other public service agencies about the social teachings of Pope Pius XI on a living wage, credit unions, and the responsibilities of industrialists, bankers, and property owners. McGuire popularized specialized Catholic Action derived from the work of the famous Belgian priest, Canon Joseph Cardijn. Based on well-organized cells among youth and workers dedicated to discerning ways to Christianize their fellow students and workers and families on a "like on like" principle, specialized Catholic Action was quite popular among priests, religious, and lay leaders. Initially sponsored by the Fourth Degree, Paul McGuire's lectures on Catholic Action also introduced the dynamic method of the Young Christian Students in France: "Observe, Think and Act." In an article on the history of the Young Christian Students in Toledo, Sister Mary Herman Corey, S.N.D., noted the significance of Paul McGuire's speech at Mary Manse College, where he presented "an enthusiastic account of the use of the *Jocist* or cell technique of Catholic Action rapidly spreading in several countries in Europe."[49] The Archdiocese of Chicago became the national center of specialized Catholic Action. Young Christian Workers and Young Christian Students were under the leadership of Monsignor Reynold Hillenbrand. Also under his inspiration, Patty and Pat Crowley founded the Christian Family Movement. Hillenbrand was a strong advocate of social justice and would on occasion join the picket lines of unions on strike.[50]

The Order's Crusade for Social Justice had no connection with the periodical *Social Justice,* published by the controversial "radio priest," Charles E. Coughlin. Ordained in 1916, Father Coughlin was a Basilian priest who taught at Assumption College in Sandwich, Ontario; because of developments in the Basilian Order, he moved to Detroit as a diocesan priest under Bishop Michael Gallagher. Two years later he received his first assignment as pastor; he was appointed to Little Flower, a recently established parish in Royal Oak, a suburb rife with Klan activity. To dispel religious prejudice and to imbue a strong sense of piety among Catholics, he successfully sought a spot on a local radio station. Coughlin was gifted with a radio voice that was second only to that of Franklin D. Roosevelt, and his program gained popularity in Detroit and later was picked up by CBS national network.[51]

He did not speak on controversial political, social, and economic topics until 1930, when he reacted to the Depression with an attack on capitalist greed, on the dominance of the "international bankers," and on the inept solutions of the Hoover administration. His answer to the moral problem posed by Communism was adherence to God's teachings of self-restraint. Throughout the 1930s his listeners sensed they had a leader who understood their own economic and social problems. At first an impassioned advocate of FDR—"the New Deal is Christ's Deal"—by 1934 he was rallying his listeners in opposition to the administration's agriculture program of crop destruction, to the influence of financial cliques, and to the official recognition of the Soviet Union. He founded the "National Union of Social Justice" and its journal *Social Justice* in 1936, the same year he and the Rev. Gerald L. K. Smith, a Protestant minister in Louisiana, and Dr. Francis P. Townsend of California founded the Union Party to oppose Roosevelt in the national election. This third-party effort was based on "living annual wage for the workers," just profit for the farmers, protections for labor unions, government ownership of utilities and other natural monopolies, and a reform of government and of taxes. After his disastrous defeat at the polls, Coughlin became disillusioned with politics, apparently alienated by the advance of what he considered to be anti-Christian conspirators among the political and economic elites. Within two years, his enemies became the international bankers, the greedy capitalists, and the Bolsheviks—each enemy being dominated by Jews. His anti-Semitism became so dominant that a photo of Hitler appeared on the covers of *Social Justice*.[52]

Several bishops were opposed to Coughlin, even before he became a strident anti-Semite. Cardinal Mundelein of Chicago, Cardinal O'Connell of Boston, and Archbishop McNicholas of Cincinnati had publicly spoken out against Coughlin. Until his death in 1937, Bishop Gallagher supported the "radio-priest." He too perceived the financiers as the principal sources of the Depression. Even after Coughlin referred to FDR as a "liar" and a "double crosser"—comments that generated a letter to Gallagher from the apostolic delegate, Archbishop Amleto Cicognani, as well as an article in *L'Osservatore Romano*—Gallagher never attempted to persuade Coughlin to tone down his rhetoric.[53] "Perhaps he didn't try," wrote Leslie Woodcock Tentler, the historian of the Archdiocese of Detroit. She explains why the bishop was hesitant to restrain the priest: "Coughlin was a phenomena greater than his programs and Gallagher was perhaps unwilling to repudiate the man whom he had long regarded as a powerful force for social justice." Though Tentler also suspects fear of a severely "savage" backlash among his followers may have affected Gallagher's reluctance to harness Coughlin, she also considers the "most likely" explanation of the bishop's approach to "lie . . . in Gallager's personality, and in his tendency to see the world in simplistic almost paranoid, terms."[54] Gallagher's successor, Archbishop Edward Mooney, was unsympathetic to Coughlin and refused to officially approve *Social Justice* with an *imprimatur*. There were periods of censorship, but he considered a stronger policy to be imprudent because it would cause a national protest among Coughlin's impassioned followers. Hence, it was not until 1942, when Coughlin's activities were considered seditious by the government, that the archbishop finally silenced the priest.[55]

Father Coughlin's radio program probably appealed to perhaps the majority of the Knights, as it did to the majority of Catholics, but there was no official public endorsement of him by the leadership of the Fourth Degree. He was considered a possible guest speaker at the 1937 anti-Communist crusade, but, because of his controversial image, he was not invited. Supreme Knight Carmody of Grand Rapids, Michigan, who may have vetoed the invitation to Coughlin, by implication repudiated the radio priest's anti-Semitism when, at the request of the Jewish war veterans, he wrote the following letter to Franklin D. Roosevelt on October 17, 1938:

> The Order of the Knights of Columbus, embracing five hundred thousand members, moved by the same sentiments of fair play and justice that have prompted it to protest on different occasions persecution by governments and fanatical groups of peoples of various faiths who sought only the enjoyment of their God-given right to worship their Creator in accordance with the dictates of their conscience, expresses the deepest sympathy for the distressed Jews of Europe, and most respectfully urges our Government to use its influence to preserve in its full meaning, force, and intent the Palestine mandate that guarantees to the Jews, now sadly persecuted in Europe, the right unhampered to seek refuge and protection in the homeland of their forefathers. In order that the bonds that bind all peoples in human fellowship may not be destroyed, we urge in the name of humanity that prompt action be taken.[56]

Carmody's letter on behalf of the European Jews and implicitly against Nazism, ran contrary to the views of most Catholics, who perceived Soviet Communism rather than Fascism as the greater evil. Bishop John Noll of Fort Wayne, founder of *Our Sunday Visitor* and an advocate of Coughlin after his 1936 attempt to defeat FDR, wrote in 1939: "There has been such a vigorous campaign against Fascism in the American press . . . that the attention of the American people has been at least temporarily withdrawn from the even greater evil of Communism."[57] Noll's position was also congenial to Coughlin's plea for a "Christian Front," aimed at galvanizing anti-Semitic groups and frequently given to violent protests against Jews. Indeed, 238 people were arrested for anti-Semitic behavior in New York City during 1939.[58]

Patrick Scanlon, managing editor of the *Brooklyn Tablet* (1917–1968), was Coughlin's most ardent champion in the Catholic press, even during the controversial years 1938–1940. Though not a member of the Christian Front, Scanlon supported the movement. He persistently saw the world locked in a struggle between good and evil. Bishop John Noll was a Coughlinite, but within the context of a fast growing anti-Coughlin consensus among the U.S. bishops, Noll feigned an objective public image. In a letter to Noll, Helen Baldwin Krippendorf reported on a meeting of liberals, such as Nicholas Murray Butler, president of Columbia University, "who do not realize they are aiding and abetting the enemies of the church." She also told him of several economists who were sympathetic to Coughlin but moving away from his extremism. Despite Krippendorf's sympathy for Coughlin she became disillusioned with his strategies. She told Noll that she sent "detailed reports to Archbishop Amleto Cicognani, the apostolic delegate, to Cardinal Patrick Hayes, archbishop of New York and to William Larkin of the Knights of Columbus asking that Fr. Coughlin be stopped before he got the Church in trouble." She did not receive a response, but she did warn Fr. Coughlin "that he was bringing trouble to the Church. No Answer."[59]

William Larkin was a prominent New York Catholic, a well-known speaker, a leading figure in the Fourth Degree, a former member of the Supreme Board of Directors, and one of the Knights who managed the war work of the Order after P. H. Callahan resigned. Perhaps one of the reasons Helen Baldwin Krippendorf did not receive a reply was that by this time Archbishops Cicognani and Hayes, and probably Larkin, were themselves in opposition to Coughlin. With no evidence of Larkin's views, it is unlikely that he would not follow the lead of his ordinary, Archbishop Hayes.

V

Martin Carmody's Deputy Supreme Knight was Francis Matthews. He succeeded Carmody after defeating a challenge candidate, Patrick J. Moynihan, a former State Deputy of Massachusetts. An active Democrat from Omaha, Nebraska, Matthews was the first Supreme Knight born west of the Mississippi. John Reddin retired from the position of Supreme Master on December 30, 1940, and he died a year later.[60] Timothy P. Galvin, past State Deputy of Indiana and a Supreme Director, was chosen as Reddin's successor. A prominent lawyer in the area of Hammond, Indiana, and a graduate of the University of Notre Dame, Galvin was highly qualified for the position; moreover, after serving as Supreme Master for thirty years Reddin had so shaped the office that Galvin could easily adapt to the position.

The pressing issues facing the nation and the church between 1939 and

1941 related to responding to the war in Europe that began with Hitler's invasion of Poland on September 1, 1939. The Roosevelt administration pursued a policy of preparedness by instituting the first peacetime conscription and by passing legislation for a lend-lease program in support of England. During the debates on these issues, Catholic lay, clerical, and episcopal leaders tended toward isolationism, convinced that lend-lease aid would lead to American intervention in the war. Many supported the "America First" movement, while some in favor of aid endorsed the Committee to Defend America by aiding the Allies. Catholic isolationists invoked the moral decadence of Europe and claimed it a virtue to oppose preparedness measures. In one of his radio programs, Monsignor Fulton J. Sheen said the war was symptomatic of humanity's corruption and represented the "judgment of God." Cardinal Mundelein of Chicago was a strong interventionist, while Archbishop Francis Beckman of Dubuque and Father Coughlin were committed isolationists.[61] Supreme Knight Martin Carmody had sought support for the Jews, but he warned against another futile intervention on the model of 1917, one that fostered in Europe an ethos of "hate and greed."[62] The 1939 Supreme Council passed a resolution in favor of nonintervention and in opposition to the administration's foreign policy, with particular reference to the repeal of the Neutrality Act.

By 1940, Supreme Knight Francis P. Matthews opposed Carmody's isolationist policy and publicly stated that he deplored the isolationism of the America First stance. In this same vein, Matthews invited Supreme Court Justice Frank Murphy to address the Supreme Council convention in August of 1941. A former mayor of Detroit and governor of Michigan, Murphy was an active Catholic. Though a member of the Holy Name Society, he never joined the Knights of Columbus.[63] In the banquet address to the convention, he was eloquent in his endorsement of the administration's policy of aid to the Soviet Union in its struggle against Nazi Germany.[64] For the Knights to sponsor an address advocating that the United States should send arms to the Bolsheviks generated a strong reaction in several spheres.

Shortly after Murphy's address, Supreme Master Timothy Galvin wrote to Luke Hart about the "caustic comment" on the Supreme Court Justice's remarks published by Patrick Scanlon. Responding to Galvin, Hart noted that he was a subscriber to the *Brooklyn Tablet* and told him that he was in agreement with the article critical of Murphy's address.[65] "I think my old friend, Pat Scanlon, was somewhat generous" in his statement in August 30 edition that simply pointed out that Murphy did not represent the "vision of most people" and since he was not a Knight his "advice was that of one from without." Hart and Galvin were deliberately not informed about the contents of the address, said Hart, but if they had known, Murphy "would not have been permitted to speak." According to Hart, Francis Matthews was somewhat duplicitous; on one occasion he told Hart that Murphy had prior approval of his address from Archbishop Mooney and on another occasion Matthews said Murphy talked with the archbishop after he had spoken and that "Mooney was in agreement with the Supreme Court Justice."[66] Though Hart considered publishing a response to Murphy in *Columbia* he decided on a more modest arrangement: a boxed statement next to Murphy's address in the printed proceedings explaining the policy of not asking for an advance copy of a manuscript or a speech, thereby removing the Order from any association with the content of such addresses. However, the simplest solution was followed; Murphy's address was not printed in the proceedings of the Supreme Council published the following October.

In a newspaper clipping included in Galvin's letter to Hart the title reads "Dr. McMahon, Notre Dame Professor Endorses Justice Murphy's stand": McMahon was also chairman of the American Catholic Philosophical Society; the previous April he had delivered an address at the Catholic Association for International Peace in which he charged the isolationists with being responsible for the chaotic condition in Europe.[67] He evaluated Justice Murphy's position as "the only one compatible with sound patriotism and Christian ethics . . . Hitlerism is the number one menace to religion, culture, and American liberty today. Aiding Russia to fight and weaken this menace is not only ethically permissible but a matter of great practical urgency."[68] By supporting Patrick Scanlon's views, which were rooted in America-First nationalism, Galvin's understanding of patriotism obviously clashed with McMahon's meaning of the term—a conflict that presaged polarizations in the postwar period of anti-Communism as well as in the culture conflicts of the 1960s and beyond.

Three months after the Murphy controversy, the nation and church were unified in vigorous response to the declaration of war as a result of the Japanese attack on Pearl Harbor. Anticipating the need for social-service efforts, the Knights of Columbus and the NCWC engaged in discussions on the development of a program. The United States K. of C. Huts program of World War I was not reinstituted in World War II simply because the National Catholic Welfare Conference had become so well organized that it proved unrealistic for the bishops to turn over the war work to the Knights of Columbus as they had in 1917. However, Matthews and Hart had met with the YMCA, Salvation Army, and the Jewish Welfare Board with the anticipation of receiving the necessary permission from the administrative board of the NCWC, chaired by Archbishop Mooney of Detroit. However, by this time the NCWC had established the National Catholic Community Service (NCCS), which worked in tandem with the federal government's United Service Organization (USO). The Order was one of several Catholic societies represented in the administration of the NCCS, with Francis Matthews the chairman of its executive committee. Hart was disappointed at these developments and eventually blamed Matthews, formerly his close friend, for his lack of leadership in establishing a Knights' war activities council independent of the bishops. He also disagreed with Matthews's commitment to the NCCS. Hart expected Matthews to take responsibility for the insurance and other programs at the home office by visiting New Haven at least one week a month. Though Hart muted his criticism of Matthews during the war, he considered his position to be almost irreconcilable with that of Matthews. However, Hart ultimately served on committees of the NCCS and placed a member of the home office on its budget and administrative staff and released members to be field supervisors; this helped to generate interest in NCCS social centers among the local councils of the Order, such as the Atlanta Council.[69]

As a member of the British Commonwealth, Canada entered the war in September 1939. A Knights of Columbus Huts program, based on the World War I model, was initiated within two weeks. Supreme Director Claude Brown of London, Ontario, was the principal organizer of the program. The YMCA, the Salvation Army, and the Canadian Legion formed the United Welfare Organization. Claude Brown, a dentist and former State Deputy of Ontario and Master of the Fourth Degree, created an ad hoc committee, which later became the executive board. Besides Brown as president, the other members were Supreme Director Francis Fauteaux of Montreal, vice president; Ontario State Deputy Philip Phelan, secretary; and State Deputy of Quebec, Ludger Faguy, treasurer. This committee administered the Huts program, which was limited to Ontario and Quebec, representing 26,000 of the total 33,000 Canadian Knights, less than 10 percent of the membership of the entire Order. On the board of directors were Bishop C. L. Nelligan, head of the National Catholic Chaplains, two other chaplains, Archbishop A. A. Vachen of Ottawa, and K. of C. representatives of the nine provinces.[70]

Two hundred Knights were involved in the program, which featured recreation centers in the large cities, morale programs in training camps, and K. of C. hostels to provide hospitality and entertainment for servicemen on furlough in England. When France was liberated in 1944, these hostels were established on the Continent. Some volunteers died during the war, including Claude Brown, and one Knight was a POW. In 1942, Bishop Nelligan wrote : "In Canada the Knights of Columbus Canadian Army huts stitch like a golden chain from coast to coast, connecting up all our military camps and a large number of our newly established training centers."[71] He was also pleased with the Knights' free distribution of statues, religious articles, stations of the cross, prayer books, and rosaries. The entire program was based on interreligious cooperation among Catholics, collaboration between French- and English-speaking Knights, and a strong organizational effort among the Knights, the hierarchy, and the government.

A month after Pearl Harbor, Supreme Master Timothy Galvin successfully introduced a proposal to the members of the Supreme Board of Directors to adopt a local Fourth Degree program entitled, "America Fights for God Given Rights." In a letter to Bishop Francis McIntyre, auxiliary bishop of New York, Galvin explained that the program was aimed at promoting among the membership and the American people the "true essence of Americanism," which Galvin stated is "a distinctively Catholic and Christian thing, pointing out that the founding fathers of our country had declared that the source of our liberties and the rights of man to be rooted in God." He cited the "language of the Declaration of Independence," and noted that this fact "is altogether too obscure in the mind of the people generally." To promote this ideal through a national publicity campaign "is bound to contribute to the national morale," and would tend to imbue the postwar reconstruction programs with Christian values that may otherwise be marginalized. "The whole program simply means studying and publicizing the place God occupies in the American system of government." Though Galvin did not refer to the Fourth Degree ceremonials that ritualize the traditional Catholic ideal of the providential mission of America, he did state that "while this program is essentially and thoroughly Catholic, we are confident it will appeal to all Americans who believe in a personal God." The Fourth Degree members were central to the plan; they were to distribute literature explaining "our thesis and its historical background." After the Fourth Degree assemblies had devoted themselves to a study of "the Christian concept of Government and its expression in our America Republic" they would sponsor public programs in the Catholic schools. Hence, it will provide "a real objective, patriotic in character, to the Fourth Degree Organization." To launch the program Galvin developed a four-part national radio broadcast featuring Archbishop Francis Spellman, J. Edgar Hoover, Clarence Manion, dean of the Law School at the University of Notre Dame, who coined the motto, "America Fights For God Given Rights," and Galvin himself. He told McIntyre that J. Edgar Hoover is "a thorough-going Christian . . . and an outstanding figure in opposition to subversive forces in American life."[72]

Because the minutes of the Fourth Degree biennial Supreme Assemblies are not extant for the period, the impact of this program is impossible to determine. However, an address by Timothy Galvin on the motto of this program was cited by the New Haven *Journal Courier* in an editorial on July 25, 1942, "It Need Not Be a Civil War." The opening two paragraphs responded to the race question; there were two ways of dealing with the question: "the enlightenedly self-interested attempt to work out what is at best a complicated and difficult problem. This method demands the realization that the future of our country is involved in the race issue." The second way was "to stubbornly refuse to consider any fact or proposal that would alter the status quo." After referring to the groups who perpetuated the Jim Crow system in the South, the editor listed some of the positive forces and cited a recent speech by the Supreme Master in Hartford; Galvin told his Fourth Degree members that "America is fighting for God given rights, and in this sign we shall conquer. . . . We believe that an abiding conviction of the justice of our cause will give Americans unconquerable courage for the fight." The editorial then concluded that if the "international cause is just, our National cause to face the race issue must be just. It can be."[73] There is no evidence, however, that the Knights dealt positively with the race issue until the mid-1950s.

Galvin's radio campaign involved Archbishop Francis Spellman, who echoed the Fourth Degree ideal contained in the ceremonials mentioned in Galvin's letter to Bishop McIntyre: "our nation is built upon a rock which is God."[74] This address seems to have presaged the Order's Peace Program, adopted in August 1943, "based upon shaping and educating public opinion to the end that Catholic principles and Catholic philosophy will be properly represented at the peace table at the conclusion of this general war."[75] Under Deputy Supreme Knight John Swift of Massachusetts, the Peace Program committee published lengthy essays from theologians, philosophers, and sociologists steeped in the natural law theory of Thomas Aquinas and launched "an ardent crusade of Christian forces to prevent the collapse of Christian Evangelization . . . and to bring God back to world government." James Gillis, C.S.P., editor of the *Catholic World*, concluded that the Order's program was superior to the proposal composed by an ecumenical group of Catholics, Protestants and Jews, because "it was more specific."[76]

The Order's role in World War II was not as socially participatory as the Canadian Huts program, but on the leadership level, Francis Matthews and Luke Hart served in the administration of the NCCS. Timothy Galvin was committed to energizing the Fourth Degree with a program of Catholic Americanism aimed at all who "believed in a personal God." Hart's crucial support for Francis Matthews in the 1939 election as Supreme Knight was based on his promise to be an activist administrator in New Haven, where he would attend to the insurance and investment interests of the Order. Since he failed to fulfill that promise, Hart opposed Matthews in the 1943 election for Supreme Knight. Though Matthews won the contest, Hart was determined to continue to lead a campaign for his defeat.

Prior to the 1945 election, Matthews had promoted a merger between the Order and the National Council of Catholic Men, a measure supported by many bishops. Luke E. Hart and others were opposed to this proposal since it would reduce the Knights' autonomy and place them under the authority of the bishops. This would have entailed a change in canonical status; the Knights of Columbus would go from an Order of Catholic men to a Catholic Order of men. Alienated by this proposed merger, Luke Hart and others were even more determined to defeat Matthews. Deputy Supreme Knight John Swift of Boston, a forceful speaker, defeated him at the Supreme Council convention in 1945. The short distance between Boston and New Haven allowed Swift to attend to the business of the home office. For personal and professional reasons Timothy Galvin resigned before the end of his term as Supreme Master. He became once again Deputy Supreme Knight, a position that did not require the commitment of time and travel. William J. Mulligan, past State Deputy of Connecticut, was appointed to fill out the term and then in August was appointed by the Board of Directors to his own term, effective in September 1945. For the first time the Supreme Master was from the Northeast. Mulligan and Swift represented Catholic anti-Communism during the Cold War and the rise of Joseph McCarthy.

VI

William Mulligan, who succeeded P. H. Callahan as the director of the Order's War Activities Committee in 1918, became a member of the Reconstruction Program aimed at ousting the Flaherty administration. This was ostensibly for its support of Supreme Advocate Joseph Pelletier during his trial for extortion as District Attorney of Suffolk County (Boston) in 1921. The Reconstruction Program had a broad platform that included greater accountability and severe restrictions on the finances of the Order. There is a touch of irony in the Board's appointment of Mulligan as Supreme Master; in 1923 he had opposed Luke Hart for election to the office of Supreme Advocate, while in 1945 Hart was the dominant figure on the Board that unanimously endorsed Mulligan for Supreme Master of the Fourth Degree. Obviously the two had reconciled their differences over the twenty-two years, as symbolized by Mulligan's anti-Matthews sentiment. In contrast to Reddin and in a sense to Galvin as well, William Mulligan did not initiate new programs for the Fourth Degree. In his first report to a Supreme Assembly, Mulligan immediately revealed his leadership style: "Many times it is said that the Fourth Degree should have a set plan of action which would promote patriotism. It is difficult to prescribe activities which would meet the approval of all assemblies. Assemblies in different dioceses are doing work in their own way and promoting patriotism for the benefit of our Church."[77] He cited three local programs each of which benefited the church and represented Catholic patriotism. The Washington General Assembly in the District of Columbia had hosted a Pan-American reception for the diplomats of Central and South America; Catholics were introduced to the Knights of Columbus "and the power and the strength and the influence for good that it [i.e., the Order] has in the United States and Canada." Mulligan also noted the same assembly's "annual field Mass at the Tomb of the Unknown Soldier," which drew over two thousand people in 1946; Cardinal Francis Spellman was the speaker on that occasion.[78]

Another local program sponsored by the St. Paul General Assembly, featured youth work with Columbian Squires, Boy Scouts, and other groups: "programs for youths of 15 years and older, that will build character, love of country, moral and physical health and the understanding of how true Americans live together." The St. Louis, Missouri, members of the Fourth Degree had been sponsoring a boys' club for underprivileged youths since 1929. Luke Hart was there at its origin; Mulligan noted in 1946 that it was partially supported by a civic program, "United Charities," and it provided club activity for 54,000 boys, representing thirty-four nationalities and sixteen religious denominations. Mulligan also listed several other Fourth Degree programs; such as the catechists for poor children in Chihuahua, Mexico.[79]

Mulligan elaborated on the elite character of this special corps of members: "Fourth Degree Knights are picked men, men of understanding, of integrity, loyalty, readiness in service. When you [Vice-Supreme Masters] meet with your Masters I would advise urging them to . . . [be certain] that the selection of candidates is carefully made." He concluded with an exhortation derived from the ceremonials. "Our patriotism should prompt us to feel a spiritual concern for our nation. . . . The Founding Fathers were aware that a nation that turns its back on God . . . is a doomed nation."[80]

Entirely absent from Mulligan's first report was any reference to the postwar anti-Communist dynamic among Protestants, Catholics, and Jews, conservatives as well as liberals, though with varying emphases and tonalities. There is no doubt about Mulligan's participation in this general crusade against the "godless enemy"; he simply deferred to Supreme Knight John Swift as the leader in the movement. Since Mulligan departed from Reddin's style of developing general programs for all the membership, he did not propose an anti-Communist project for each assembly, but rather encouraged it to adopt its own. In other reports to the Supreme Assembly he followed the model of his initial address by listing vital projects of local assemblies most of which originated in the Reddin era, 1910–1940. Subsequent Supreme Masters adopted the Mulligan principle of local, rather than national or international, initiatives. Since the Supreme Knight was the primary agent in fostering the ideals of American patriotism and Catholic citizenship, much of the remainder of this chapter focuses on Swift's speeches on the threats of Communism both at home and abroad.

VII

Despite the strong tendency toward isolationism among Catholics, there was little dissent once the war began. David O'Brien reports that of the 11,887 conscientious objectors during World War II only 135 were Catholic, a figure far out of proportion to the relationship between Catholics and the general population.[81] There was also very little Catholic opposition, including among theologians, to the strategy of saturation bombing of cities, which was in violation of the principle of non-combatant immunity; the policy of unconditional surrender in the Pacific war was questioned by some bishops, but the use of atomic weapons was considered to be the tragic blow at the principle of non-combatant immunity. A growing debate among theologians and bishops on the use of atomic bombs was carried out in the Catholic press. Perhaps for the first time, the conservative Patrick Scanlon, managing editor of the *Brooklyn Tablet,* and John Cogley, editor of *Commonweal,* agreed; both affirmed the immorality of the nuclear bombing of Hiroshima and Nagasaki. Archbishop Spellman was concerned about the imbalance between the unconditioned-surrender policy imposed upon Japan and the principle enunciated by Pope Pius XII, "peace with justice."[82] Among the American bishops there was near unanimity on Spellman's warning of the advance of the Soviet Union in postwar Europe. In 1947 the domination of the Soviet Union in Eastern Europe and its attacks upon the church elicited strong anti-Communist response by the American hierarchy.

During the Cold War, Marian devotions, particularly the continuation of the devotion to Our Lady of Fatima, included prayers for the conversion of Russia that were said at the end of daily masses throughout the nation. David F. Crosby, S.J., captured the development of a "new" anti-Communism.

> In the final year of the war Catholic anti-communism entered a new phase; what had previously been only one of a huge number of concerns became a way of life. American Catholics had only one thought in their minds—the preservation of their church from the Marxist marauder. . . . American Catholics had a new obsession and they would receive nothing but encouragement from a large part of the American Press and electorate . . . anti-Communism had become a common denominator, the bulwark of both Americanism and authentic Catholicism.[83]

Though Crosby was given to emotive rhetoric, the Knights of Columbus, particularly the Fourth Degree, had been identifying patriotic Americanism and authentic Catholicism since their origin. As early as January of 1946 Supreme Knight John Swift spoke out on the American capitulation to Soviet expansion with reference to "Godless Russia's" disregard of the Atlantic Charter by "enslaving millions of our fellow Catholics." Because of its "shameless appeasement" America had "failed to uphold American ideals."[84] Swift's report to the August 1946 convention of the Supreme Council was a distinctively Catholic anti-Communist manifesto, a lengthy description of "the Satanic scourge" of Bolshevist imperialism, the Marxist-Leninist philosophy and the widespread penetration of Communists in government, labor unions, and college faculties, all buttressed by hundreds of Communist-front organizations."[85]

As a sign of the commitment to enlighten citizens on the dangerous character of Communism, the Order sponsored full-page advertisements in twelve large metropolitan daily newspapers in the United States and Canada. These ads not only elaborated on the dangers of the expansion of the Soviet Union but also offered free copies of Monsignor Fulton J. Sheen's pamphlet *Communism, the Opium of the People.* To follow up on his charge of U.S. appeasement, John Swift successfully urged the Supreme Board to establish "The Knights of Columbus Crusade for the Preservation and Promotion of American Ideals."[86] Analogous to the Crusade for Social Justice of 1938, this postwar program also featured a national tour by George Hermann Derry to energize local councils through discussion programs. He eventually published his *Manual for Discussion Groups* in 1947. The crusade imagery evokes a millennial struggle between the forces of darkness and light, the enslaved and the free. The Catholic component of the American Ideals Program was expressed theoretically. The principal documents of American idealism were the Declaration of Independence and the Bill of Rights, as well as the speeches of Adams, Jefferson, and Lincoln, documents that resounded with the natural law theories of "our Suarez and St. Thomas [Aquinas]."[87] The natural law was the basis of Catholic moral philosophy, the glue of conscience that holds society together. It was also symbolic of the Catholic foundation story of the nation, based on natural laws, the historical memory that bestows a sense of authority to the Order's proponents of the Preservation and Promotion of American Ideals in its conflict with the godless communists, their sympathizers and the secularists who eliminate God from the American creed. Contrary to those historians who perceived John Swift's plan as rationalizations for the defense of capitalism, the Order's crusade was not simply the promotion of political and religious ideals. It was also advocating the right "to a job, to a family living wage, to collective bargaining, and to strike, to Joint Management, enroute to Joint Ownership of Industry."[88]

While this plan was evolving, the rights to joint ownership, to all forms of social security were guaranteed. Steeped in principles of the papal encyclicals and the social reconstruction platform of the bishops' 1919 program—composed principally by Monsignor John A. Ryan—this rights language distinguished the Knights' crusade from the programs of other Catholic conservatives who were both protectors of capitalism and crusaders against Communism. In opposition to these conservatives, the Knights plan listed among the "abuses of unrestricted capitalism: unfair distribution of wealth, 'Rich are getting richer, and the poor are getting poorer' . . . the wretched conditions of industrial workers in many parts of the world . . . unemployment . . . and 'Economic Royalists and stubborn opponents of all reform." In contrast to the principled arguments against the apologists of capitalism, Swift's plan appears at first to have been in line with typical reactionary anti-Communist rhetoric. However, on Swift's list of enemies were also the self-serving Anglo-Saxon elites, "High brow fellow travelers" who were "culturally veneered, powerfully influential, and reportedly above suspicion." Some of the elite groups were: "Millionaire 'angels,' the do gooders . . . crackpot idealists, dreamers, 'perfectionists'. . . *self-styled* 'Intelligentsia' . . . pretentious white collared Communists."[89] These labels also reveal the Knights' populism particularly nurtured in John Swift's Boston, where the conflict between Irish-American Catholics and the Anglo-Saxon elites was played out with dramatic intensity, a political and social caldron where each group fired the coals of religious and patriotic identities.

The Order's crusade gained momentum in 1947–1948, culminating in over thirteen hundred discussion groups in local councils. To garner vast public support for the Order's anti-Communist and social-justice campaign in the spheres of public opinion, it designed a series of six fifteen-minute radio dramatizations, "Safeguards of America," along with the same allotment of time for "Foundations of Our American Ideals." "Safeguards" opened with a description of political, social, economic, and religious life in the Soviet Union and concluded with a treatment of the struggle against communist subversion in the United States. The "Foundations" series depicted the natural-law sources of American idealism and the divine origins of authority, the notable significance of religious liberty, and the contest between the nobility of democratic freedom and the ignominious character of Communist tyranny.[90] A third series, "The Future of America," focused on the role of the United States as a "moral leader in the family of nations, the great benefactor of the human race."[91] Bernard Rubin in his "Broadway Beat" column in the *Daily Worker*, the publication of the American Communist Party, portrayed the forthcoming "Safeguards" and "Foundations" programs as "K of C Plans Big Radio Hoax on Communists." He predicted that "this fantastic hoax will be the signal for the greatest crackdown and terror campaign on unions, free speech, liberals, Communists that this country has witnessed in recent times."[92] The Order's *Knights of Columbus News* regarded Rubin's comments as clearly indicating that the radio program was "hitting the Commies where it hurts" and wondered "which dream book Comrade Rubin used for some of the colorful details of the story."[93]

Motivated by their patriotic duty, the Knights did warn in their radio programs of Communist front organizations, but they also defended the First Amendment freedoms. In a resolution passed at the Supreme Council convention of 1947, the Order warned of the "beachheads of corruption and disloyalty" among government employees, union workers, teachers, and professors. It urged a Congressional investigation to expose and defeat this conspiracy.[94] Thus, the Order's anti-Communism predated Senator Joseph R. McCarthy's vigorous pursuit of Communist subversion in many spheres of American life. The charges of "witch-hunt" tactics, of demagoguery, and of deceit gave the term "McCarthyism" a permanent place in the lexicon of American politics. Later articles in *Columbia* and resolutions of the Supreme Council indicate the Knights' support of McCarthy's Senate hearings, and their defense of him against his detractors. Many other Catholics, as well as Protestant and Jewish groups, also perceived McCarthy's campaign to be a necessary means to rid the nation of Communists and their "fellow travelers."

In 1945, some years before the advent of McCarthy, the National Catholic Welfare Conference assigned Father John Cronin, the Sulpician sociologist in the Social Action Office to design and evaluate a survey of American bishops on the presence of Communist infiltration in the areas of their dioceses.[95] In a recently published collection of documents, *Public Voices: Catholics in the American Context*, one document is the response of Bishop Joseph Hurley of St. Augustine, Florida, which reveals the extent of the survey as well as the general assumption that there was widespread Communist infiltration. One of Cronin's questions asked for a list of names and backgrounds of "present officers, followers and sympathizers, . . . of those Communist minded persons." Bishop Hurley responded in detail to the questions. Cronin attempted to present the results of the survey to Senator McCarthy. David F. Crosby explained the Sulpician's motivation: "Cronin believed that a restrained and scholarly approach would impress the senator, but was due for a rough surprise. Once or twice a month he and his aides delivered a packet of information about people in government they believed worthy of investigation. To their acute disappointment, however, McCarthy completely ignored their information and continued to churn out wild accusations and garbled pieces of misinformation."[96] Hence, the pro-McCarthy stance of the leadership of the Knights, including that of Supreme Master William Mulligan, was in accord with the NCWC's deep concern with Communist subversion in the United States.

There were several Catholic opponents of the content, strategies, and tactics of McCarthy. Leonard Schmidt, McCarthy's opponent in the 1952 Republican primary, was a member of the Knights of Columbus and also in the progressive wing of the Wisconsin Republican Party. Allied with Schmidt's anti-McCarthy position were such leading American Catholics as

George Shuster, former editor of *Commonweal* and president of Hunter College; Jerome Kerwin, a political scientist at the University of Chicago; and Auxiliary Bishop of Chicago, Bernard J. Sheil. William F. Buckley, Jr., the most well-known conservative Catholic intellectual, defended Joseph McCarthy and wrote a 1964 polemic with Brent Bozell, *McCarthy and His Enemies*.[97] Recent publications based on the KGB files illustrate the significance of Communist penetration in government, unions, and other spheres of life, and verify McCarthy's fears of a Soviet conspiracy. Others responded with evidence and noted that the significance of McCarthyism—that is, "witch-hunt" demagoguery— should not be revised by these revelations made by conservative historians. David F. Crosby, S.J., the historian of Catholics and McCarthyism, evaluates the Knights' endorsement of the Senator even during the crisis of the Army hearings that marked the final stage of his anti-Communist campaign. Crosby concludes: "The Knights' pro-McCarthy policy was completely congruent with their long history of political conservatism, their failure to support civil rights legislation, their flag-waving patriotism, and their abiding distaste for Protestants, liberals, and intellectuals of every persuasion."[98] This history of the Fourth Degree stands as a refutation of Crosby's careless generalization. Because his work was published before my 1982 book on the history of the Kinghts, he was unaware of the ecumenical vision of the Commission on Religious Prejudices, the publication of notable scholars by the Historical Commission—Samuel Flagg Bemis, Allan Nevins, W. E. B. DuBois, the significance of George Hermann Derry, the social justice lecturer during the Great Depression and the Cold War, and John Swift's patriotism based on America ideals, with a blend of social-welfare reformism and anti-Communism. Hence, Crosby's critique was off the mark.

VIII

On the 1950 jubilee of the Fourth Degree, William Mulligan reflected on its historical programs: the free lecture movement to warn of the perils of socialism and communism; the World War I program in support of the K. of C. Huts; the Historical Commission "to put a stop to the perversion and falsification of American history"; the essay contest, Catholic Action, and the retreat movement. On December 4, 1949, on the eve of the jubilee, the Fourth Degree was established in the Philippine Islands. Father George Willman, S.J., who is considered the second founder of the Order there, was appointed Special Master, and he led the exemplification or initiation of 160 candidates.

Mulligan stressed the present and future work of the Fourth Degree, simultaneously patriotic and religious. However, because "a war is being waged to secularize all American life, the permanent estrangement of those words 'patriotic' and 'religious' is being attempted." Mulligan criticized those "zealots" dedicated to popularizing a "doctrine" that the human person "is no more than the creature of society, subjected to the society for existence, identity, and rights," rather than "a creature of God." Mulligan reminded the members that God is the source of all rights and identity, "freedom under God and unto God is the [citizen's] . . . birthright. . . . Genuine Americanism and the Christian religion are historically and in character closely akin."[99]

Mulligan perceived the world divided between totalitarian dictatorship and freedom, but with a domestic danger of a "drift toward secularist collectivism," America can nevertheless rally the people to the vindication of "freedom, justice and good, and godly living." If the tendency toward secularization maintains its strength, then "the greatest work of the Fourth Degree now awaits us: To renew the soul of the country we so dearly love, to reinvigorate American society with knowledge of and dedication to things that are of God's, to proclaim afresh and to apply the sovereign truths, values, and strength wherein are found the greatness of a people, their security at home and their power of constructive leadership abroad."[100]

According to John Swift and others, there was an antisecularist dimension to the Order's anti-Communism. One of the major reasons for the advancement of Communism, said Swift, was "the de-Christianized conscience and paganist heart of modern man." In contrast, Swift extolled the traditional ideals of the Fourth Degree by invoking the providential role of Catholicism in the foundation and development of this "almost chosen people." He called upon "all God created and God redeemed individuals [of all faiths] to be proud of our heritage, our American ideals, our American contributions. Together we can save America and save the World."[101] Such an ecumenical plea for promoting the ideals of Americanism presaged the thesis of the Jewish sociologist Will Herberg, whose book *Protestant, Catholic, and Jew* had achieved great popularity in 1955. The once historically conflicting faith traditions were now unified in their Americanism. "By every realistic criterion the American way of life is the operative faith of the American people."[102] This is the notion of civil religion that was representative of a religious revival in the mid-1950s. In contrast were the Protestant and secular forms of anti-Catholic militancy regnant during the postwar period and particularly forceful during the campaign of John F. Kennedy, the second Catholic to seek the office of President of the United States.

5

NEW FORMS OF ANTI-CATHOLICISM, A CATHOLIC PRESIDENT, THE NEW PATRIOTISM, 1950–2000

I

WHEN PRESIDENT HARRY S. TRUMAN announced the appointment of Mark W. Clark to be the U.S. Ambassador to the Vatican (October 20, 1951), it generated a severe reaction among leaders of many Protestant groups concerned with possible abuse of the disestablishment clause of the First Amendment. President Franklin D. Roosevelt's 1939 appointment of Myron C. Taylor as his "personal representative" to the Vatican had caused a similar backlash among the same groups concerned about "violations" of separation of church and state. The National Council of Churches, the National Association of Evangelicals, as well as the *Christian Century* were impassioned in their opposition to Truman's appointment of the Episcopalian General Clark. G. Bromley Oxnam, a Methodist bishop, considered the national election to turn on the issue of the ambassador to the Vatican. A Congregationalist clergyman from Milwaukee reportedly told his parish to "vote for Protestants who will uphold the Protestant tradition."[1] The appointment of the ambassador did not affect the election of Dwight Eisenhower in 1952, particularly because, in the heat of controversy, Clark had his name removed from consideration. Despite the apparent victory for the purported "protectors of the First Amendment," there were significant pro-appointment editorials in the *New York Times* and the *Washington Post,* as well as endorsements of the ambassador by two prominent historians, Edwin S. Corwin of Princeton and Arthur Schlesinger, Jr., of Harvard.[2] The opposition to Clark presaged the Protestant opposition to the election of John F. Kennedy, a coalition that also included Protestants and Other Americans United for the Separation of Church and State, the POAU, founded in 1948.

As early as 1944, the *Christian Century* had published a series of articles by Harold E. Fey, a principal figure in the POAU, warning its readers, mostly Protestant clergymen, that Catholicism was becoming a dominant force in American life. The *Christian Century* and the POAU represented another phase in the continuous conflict over the role of Catholicism in America. This chapter opens with this phase of the conflict, one that culminates during the election and administration of John F. Kennedy. The second part focuses on the culture wars symbolized by the Knights' ideals of patriotism as opposed to new forms of patriotism by antiwar protesters and other dissidents in the 1960s and early 1970s. The 1973 Supreme Court decision *Roe v. Wade* also entailed two conflicting interpretations of the Declaration of Independence, particularly the meaning of *life*, liberty, and the pursuit of happiness, as rights endowed by the creator. The book concludes with the Fourth Degree's effort to pass a constitutional amendment to protect the flag from desecration, the final conflict of the century, abundant with symbolic images of patriotism.

II

The prominent editor of the *Christian Century*, Harold E. Fey, wrote an eight-part series on the subject "Can Catholicism Win America?" After underscoring "the powerful agencies" accelerating the process of "homogenization" of American society—"universal education, universal conscription, universal radio, universal press"—Fey considered the "relationship between Catholicism and our emerging American culture." The nearly twenty-three million Catholics, three times more numerous than members of the Methodist Church, were particularly challenging because "these American citizens are subject to the spiritual direction of an Italian Pontiff who represents a culture historically alien to American institutions."[3] The social Americanization of immigrant Catholics, no longer hindered by their traditional "inferiority complex," has meant the growth of a nationally unified church, represented by the National Catholic Welfare Conference, and indicative of a new phase, characterized by a bold and aggressive assertion of power, "to make history—American history." According to Fey, the inherently antidemocratic tendencies of the American Roman Church have been expressed in American policies such as helping to "defeat democracy and enthrone clerical fascism in Franco's Spain" and in "affecting our dealings with Mexico."[4] Fey also lamented the Catholic influence to end prohibition of the sale of alcoholic beverages and the power of the Legion of Decency in promoting "numerous pro-Catholic films."[5] The rhetoric of this opening article reveals Fey's methodology, a blend of factual narrative and an exaggeration of Catholicism's power and influence to the point of distortion. For example, many American Catholics were alienated by the church burnings initiated by the forces of the Spanish Republic, but they did not necessarily support the Franco regime's stance on the unity of state and altar. Hence, the policy in the Spanish Civil War was not simply representative of American Catholicism's tendency toward authoritarianism. But to nuance the complexity of those conditions would not have served Fey's purpose. However, he was also critical of the mindless, anti-Catholic bigotry of the American Protective Association and of the "shameful record of Protestant support for the Ku Klux Klan and for a succession of unorganized anti-Catholic bigots."[6] He defended the freedom of the NCWC to pursue its own aims in affecting public policy. But also he urged thirty-six million Protestants to repudiate the three traditional factors inhibiting unity, "individualism, . . . localism and atomistic pride. Then Protestants would become a major force in shaping the emerging American Civilization."[7] In the contest for "the soul of the American civilization" he portrayed the twenty-three million American Catholics in lock-step with the forces of "ecclesiastical fascism" in Spain and as co-conspirators with the anti-freedom forces of the Vatican that threaten Protestant cultures.[8] The subtext of these eight articles in a mainstream religious weekly is the contest between Protestants and Catholics over the historical memory and meaning of American-democratic identity.

The patriotism of the Fourth Degree and the concurrent promotion of the American Catholic heritage were energized by its opposition to American Protestant historical memory. Fey elaborates on that memory:

> Our sixteenth century forebears were compelled to brush aside the priestly facade of medieval Christianity patterned after imperial Rome to recover the central structure of living faith which was given to the world in first century Palestine. We can do that better than they, thanks to modern scholarship. We are also better equipped to appraise the peril which the authoritarian principle holds for modern society. We have better reason to know that the thing which made our fathers break with Rome is today far more important than

> are any of the issues which separate Protestant from Protestant. The faith which once molded the pattern of American national life, and has also shaped the character of other cultures, still lives.[9]

Fey's fear of the prospect of Catholic dominance in the making of American culture appeared to have been supported by the Supreme Court decision affecting the separation of church and state, *Everson v. Board of Education* (February 10, 1947), which allowed parochial school children to be transported to their schools on public-funded buses. A scholar of American Protestantism described the decision: "Of great portent for the future, the court again invoked the Fourteenth Amendment [due process clause] to the states and went into extensive detail about the meaning of the First Amendment guarantees of religious liberty citing the words of Jefferson . . . [on] the Wall of Separation between Church and State."[10] The court concluded that New Jersey's busing policy did not represent a breach of that wall. As a result of the Everson decision and of the growing fear of Catholic influence in the spheres of public policy allied with the "alien power" of the Vatican, sixty Protestant leaders issued a manifesto on "the Separation of Church and State" in November 1947. Referring to itself as Protestants and other Americans United for the Separation of Church and State (POAU), its manifesto was "anti-Catholic only in the sense that every Catholic is anti-Protestant."[11] The principal officers of the POAU were Baptists who had organized a national Joint Conference Committee in 1945 composed of the American Baptist organizations—Southern, Northern, National, and National, Inc. Roosevelt's appointment of Myron Taylor as his representative[12] to the Vatican had led to the formation of the Joint Conference Committee opposed to expenditure of public funds for any ecclesiastical institution. The POAU indictment of American Catholics for undermining the constitutional guarantees of separation of church and state generated a response from several sources. Among the Knights of Columbus, Supreme Knight John Swift replied to the POAU manifesto with a press release notifying the public that the manifesto was an attack on the patriotism of Catholics, Protestants, and Jews "who do not subscribe to its biased and inaccurate interpretation of the First Amendment." A Bostonian who had experienced the contentious relations between Protestants and Catholics, Swift referred to the manifesto as another form of "religious bigotry."[13] His defense of the patriotism of the three principal religions—Protestant, Catholic, and Jew—underscored the broad sense of citizenship promoted by the Fourth Degree and simultaneously relegated the POAU to the status of a sectarian fringe group.

In 1948, John Donahue, editor of *Columbia,* caricatured the POAU as the "P.U. and Co." and severely criticized "the self-appointed guardians of the First Amendment." He extolled the Knights' defense of federal aid to all schools because the parochial school was a vital source of strength in the battle against materialism and secularism.[14] The 1949 Supreme Council adopted two resolutions implicitly aimed at the POAU manifesto. The resolution "on Church and State" simply stated that the "wall of separation" was "far fetched, unwarranted, and prejudicial." It merely prohibits laws "respecting the establishment of religion." To invoke the wall of separation as the rationale for prohibiting Catholic students to be bussed to schools, was to mislead "people . . . into accepting a figure of speech as a principle of law." The Knights' resolution on federal aid to education was complemented by the assertion: "Catholics support unequivocally the principle of the separation of Church and State."[15] Indeed, the Fourth Degree ceremonials celebrated the First Amendment as the source of the Knights' Catholic citizenship, their republicanism, and their commitment to the rule of law. The delegates to the 1949 Supreme Council convention were predominantly Fourth Degree Knights and dedicated separationists. The ceremonials also portrayed Charles Carroll of Carrollton, the Catholic signer of the Declaration of Independence, and Bishop John Carroll of Baltimore. Despite the Carrolls' explicit endorsement of separation, some Catholic apologists traditionally evaluated such endorsements as necessary adjustments to American religious liberty; the teaching of the church was that the provisional character of these adjustments was practical and acceptable as a hypothesis. The unity of church and state was the thesis, the principle that guarantees the state's protection of the church's teachings and its role in education and in other spheres of morality. The effectiveness of this thesis-hypothesis argument was considered basic to the Catholics' provisional acceptance of separation of church and state. The Catholics in the pews never distinguished between hypothesis and thesis; they simply embraced separation of church and state as American patriots proud of religious liberty. The Fourth Degree ceremonials clearly extolled these principles. Of course, Protestants were eager to refute these American Catholic claims by referring to this teaching of the church, particularly in regard to the Vatican's support of Franco's Spain where church and state were united.

John Courtney Murray, S.J., criticized a powerful cardinal in the Vatican for his support of Franco's church-state policy, criticism that led his Jesuit superiors in Rome to forbid him to write on the topic.[16] However, the 1959 election of Pope John XXIII left Murray free to write on church and state issues. In 1960 he published his views in support of the First Amendment, *We Hold These Truths.*[17] The book was the basis for his role in the preparation of the Decree on Religious Freedom passed by the Second Vatican Council in 1965.[18]

In 1947 Murray commented on the Everson decision, particularly in relation to Thomas Jefferson's wall of separation as a precedent. Writing in *Columbia,* he referred to the proponents of the wall as advocates of a "barrier deflecting American democracy toward a disastrous development alien to its primitive spirit . . . [deflecting] all government aid singly and solely toward the subsidization of secularism as the one national 'religion' and culture, whose agent of propagation is the secularized public school."[19] Murray's reference to the original spirit of American democracy revealed his understanding of the natural-law basis of the new republic. This was the kernal of his argument for a historical and developmental understanding of the separation of church and state and religious liberty, an argument that became foundational for the Declaration on Religious Liberty.

The POAU's hostility to what its leadership perceived as the threat of Catholic dominance included the Knights' Catholic advertising program, which originated in Missouri and became a national program in 1948. In its *Church and State Newsletter* the POAU published an accurate introduction to the program, which placed ads in secular newspapers and other periodicals encouraging inquiries about the church. Though it doubted the statistics substantiating the new Knights' program as a success, the newsletter told its members: "We of the P.O.A.U. consider this [program of the Knights as a] challenge to redouble our efforts to acquaint every thinking person in this great democracy with the principles of the Manifesto. Ecclesiastical totalitarianism is as menacing as political totalitarianism."[20] In a newsletter published three years later, the POAU warned its readers of the "spurious" Fourth Degree "Knights of Columbus Oath . . . which is being distributed in some communities." However, it prefaced its warning, "to be aware of the forged document," with the disparaging remark: "an organization which has expressed its admiration of 'Catholic Spain' can be justly criticized on several counts."[21]

As the POAU was mounting a continuous barrage of criticism aimed at "ecclesiastical totalitarianism" it was also promoting the book and lecture tour of Paul Blanshard, one of the "other Americans" in the "Protestants and Other. . . ."[22] A former congregational minister, then a Unitarian author, and a lawyer with experience in the New York City government and in the federal State Department, Paul Blanshard's 1947 articles in the

Nation on the inherent conflict between Roman Catholicism and the American ethos were well received and later published as a book, *American Freedom and Catholic Power*. Though he claimed to be free of anti-Catholic bigotry, historian Barbara Welter's 1987 essay "From Maria Monk to Paul Blanshard" united the two authors as anti-Catholic. Despite the 125-year separation between the publication of their books, they shared much in common: the abusive power of the clergy, the church's subjugation of women, particularly the unnatural character of women religious, the denial of the true scriptures, and the arrogance and separatism of the church in the United States, exemplified by the parochial school.[23]

In his "Personal Prologue: The Duty to Speak," Blanshard, whose brother was a professor of philosophy at Yale, notes his indebtedness to a "panel of experts which included George LaPiana, professor emeritus of Church History at Harvard who had been vice-rector of a Pontifical College in Rome, Giovani Pioli of Milan and Edwin McNeil Poteat, the former president of Rochester-Colgate Divinity School."[24] Though these were highly regarded figures in the academic world, both LaPiana and Pioli were former priests with biases against "Catholic power." Poteat was serving as president of the POAU.

In an insightful study, "The American Intellectual Imagination, 1928–1960," John McGreevy explores the widespread bias among prominent liberals who were pro-Blanshard and therefore allies in opposition to Catholic power; among them were John Dewey, Louis Mumford, Walter Lippmann, and associates of Paul Blanshard's brother, Brandon, the philosopher at Yale. McGreevy cites Dewey's praise for Paul Blanshard's "exemplary scholarship, good judgment, and tact." A reviewer in one scholarly journal noted Blanshard's "power of scholarly documentation, [and his] . . . restraint in presentation."[25] But Blanshard's mask of scholarship did not disguise his principal intention—to expose the Catholic Church as a modern dictatorship with bishops and priests in lock-step with "the world monarch who rules a synthetic moral empire that oversteps and penetrates the sovereignty of all earthly governments."[26] Because of their putative subservience to a foreign power, American bishops should be listed as foreign agents by the federal government, argued Blanshard.

He inaccurately described the bogus Fourth Degree oath as originating in the South and circulating in the Southwest. He then accused the Knights of exploiting the circulation of the oath. "Unhappily, this type of anti-Catholic fanaticism—the oath is purely imaginary and has been proved so in court on a number of occasions—has produced a counter-fanaticism in the

K. of C. Its propaganda persists in the illusion that critics of Catholic autocracy are somehow attempting to revive the Ku Klux Klan and destroy the liberties of the Church. The priests encourage [the Knights to cling to] this criticism, since it is a valuable stimulant to partisan spirit."[27] It is ironic that Blanshard's criticism of priests' fostering a partisan spirit is exemplified in his own works, which are composed in an extreme polemical style and from a partisan point of view. Without a reference to documentation for either the Knights' exploitation of the Fourth Degree bogus oath, or for the priestly domination of the Knights in that process, one can only conclude that Blanshard's "analysis" derives from the overriding bias of his book. Far from exploiting the bogus oath, the Fourth Degree and the Order quietly threatened libel in a letter to the publisher rather than launch a public attack. Blanshard concludes the section on the oath with a patronizing remark: "Aside from this partisan spirit, and the uses to which the Order is put by the hierarchy, the K. of C. is simply one more fraternal order, composed of men who love plumes, their country, and a good time."[28]

The Knights' Catholic Advertising program and its Religious Information Bureau, which had come under attack by the POAU as a form of "ecclesiastical totalitarianism," was also subjected to Blanshard's critique. First, he mistakenly pointed out that the intention of the program was "to counteract the effect of reactionary dogmas upon the American non-Catholic public." Then he accused the Knights of using a tautological methodology; in the attempt to "destroy misconceptions" the ads state the truth about a dogma by repeating the real truth in different wording; Blanshard said the Knights' ads were intended "to disguise the worst feature of their faith by adroit double-talk."[29] To illustrate his interpretation he placed the Knights' advertisement on one side of a page opposite "the wording of the actual doctrines of the Church . . . contained in Catholic sources."[30] At the top of one column Blanshard's heading is "The Erroneous Ideas as advertised by the Knights of Columbus," and on the other side, "What the Hierarchy Actually Teaches." In opposition to the Knights' "erroneous belief" that the pope "should not have political power to rule America," Blanshard's "actual teaching" is: "He should rule America in moral, educational and priestly rights."[31] The so-called actual teaching does not really match the "Knights' Erroneous Ideas." The entire list of fourteen ideas and teachings are equally mixed. On the one hand, the Knights are marionettes of priests and are simple yahoos who "love plumes" and fun; but on the other hand they are skilled manipulators of religious rhetoric.

The Catholic community in America, so threatening to the POAU and

Paul Blanshard, experienced significant population growth that effected qualitative change during the period from the close of World War II to the opening of the Second Vatican Council; between 1945 and 1962 the population grew from twenty-four million to forty-four million. This increase placed a strain on parochial and diocesan education, while the G.I. Bill of Rights, which guaranteed a college education for veterans, was a program that nearly quadrupled enrollments in Catholic colleges and universities by 1950. Though the Catholic middle-class was expanding, Protestants continued to dominate the top positions in the corporations as well as in the manufacturing, mining, and financial spheres of the economy. David O'Brien wrote: "Polls showed that . . . [Catholics] like most Americans, believed almost unanimously in the basic doctrines of Christianity and they seemed not to question such controversial Catholic teachings against birth control and the infallibility of the pope. If the historic goals of the American Church were to preserve the faith of immigrants and their children to win a secure place in American society, these goals seemed to have finally been achieved."[32] Concurrent with these developments of social assimilation and religious practice was the persistence of Catholic separatism, represented by the many Catholic organizations of teachers, physicians, nurses, lawyers, philosophers, sociologists, and journalists, buttressed by a wide array of Catholic devotional societies in parishes and dioceses. This social and religious subculture, which originated in the nineteenth century, was experiencing strains in the 1950s that emerged clearly only after the Second Vatican Council. The ethos of the sixties and Vatican II effected a rapid unraveling of many strands of this subculture. However, in the mid-fifties the development of the suburbs and of new Catholic parishes brought about significant change. As historian Jay P. Dolan remarked, the parish cannot sponsor Corpus Christi processions in a suburban cul de sac.[33] The Cold War was a dominant factor throughout the period. But there was another Cold War, the arctic air surrounding Protestant–Catholic relations. Indeed, the *Christian Century's* editorial in the June 11, 1950 issue dealt with the question "Is the Cold War a Holy War?" According to the editor, it appeared that U.S. foreign policy was being adeptly formulated by Pope Pius XII, taking advantage of the naiveté of American anti-Communism and directing it toward his principal foreign policy goal, a "Catholic Western Europe."[34]

Such suspicions were represented not only by the news releases of the POAU, but also by the Protestant and the Catholic weeklies on such issues as federal aid to education. Moreover, there were the perennial issues of loyalty to the Vatican and the many Marian devotions. Pope Pius XII in 1950 proclaimed the dogma of the Assumption and in 1954 led the centennial celebration of the dogma of the Immaculate Conception. Marian shrines at Lourdes, LaSallette, and Fatima were sites of growing devotionalism and pilgrimage by Americans during an era of economic prosperity. The *Christian Century* regarded the definition of the bodily Assumption of Mary as symbolic of the church's "opposition to all the canons of scholarship as that discipline is today understood. This would give added ammunition to the Kremlin eager to pursue its battles against all religions that it considered to be contrary to science and reason."[35] As mentioned earlier, the POAU, Paul Blanshard, and the *Christian Century* had all criticized the Knights' Catholic Advertising campaign and its Religious Information Bureau. Actually Luke E. Hart, who was present at the inception of the program in St. Louis, considered it to be a means of reducing Protestant–Catholic tensions.

> In sponsoring this advertising program the Knights of Columbus is performing direct and highly essential service to the Church . . . a service which is performed by no other agency . . . our advertisements go into the homes of those who will not visit a Catholic Church. They reach people who do not read our Catholic literature, magazines, and newspapers. . . . They correct false notions about our faith. They discredit long-standing anti-Catholic propaganda and refute current falsehoods which are calculated to turn decent people against us. They compel even those who will not join us to respect us. They bring Catholic teaching right out into the open, where people may accept or reject as they wish . . . but where no person of common sense and fairness can misunderstand or misinterpret it.[36]

It appears that any form of the Knights' public Catholicism was subjected to distortion by the Harold Feys and the Paul Blanshards.

III

The Knights' anti-Communism and antisecularism were founded on the patriotic idealism linked to the providential mission of the United States. Just as the Declaration of Independence includes the phrase "endowed by our Creator" with natural rights, so the Knights vigorously promoted amending the Pledge of Allegiance to include "under God" after the phrase "one nation." The initiative to amend the Pledge began in April 1951 when the Board of Directors adopted a resolution mandating that the new pledge be formally recited in each of the 750 Fourth Degree assemblies. The next year the Supreme Council passed a resolution urging Congress to amend the pledge; copies of the resolution were sent to President Eisenhower and to Vice President Nixon. Congressman Louis C. Rabaut of Michigan introduced the bill, which was eventually passed, and the president signed it into law on June 14, 1954, Flag Day.[37] Later Dwight D. Eisenhower wrote a congratulatory letter to Luke E. Hart gratefully acknowledging the Knights' "part in the movement to have the words 'under God' added to our Pledge of Allegiance. These words 'under God' will remind Americans that despite our great physical strength we must remain humble."[38] The Fourth Degree's commitment to religious patriotism was now in opposition to the secular patriotism proferred by liberals such as Paul Blanshard and the editors of the *Nation*, who sought to remove references to God from the public language of American life.

In opposition to foreign-policy developments that appeared as capitulations to secularism or communism, the Order's Catholicism became confrontational during the Hart administration. He called upon Eisenhower to bring the issue of the Hungarian Revolution of 1956 to the United Nations Security Council. Though Secretary of State John Foster Dulles had been articulating the "idealistic" language of "liberation" of the "captive" people behind the iron curtain, in actual situations, such as the uprising in Budapest, pragmatism prevented the implementation of that policy.

In 1956 Hart's anti-Communism and the concern for the status of the church led him to oppose the prospective 1957 visit to the United States by Marshall Josip Broz Tito, president of Yugoslavia. Though it was only rumored that Tito would be visiting the United States, Hart was convinced that he would indeed make the journey; hence on December 19, 1956, he wired President Eisenhower of "his amazement that he should consider inviting to the country the jailor of Cardinal Stepenac, the persecutor of religion, and the accomplice of the murders of Budapest, who put an end to the revolution."[39] Eventually Hart met with Undersecretary of State Robert T. Murphy, a Catholic and "one who was in sympathy with our viewpoint."[40] With several political allies and with support from anti-Tito protest, some two weeks later it was announced that Tito would not be visiting the United States. Later Hart claimed the success of the anti-Tito forces was due to the patriotic leadership of the Knights of Columbus.[41]

The Knights' public Catholicism received national attention during the seventy-fifth anniversary of Founders' Day, March 29, 1957, an event that was highlighted by the formal dedication of the statue of Father Michael J. McGivney in his hometown, Waterbury, Connecticut. Sculpted by a Boston artist, Joseph A. Colleti, the statue portrayed the founder "garbed in a simple cassock and cloak" with his left hand holding "the book of the gospel" while his other hand "reached heavenward to represent the Kingdom of God," said Colleti.[42] Adorning the pedestal were bronze reliefs depicting the four degrees of the Order: Charity, Unity, Fraternity, and Patriotism. *Life* magazine of May 27, 1957, featured the Knights' celebration of their jubilee in an article that was initiated by Luke Hart. He had convinced the editors to publish the piece because in 1956 they had published such an article on the Masons.[43] Like the latter, the story on the Knights was a pictorial essay. Among the photos selected were those of the Fourth Degree that were placed on the cover as well as within the article. Their regalia was so distinctive that it appeared as if all members wore this formal wear. However, the Squires, the Columbettes (an unofficial women's auxiliary), and various photos of Luke E. Hart and others brought to the attention of one million readers the fraternal, insurance, and investment features of the largest Catholic lay organization in the world.[44] Evident throughout this historical year was the pervasive quality of Luke Hart's leadership; in a real sense, he actually directed the Fourth Degree. Despite the fact that Supreme Master Mulligan was a native of Connecticut, his principal role was limited to the quarterly meetings of the Board of Directors.

Luke Hart was gratified by the events in Cuba during the Order's golden jubilee there in 1959, the first year of the Castro administration. Many Knights had participated in the struggle against the Batista regime, a political stance that prompted hope that Castro would attend the Fourth Degree banquet in honor of the golden jubilee; instead he sent one of his aides, who was treated to several speeches on Catholic patriotism.[45] One past State Deputy spoke on the Knights' role in the revolutionary army to dispel rumors of the Marxist character of the new government. Similar rumors were denied in an article in *Columbia* in March 1959.[46] But within a year after this article was published, Castro's administration had become publicly a Communist regime. This brought about a rapid stream of emigrants, many of whom were Fourth Degree Knights. These exiles established in Miami the Our Lady of Charity Council; soon there was a shrine of Our Lady of Charity, a devotion originating in Havana which became a popular pilgrimage site in Miami for exiles and their families.[47]

The Fourth Degree's patriotism, conceived and developed in opposition to several forms of anti-Catholicism, was based on the compatibility between Roman Catholicism and American democracy. This patriotism was energized by the 1959 election of Pope John XXII and the 1960 election of John F. Kennedy. Two anti-Catholic caricatures were thus exposed as shams. The warm, good-hearted openness of Pope John dispelled the anti-Catholic myth that portrayed papal power in terms of world conquest; while the generally esteemed leadership qualities of John Kennedy put to rest the bias that a Catholic President could not be loyal to American democracy and Roman Catholicism.

In his famous address before the Greater Houston Ministerial Association, Kennedy referred to Communism ninety miles from our shores and also to the impoverished children he had witnessed in West Virginia, but those issues were "obscured by the religious issue, because I am a Catholic and no Catholic has ever been President."[48] In opposition to Kennedy was a long line of Protestant leaders, led by Norman Vincent Peale, who had been organized as the National Conference of Citizens For Religious Freedom a few days after Kennedy announced his decision to run for the Democratic nomination.[49] One Protestant pastor remarked that Khrushchev and Kennedy were comparable, as both were "captives of a system,"[50] an echo of Paul Blanshard's *Communism, Democracy and Catholic Power.*[51] In 1960 Blanshard published *God and Man in Washington*,[52] an allusion to the book written by the leading Catholic conservative, William F. Buckley, Jr., *God and Man at Yale.*[53] Blanshard challenged Kennedy to state his position on canon 1374 obliging parents to send their children to Catholic schools under pain of excommunication. Though Blanshard understood that few bishops rigidly enforced canon law on this issue, he was relentless in exposing the contradiction. He later was convinced that Kennedy was indeed a separationist, and in a book edited by him, *Classics of Free Thought,* Blanshard included Kennedy's address to the Houston Ministers' Meeting.[54]

In his address to the Houston ministers, Kennedy responded to the Protestants. "I believe in an America where separation of Church and State is absolute . . . where no church or school is granted any public funds or political preference. . . . I believe in a president whose views on religion are his own private affair, neither imposed on him by the nation nor imposed by him as a condition of holding that office."Kennedy assured his audience that he believed in a "Presidential office [that] is not limited nor conditioned by any religious oath, ritual or obligation."[55] This and other public explanations of Kennedy's privatization of his Catholicism greatly reduced fear of a Catholic President. Even before the address, a leading figure in the POAU, Methodist Bishop G. Bromley Oxnam, along with eleven Protestant leaders, published an open letter "To Their Fellow Pastors in Christ," which asserted their conviction that the candidate's faith should not disqualify him from consideration, though they themselves were not sympathetic to Catholicism.[56] Even without this tepid advice to disregard the danger of the candidate's Catholic identity, Kennedy would have been victorious in the crucial West Virginia primary. Since the state was 95 percent Protestant, Kennedy's victory over Hubert Humphrey by 61 percent to 39 percent of the Democratic voters was so decisive that Humphrey resigned with characteristic grace.[57]

John Kennedy's election victory over Richard Nixon was much narrower, around one percent of the popular vote. Nixon did not exploit the religious issue, nor did Kennedy stir up the caldron of interreligious strife by departing from his Houston address. However, religion was obviously a factor as voters entered the polls. Lawrence H. Fuchs, author of *John F. Kennedy and American Catholicism*, stated: "Since Protestant-Catholic tensions in American had actually become more complex and deep in many respects in the 1940's and 1950's than they had been in the 1920's, Kennedy's victory was a triumph of reasonableness and fairplay."[58] Luke E. Hart was one of the two million or so Catholic Republicans who voted for Kennedy in 1960. Four and a half million Protestant Democrats voted for Nixon.

John F. Kennedy was a Fourth Degree Knight; it is therefore not surprising that during the campaign the bogus oath of the Fourth Degree circulated throughout the nation. Though the POAU and Paul Blanshard had published warnings about the oath, during the few months before the election Hart and the chief legal officer of the Order, Supreme Advocate Harold Lamboley, had to spend "a tremendous amount of time" responding to the many publications of the oath.[59]

The Knights' policy toward publishers of the oath did not entail legal prosecution unless the printer or publisher refused to retract, apologize, or give assurance that it would discontinue its publication. The Order did prosecute W. L. King, an ordained minister who was the publisher of *The Voice of the Nazarene* (Elizabeth, Pennsylvania), which circulated thousands of copies of the oath. On September 16, 1960, a court in Pennsylvania issued a temporary injunction.[60] Publication was so extensive that *Time* reported on the history of the oath, "an old and notorious piece of anti-Catholic propaganda," and noted its widespread circulation in many states.[61] The appearance of the oath in 1960 challenged the patriotism of the Order and prompted Hart to proceed with caution rather than fan the flames of anti-Kennedy bigotry. However, Hart certainly did not allow the unrepentant anti-Catholic publishers to define who is a true American and whose image of America was to prevail. In his campaign against the bogus oath of the Fourth Degree, Hart consulted with the leaders of the Anti-Defamation League of B'nai B'rith. "They were quite pleased with the way in which we have undertaken to suppress the oath. They have a very kindly feeling for Catholics because they feel that both groups are discriminated against and it is their opinion that the vast majority of the Jewish people will vote for Kennedy."[62] Hart's enthusiasm for Kennedy was not affected by the latter's close ties to the "so-called liberal element," because he understood that he would be guided by his father, Joe Kennedy: "And that is pretty much a guarantee that he would keep his feet on the ground."[63]

On October 11, 1962, Hart visited Kennedy at the White House, where he presented him with a framed copy of the Pledge of Allegiance featuring the "under God" addition. In 1946 John Kennedy had been initiated into Bunker Hill Council No. 62 in Charlestown, Massachusetts, and in Bishop Chevrus General Assembly Fourth Degree in 1958. Hart invited him to address the States Dinner during the Supreme Council convention in Boston in August 1963. He reminded him that his grandfather, John F. Fitzgerald, when he was mayor of Boston, addressed the convention's dinner in 1913. Kennedy said he would "try to accept if his schedule permits." The article on the Hart–Kennedy meeting featured in *Columbia* reported that Hart presented Kennedy with "a lapel emblem of the Fourth degree" and that Kennedy expressed "much interest in and familiarity with our Order's activities." Accompanying Hart were the then present and former Vice Supreme Masters of Calvert Province, centered in Boston, Angelo Catucci and his father, Henry Catucci.[64]

The day after the visit Hart delivered his Columbus Day address over more than 750 radio stations. Placing the role of Columbus at the juncture of a new era of migration from Europe and the development of a new nation, Hart asserted the meaning of the Declaration of Independence, as it is related to the "under God" amendment and the general providential mission of the United States: "the first two paragraphs of that magnificent charter acknowledges our dependency upon God." Following this opening statement that "men are endowed" by their Creator with certain inalienable rights, Hart quoted—"with a firm reliance on the Protection of Divine Providence, we mutually pledge to each other our lives, our fortunes, and our sacred honor." To preserve these ideals "shared alike by Columbus and our founding fathers" it is necessary, said Hart, "to read and study history, whether it be recorded by a Columbus or a Washington or embodied in the customs and institutions which identify it. . . . Nothing strengthens the patriotic fervor more than the study of history." This address concluded with a long narrative on the important ways to inculcate in the nation's youth the "ideals of civil and religious liberty for all time."[65]

Thirteen months after Luke Hart visited with the president, John F. Kennedy was assassinated in Dallas, a tragedy permanently etched in the memory of millions of people from many nations. Hart issued a statement dated November 22, 1963:

> The Members of the Knights of Columbus are overwhelmed with grief at the loss occasioned by the assassination of President Kennedy, the most distinguished member of our Order. He was kindly, considerate, patient, and understanding. His qualities of heart and mind were befitting the magnificent attainments of his remarkable career. In the light of the most searching scrutiny he met every test, intellectual, cultural, humane, religious, patriotic. Our hearts go out in sympathy to his stricken family, to our nation and to all mankind. May his soul rest in peace.[66]

Pope John XXIII's death on June 5, 1963, and John F. Kennedy's on the following November 22, marked the passing of the two significant leaders who elicited the deep sense of pride and loyalty among their co-religionists. Hart wrote that this pope's "warmth and amiability, combined with the depth and brightness of his vision, captured the imagination of Catholics and non-Catholics and unbelievers."[67] Luke Hart and Deputy Supreme Knight John W. McDevitt, a native of Malden, Massachusetts, who inducted John Kennedy into the Fourth Degree, attended his funeral. Hart recalled the experience. "As a representative of the Order, it was my privilege to be the only layman seated in the sanctuary during the funeral mass. . . . His death was a terrible loss to his wife, children, his parents, brothers and sisters. It was also a great loss to our country, our Order, of which he was its most distinguished member and to all mankind." He concluded with sentiments congenial to the ideals exemplified in the ceremonial of the Fourth Degree: "But he had not lived in vain. He demonstrated a truth which Catholics have asserted since the founding of the Republic, i.e. that a Catholic might be President of the United States. And that a Catholic President would prove to be worthy of that high honor."[68]

Published in January of 1964, this memoir of the Supreme Knight's experience at the funeral of John Kennedy was his last public statement. The eighty-four-year-old Supreme Knight died on February 19, 1964. One of the crucial issues on his agenda was the civil rights problem facing the Knights of Columbus. Indeed, the Order had been accused of racism. In response he observed that the application for membership had never included inquiries as to the applicant's race or color, and that members of a local council voted on the candidate according to their consciences, with five negative votes constituting rejection of the applicant. Of course this system was vulnerable to a small minority upholding the traditional color line. The Supreme Court decision *Brown v. Board of Education* (1954), delegitimated the "separate but equal" principle in public education and was a catalyst for the subsequent acceleration of the civil rights movement. When the American bishops spoke out on the issue of racial justice, Luke E. Hart explicitly urged the councils to desegregate, but he did not urge then to abandon the five-negative-vote rule. The leading Catholic interracialist, John LaFarge, S.J., said that the Order of "the Knights of Columbus badly need a new and enlightened policy . . . even though fragments of its honor are saved by the interracialist membership of some of its councils."[69] There were integrated councils and Fourth Degree assemblies, but since Hart refused to take a survey there were no accurate statistics on the extent of integration—but it was certainly not a high figure. The precipitating factor that led to consideration of reform of the system was the crisis in the Chicago Council when six officers resigned because a black applicant was rejected clearly on the basis of his race. This generated criticism among church leaders in Chicago, criticism that moved Hart to announce a full airing of the issue at the Supreme Council in August of 1964.[70] Since Hart died six months before the council, it was left to John W. McDevitt to deal with the charges of racism and the demands for reforming the voting system.

Born in 1880, Hart had witnessed the advance of Jim Crow segregation in St. Louis, a southern city until economic and social forces effected its change to a Midwestern metropolis. He had been a Supreme Officer for forty-two years, Supreme Advocate from 1922 to 1953, and Supreme Knight from 1953 to 1964. He died just eight months before Vatican Council II passed the Declaration on Religious Liberty, a cause close to Hart's public Catholicism. He was strongly identified with the Order for so many years that his name became synonymous with the Knights of Columbus, and he left a significant legacy to McDevitt: over one million members and over one billion dollars of insurance in force. Hart had become a Fourth Degree Knight during the era of John Reddin. This was evident in his promotion of the idealism of the providential mission of America as embodied in the Declaration of Independence. His Americanism was not imbued with the evangelicalism characteristic of John Reddin's leadership. Hart's Catholicism was unaffected by public zeal and was in a sense comparable to John Kennedy's private religious style.

IV

John McDevitt, a former teacher, principal, and superintendent of schools in Walden, Massachussetts, represents a new generation of leadership. He was the first Supreme Knight born in the twentieth century. His style of leadership was characterized by moderation in fraternal affairs and on racial issues. He revised the Third Degree ceremonials and reformed the voting system on rejecting applicants from five votes to one-third voting—and finally a majority rejection or approval. He thus removed obstructions to the desegregation of the local councils. He was an impassioned critic of the counterculture of the 1960s; and he supported the war in Vietnam until the early 1970s. On ecclesiastical and moral matters he expressed his deep commitment to the magisterium, particularly on the issues of divorce, birth control, abortion, and pornography.[71] Hart had offended many bishops, but McDevitt regained their confidence, and before he appointed a Knight to the Board of Directors he consulted with the prospective director's bishop.

Called upon to speak on many occasions as an educator, McDevitt was a skilled orator with a compelling and direct style laced with the apt metaphor to convey a clear argument. For example, in reference to general Catholic assimilation into American society, McDevitt stated that because "the Church has taken firm root and has become the leading Christian body in the land . . . , it is high time we abandon the concept of our Order as mainly a fortress to protect us from the hostile world. We are not a besieged minority." Perhaps he was revealing his roots in Boston Catholicism, but this fortress image does not represent the Order's history, particularly that of the Fourth Degree. The Order was never considered a fortress but rather as a tributary of the mainstream of American society.[72] He may have been referring to the spirit of ecclesial updating, that is, *aggiornamento;* but he did extol the general ethos of the Second Vatican Council in its openness to the modern world, which entailed the demise of the fortress mentality. He likened the Constitution on the Church in the Modern World (*Gaudium et Spes*) as a "veritable banquet table from which our councils can choose additional programs to fit their interests and capabilities."[73] His views appear to have reflected a consensus in the Order, with the exception of the revisions of the ceremonials for the three degrees which stirred dissent.

Complementing the social and political assimilation represented by the election of John Kennedy was the Second Vatican Council, symbolic of a new era of religious maturity and self-confidence. In general, the sixteen documents of Vatican II "revitalized understanding of the Church's nature and mission in the modern world," wrote theologian Patrick W. Carey. "The documents on the liturgy, church, revelation, the church's relationship with the modern world, ecumenism and religious liberty are the most significant of the sixteen."[74] As the changes of the Second Vatican Council were implemented in the "second 1960s" (that is, 1965–1974), cultural trends profoundly affected that process. The civil rights movement entered a more militant phase; the Vietnam War intensified; the women's movement initiated a new consciousness and proposals for reform in church and society; renewal and reforms of the religious life polarized many congregations; there were generational differences that tended to affect the interpretations of many of these political, social, and religious developments; and the appearance of the counterculture had an impact on college campuses and in the general emergence of a spirit of dissent and protest. The events of the year 1968 are clearly illustrative of the profound changes occurring in church and society: the assassinations of Martin Luther King, Malcolm X, and Robert Kennedy; urban riots; the violence at the Democratic Convention in Chicago; student confrontations at Columbia University and other campuses throughout the nation; the Tet offensive against the South Vietnamese troops; and the publication of Pope Paul VI's encyclical *Humanae Vitae* and the resistance to the encyclical led by Charles Curran, the priest moral theologian at the Catholic University of America, and many other theologians in several dioceses.

The convergence of these events represented the sharp division between the idealism of the first phase of the 1960s and the cynical realism of its second phase. The change related to antiwar protest, to student confrontations with university authorities, and to the counterculture generated a style of patriotism based on the realism of dissent, which was in sharp contrast to the idealism of traditional patriotism embodied in the Fourth Degree's assertion of the universal truths of the Declaration of Independence. In opposition to both the cultural sources of patriotic dissent and of theological dissent, McDevitt reaffirmed the Knights' loyalty to the authority of the founding fathers and to the church's magisterium. The clash between the new and the traditional patriotism was a conflict over the meaning of America, while the conflict between the religious dissent and the Order's sense of authority was a struggle over the meaning of church in American Catholic life.

In his first address after the publication of *Humanae Vitae,* McDevitt's rhetorical imagery is akin to one of Avery Dulles's models, "The Suffering

Servant."[75] "Today our Church is suffering a form of modern Gethsemane," as it is confronted with "[e]rroneous interpretations of traditional Catholic teachings," with the demand that the church "ease its rules because its people have expressed a desire for less discipline" and with "many people today who are advocating liberal abortion laws, even the acception of homosexuality." He was confident that the Order would generously support their "spiritual shepherds" in the defense of the "traditional discipline of the Judeo-Christian concept." As a practical measure to promote the encyclical on *Human Life,* McDevitt announced that in response to Cardinal Patrick O'Boyle's request, the Order would sponsor the booklet entitled "Sex in Marriage," supporting the traditional views on birth control. To sponsor this manual was "a service to the Church universal and to Catholics everywhere," particularly to dispel "doubts" in the minds of the laity. Hence, the Order published a first printing of seventy thousand copies.[76]

Reflecting the general cultural trends in society, John McDevitt expressed a sense of idealism in the early phase of his administration. Though his rhetorical style revealed a polemical edge, his 1966 Columbus Day radio address was a theoretical piece on freedom and responsibility under the title "Crisis of Authority." As one who led the Knights to racially integrate their councils, he viewed local resistance to desegregation as symbolic of a "warped view of liberty that would sacrifice the interests of the nation to satisfy the whims of a locality. It is a warped view of liberty that would penalize the aspirations of a broad movement and infringe on the rights of the many to satisfy the inordinate desire of a few individuals." McDevitt implied that this distorted notion of liberty aimed at obstructing civil rights was tantamount to redefining the foundational principles of law, the basis of patriotism. However, McDevitt listed several other groups who represented the crisis of authority, such as the student radicals: "Suddenly we find students trying to usurp the role of teachers and administration. . . . Apparently they want every resource of the pursuit of wisdom that will not interfere with their pursuit of pleasure, fancy or a vacation." McDevitt expressed sympathy with the "objective of many movements for civic, social and racial justice." But he also expressed dismay at the means used to achieve these goals, means such as various forms of civil disobedience: "flouting of civic authority is a double-edged sword. It may wound a good cause more than it helps it." McDevitt's views on the crisis of authority were based on a "universal . . . sense of the word [authority]" comparable to the universal character of the ideals of American patriotism.[77] He called for a balance of authority and freedom: "Freedom becomes excessive when it challenges the proper restraints of legitimate authority." Though he defends the right to "dissent with those in authority . . . but it is not given to us to violate the law simply because we disagree with it." To think otherwise is to advocate anarchy. "True liberty and freedom enable us to recognize our dignity and that of our fellow man as children of God and citizens of our respective lands." McDevitt, true to the ideals of the Fourth Degree, concluded on a patriotic note:

> May we be reminded that patriotism is not an outmoded virtue but a legitimate extension of our Fourth Commandment which tells us to honor our father and mother, so should we honor our native land. . . . May the sole motive of each one of us be to serve God and his Church, walking manfully with the assurance that in his good time the Lord will truly bless our efforts to be loyal and true sons of God and country.[78]

In response to the polarization in church and society as well as in response to those who criticized the mission of the Knights, John McDevitt stated: "We are both progressive and conservative and we are neither." The progressive character was expressed in the Knights' "efforts to shake the country free from prejudice . . . to create conditions which will give every American the chance to obtain decent money . . . to eliminate poverty [and to foster] interreligious and interracial understanding." Their conservatism was represented by their deep commitment to Judeo-Christian morality; by their Catholic patriotism, which targeted the secularism that would remove God from society; by their strong loyalty to their bishops and to the pope; and by their utter disregard for "the haughty harangue or deceiving sophism of Father so and so's latest recital on 'why I left the Church.'" The Knights were progressive on social issues, conservative on cultural and ecclesial issues, and neither when it came to their persistent reliance upon the hierarchy "for teaching, sanctifying and guidance of the church."[79] Programmatically, the Knights adopted interracial projects of the LaFarge Institute and helped to fund CARA—Center for Applied Research in the Apostolate—seeking new approaches to effective ministry suitable for the needs of contemporary Catholics. Hence, the McDevitt administration was dedicated to mediating the traditions of the Order in the modern world, and thereby preserving Catholic fraternalism during a period of accelerated change. A major factor in this adaptation was the modernization of the insurance program, which allowed the Order to enlarge its charitable gifts, such as funds for expanding the range of the Vatican's communications system, an expansion that continued into the twenty-first century.

The Fourth Degree's patriotism developed in competition with those groups which had described American identity exclusive of Catholics. Since Masons had been active in many anti-Catholic organizations, from membership in the American Protective Association to sponsorship of the work of Paul Blanshard, members of the Fourth Degree tended to sharpen their own patriotic identity in competition with the Masons over the historical memory of the Catholic contributions to American life. In the 1960s, when both the Masons and the Knights shared a common enemy—political and social protests and the "Woodstock" counterculture—they were able to shed their traditional antagonism, symbolized by the meeting between John McDevitt, his Deputy Supreme Knight Charles Ducey, and Harold Lamboley, Supreme Advocate, and their counterparts in the Masons: John M. Newbury, Sovereign Grand Commander of the Northern Jurisdiction of the Scottish Rite of Freemasonry; Frank C. Staples, Grand Master of the Masons, State of New York; Irving Partridge, Deputy for Connecticut, and several other officials. At the "fraternal summit" the leaders considered ways both societies could join forces to "combat and overcome the forces whose degenerative influence is becoming a crippling menace to our way of life." The Knights and Masons expressed their common commitment to promote patriotism, programs in good citizenship, and respect for constitutional law and order, as well as educational projects that promised to imbue the nation's youth with these values.[80] Meetings with Masons continued into the twenty-first century.

As Supreme Knight, Luke E. Hart was consistently proud of the Fourth Degree and praised Supreme Master William J. Mulligan for his successful promotion of new members. He was particularly edified by "the world-famous color guard" and noted Mulligan's commitment to keep the guard "on a dignified plane so that it has become an identifying symbol of the Degree and has gained for it the respect and admiration of everyone, Catholic and non-Catholic."[81] John McDevitt proposed a reform of the Fourth Degree that would open the assembly meetings "to our family and friends as we conduct non-degree activities," a reform that embraced the councils as well.[82] In response to those who criticized the Knights as simply a men's society, McDevitt and his successor, Virgil C. Dechant, initiated measures that underscored the Order's family character, by incorporating wives and children in their programs.

In anticipation of the bicentennial of the nation in 1976, John McDevitt's Columbus Day address was entitled "In God We Trust." Just as Columbus's life represented such a trust, so the men who gathered in Philadelphia in 1776 as delegates of the thirteen colonies expressed the trust in the document they approved. "The remarkable future of this declaration is that it is more a declaration of the dependence on God than of independence of man. The former is mentioned three times; God four times . . . God as [the] source of all democratic rights."[83] He went on to cite George Washington's Farewell Address, with its commitment to the ties between religion and morality. Later he quoted from Lincoln's call for God's assistance as he left Springfield, Illinois, for his inauguration in 1861. He told of how the Secretary of the Treasury, Solomon P. Chase, in commemoration of Lincoln's commitment to the motto, placed "In God We Trust" on the coinage. It became the national motto in 1956, the year after Congress had the motto put on all currency, both paper and metal. This religious dimension of patriotism is, according to McDevitt, the source of unity, but in a society driven by enmity, there is "dissension and confusion over national objectives." He also noted that "without God and his morality there can be no civilization and culture." He referred to "the so-called humanists" who need to free themselves from God "but end up being slaves to themselves." In contrast, belief in God connects the believer to humanity as well as to Divinity, connections that lead to the solution of the "crisis-ridden era."[84]

During World War II, Supreme Master Timothy Galvin promoted a Fourth Degree campaign among the assemblies that would instruct the public that the United States and Canada were fighting in defense of "God-given rights." In the predominant polarization of the 1960s and 1970s, McDevitt's addresses on God and country were echoed by the conservative leaders of church and society who shared the belief that in proclaiming the idealism of Catholic patriotism; the Knights and many coreligionists were trumpeting calls for hope and trust in God. After nearly thirteen years as Supreme Knight, John W. McDevitt retired at the mandatory age of seventy at the end of the calendar year of 1976. In honor of the bicentennial of the Declaration of Independence, in commemoration of his administration, and in gratitude for his leadership, the Fourth Degree established the John W. McDevitt Fund for Religious Liberties.

Over the years the Fund has supported some church-state court cases such as a 1984 case in Canada involving Catholic education. McDevitt frequently invoked First Amendment liberties in an effort to balance the individual's rights in a democracy with the government's authority to safeguard society from the abuses of those freedoms during crises of civil disobedience. Throughout its history the Fourth Degree ritualized the ideals of both the Declaration of Independence and the First Amendment in its initiation ceremonies. The Fourth Degree experienced steady growth during the

McDevitt years: 1964—165,000; 1976—171,500 members. Considering the decline in volunteerism during the 1960s and early 1970s, such an increase was no small achievement. The Order grew by nearly 100,000 during this period to reach 1.1 million members. Under the direction of the then Supreme Secretary Virgil C. Dechant, the insurance program nearly tripled. During the latter's twenty-three years as Supreme Knight the Order grew to 1.65 million members, while the insurance program increased from three to forty billion dollars in force.

V

There was no question that Virgil C. Dechant would be the board's choice to succeed John McDevitt when it met on January 22, 1977. Entering the Order at age eighteen, Dechant rose rapidly; he went from Grand Knight of St. Augustine's Council in Liebenthal to State Deputy of Kansas in a matter of eleven years. At age twenty-nine he was one of the youngest State Deputies in the history of the Knights. Dechant's success in both insurance and general membership campaigns earned him the recognition of Supreme Knight Luke Hart, who, after assigning him to the chair of the Good of the Order committee, recommended him to serve on the Board of Directors. Shortly after Dechant became a Supreme Director, Hart died. In 1966 Dechant was elected to serve as Supreme Master of the Fourth Degree, while he was also Assistant Supreme Secretary. He served in these positions for little over a year when he became Supreme Secretary. Virgil Dechant succeeded William Mulligan as Supreme Master, who had retired in 1965. He inherited a program to support the needs of retarded children, one that was passed in 1964 in commemoration of John F. Kennedy, whose family was and still is deeply committed to that charity.[85] The program was absorbed into the general charities of the entire Order and was later incorporated into the charity for the Supreme Chaplain Bishop Charles P. Greco's homes for retarded children. It also supported the Special Olympics, under the direction of Eunice Kennedy Shriver and her husband, Sargent Shriver, the first director of the Peace Corps.

Traditionally, the candidates for the Fourth Degree wore white ties and tails at initiation ceremonies, symbolic of their dignity as Sir Knights; they also tended to be of the ascending middle class. For many years there were resolutions passed by several Provincial Assemblies requesting a change to tuxedo as the standard formal wear, but it was consistently rejected at the Supreme Assembly level. As a young man raised on the plains of Kansas, and as a representative of a new generation, Virgil Dechant was the first Supreme Master to endorse modern formal wear at the biennial meeting of the Supreme Assembly in 1966.[86] His commitment to modernization was illustrative of his general administration as Supreme Secretary and Supreme Knight.

Virgil Dechant's background as a seminarian at the Pontifical College Josephinum in Worthington, Ohio, was clearly evident in the Marian piety imbued in his administration: the distribution of more than a million rosaries, the circulation of several pictorial renderings of Mary—both historical classics and local popular icons. His business experiences in the automotive and farm-equipment agency and in wheat farming were woven into the cloth of his identity as a committed Catholic layman with seasoned skills in motivating fraternal volunteers, and local and general insurance agents. He also led the Board of Directors to fund several projects: among them was the Vicarious Christ Fund for the pope's personal charities; the Vatican's communications programs; the restoration and renewal of several sections of St. Peter's Basilica; the needs of local bishops and the National Conference of Catholic Bishops; vocations, and pro-life activities; and other family programs. His ethnic roots as a Volga-German and his participation in many significant public events yielded a strong sense of history, represented by the establishment of the Order's museum and archives, now located in a separate building, and by sponsoring a history of the Order, *Faith and Fraternalism,* as well as supporting this history of the Fourth Degree. John W. McDevitt was the educator, who seldom spoke in personal terms; Virgil Dechant draws upon his personal experiences in his speeches, experiences that reveal him as a committed Catholic fraternalist, a modernizer of the fraternal insurance and investments, and an effective communicator. Both Supreme Knights expressed their strong loyalty to the church's magisterium and to the Order's traditions, including Catholic patriotism and citizenship. His engagement in the civic life of the nation revealed Virgil Dechant's style of public Catholicism: he developed a set of priorities congenial to his worldview as the designated leader of the Knights of Columbus.

During the first fifteen years of his administration, the nation took a turn to the right. Though there was considerable social change, such as the urban crises related to severe drug problems, high crime rates, homelessness, loss of confidence in public schools, the so-called "Reagan revolution" symbolized a revival of traditional values of rugged individualism, of the sanctity of home and family, patriotism, and the scripted images of the foundation stories, "redeemer nation," and the "city on a hill." There was also a strong endorsement of the inherent benevolence of private spheres of activity: the market economy and volunteerism, the restraint of government expressed in the popular dictum, "government is not the solution it is the problem," the efforts to reverse *Roe v. Wade,* to promote prayer in public schools, and to support some form of tax relief for parents of children in private schools. The Iran hostage crisis that haunted Jimmy Carter and the general "malaise" he addressed during his administration stand in stark contrast to the optimism, however defined, of Ronald Reagan's invocation of traditional patriotism.

George Bush's campaign for president against Michael Dukakis entailed a defense of the American flag against those who demonstrated disrespect and derision. Bush criticized Dukakis for his membership in the American Civil Liberties Union (ACLU), which included on its agenda removal of "under God" from the Pledge of Allegiance.[87] Bush's campaign for volunteerism, the "Thousand Points of Light," was endorsed by the Order, which established its own Points of Light program. Not since the 1950s was the general direction of the Knights of Columbus so clearly in harmony with the regnant political ethos than it was between 1980 and 1992. Though Jimmy Carter expressed a distinctive patriotism, he did not convey the traditional idealism so evident in the Reagan-Bush years. The invasion of Grenada during the Reagan years and the invasion of Panama and "the Desert Storm" war against Iraq in the Bush years were viewed by some Americans as strong countermovements to what was considered the tragic demoralizing consequences of the war in Vietnam.[88]

The Fourth Degree's patriotic programs during the Reagan-Bush years included a $50,000 grant in 1983 to the U.S. Military Ordinariate for its project to establish a chaplaincy office responsible for ministry to the armed services and their families as well as to the diplomatic personnel in the European theater.[89] This was followed by a $20,000 grant to the Canadian military vicar for ministry programs for military personnel located in the various provinces of Canada.[90] An entirely distinctive program was the "To Be A Patriot" award, presented annually to the top three assemblies of the Fourth Degree for their innovative and effective projects that reveal a commitment to patriotism. The program was initiated during the administration of Supreme Master Alfred N. Nicolas of Corpus Christi, Texas. For example, in 1987 the awards were presented to the John XXIII Assembly, Pentican, British Columbia, for its Canadian Citizenship Classes; to Monsignor Charles N. Kennedy Assembly, Lancaster, California, for the "History of Our Flag" ceremony on Flag Day; and to the Captain Francisco de Ibarra

Assembly, Durango, Mexico, for the Memorial Mass in honor of Mexican independence and the heroic role of the prominent Catholic, Augustin de Iturbe.[91]

The international character of the Fourth Degree is further illustrated by the three awards presented in 1991: Marian Assembly, Rensaleer, Indiana, "Remember Our Veterans"; Maharilka Assembly, Quezon City, Luzon, for its essay contest on Filipino heroes and patriots; Missoula Assembly in Montana, for its distribution of flags that had flown on top of the United States Congress.[92]

In anticipation of the centennial of the Statue of Liberty in 1986, President Ronald Reagan appointed Lee A. Iacocca, the president of the Chrysler Corporation, to be chairman of the Statue of Liberty-Ellis Island Centennial Commission in 1983. In a letter to Virgil Dechant, Iacocca noted that this is "the first federal commission to appeal to the private sector for total funding."[93] The chairman explained the aims and objectives of the project:

> Our goal is to restore and preserve our national symbol, the Statue of Liberty, as well as the symbol of the immigrant tradition of this nation, Ellis Island, and to celebrate both of these monuments through a Liberty Centennial. We hope this will rekindle the spirit of liberty in the hearts of all Americans. In leading an organization dedicated to strong ideals and civic citizenship, we seek your involvement in this purpose.[94]

The Fourth Degree Historical Commission, established in 1921, was headed by Edward McSweeney, an immigration commissioner on Ellis Island, who was, as mentioned earlier, a vigorous opponent of the Americanization programs of the early 1920s that relegated immigrants to a hyphenated, "mongrelized" status. The Historical Commission was a source of pride among the Supreme Masters John Reddin and John Mulligan. As Mulligan's successor, Virgil Dechant, who had learned some German at home and who, as mentioned earlier, attended the Pontifical College Josephinum, founded for German-speaking students, was proud of the immigrant character so dominant in American Catholic life. He was also imbued with civic ideals of Catholic patriotism and citizenship that were central to the initiation into the Fourth Degree. Hence, he turned to the membership of the patriotic degree to achieve a million-dollar commitment. With one-third of the total pledged by September of 1985, Virgil Dechant wrote to the chief officer of each assembly, the Faithful Navigator, a strong motivational letter: "I am well aware of the *esprit de corps* of our Fourth Degree members. Now that we have . . . a national project, under the leadership of Supreme Master Alfred N. Nicolas, I know we can count upon your assemblies' active support . . . to give concrete expression to this patriotic cause."[95] In his report to the 1987 Supreme Council, Virgil Dechant said that though the fund-raising efforts fell short of the one-million-dollar goal by $240,000, the balance was drawn from the Fourth Degree fund. He concluded with thanks for all those Sir Knights "who worked so diligently on behalf of Lady Liberty." It was a source of gratification for the Fourth Degree of the Knights of Columbus to be included in the Torch Club, limited to contributions of a million or over. There were two other fraternal societies also in the club: the Benevolent and Protective Order of Elks and the Freemasons of North America. Just as the school children of France funded the gift of the Statue of Liberty, it was appropriate for America's school children to have contributed enough to be listed in the Torch Club.[96]

At the core of the Fourth Degree initiation ceremonies were the dramatic stories of the founders of churches and dioceses that constitute the American Catholic heritage. Local Catholic monuments include cathedrals that sacralize cityscapes in the United States, Canada, Mexico, the Philippines, and other nations where the Fourth Degree flourishes. Over the years, Fourth Degree assemblies have contributed funds to the renovation of these churches. Therefore, the Fourth Degree fund contributed $100,000 for the restoration of the Cathedral of the Immaculate Conception in Denver in anticipation of World Youth Day and the visit of Pope John Paul II. In the wake of the tragic bombing of the federal building in Oklahoma City, which severely affected the Cathedral, the Fourth Degree contributed $100,000 to the archdiocese for repairs to the Cathedral of St. Joseph. To the Cathedral of the Madelaine in Salt Lake City the Fourth Degree provided significant assistance for renovation.[97]

Supreme Master Albert Nicolas, who led the campaign to raise funds for the restoration of the Statue of Liberty and Ellis Island, died in 1987, before the completion of the project. His successor as Supreme Master was Hilary Schmittzehe, Supreme Director from Missouri.[98] A former State Deputy, Schmittzehe has been committed to the Order's program for the mentally retarded on the state and national levels. He is the founder and president of one of the largest employers and protective agencies for the mentally challenged in the Midwest. He and an Illinois Knight initiated the Tootsie Roll campaign for the mentally retarded in Missouri. The Knights in thirty states have raised millions for this special program. Hilary Schmittzehe, with the strong encouragement of Virgil Dechant, also began a Back-to-Basics project to bring uniformity to the governance system that was the responsibility of the Vice Supreme Masters and District Masters. The "Basics" dimension of the project was the implementation of a policy of uniformity for the regalia of the Color Corps and the Honor Guards, the most visible presence of the Order at church and civic events.[99] As part of the campaign it became known as the "Knights on Main Street."[100]

After World War II, democratic expressions of patriotism were evident in the diversified style of uniform or regalia worn by Color Corps and Honor Guards, ranging from Eisenhower Jackets in Missouri to veterans wearing their medals on the uniforms of their service. Though some wore the chapeau and baldric in formal attire it appeared to many as conveying an aristocratic image. This democratic spirit culminated in the successful change from white-tie and tails to the tuxedo when, as mentioned earlier, Virgil Dechant was Supreme Master. There was some local resistance to the Back-to-the-Basics reform. But by the time he retired from office in 1991, Schmittzehe's project had achieved a consensus. He will be remembered not only for his standardization of the Fourth Degree regalia but also for his role as chair of the ceremonials committee of the Board of Directors, charged with a return to the traditional Third Degree with some modifications. To assure that there were no instances of unruly behavior by those leading the ceremonials, the degree teams were not allowed to fulfill their responsibilities until after they had been certified. Virgil Dechant worked closely with Schmittzehe and publicly praised his leadership as a fraternalist and as a gifted motivator for reform. This work was a reflection of the general trends toward standardization[101] and centralization during the Dechant administration. Schmittzehe's successor was Darrell Beck, Supreme Director from Illinois. During his period in office, 1992–1996, he administered the new Civic Award, which, said Dechant in 1992, "was a program which recognizes assemblies that report to the Supreme Office at least four varied patriotic projects conducted during the fraternal year [based on the fiscal year]. Each 142 winning assemblies [there was a total of 1,954 assemblies in 1992][102] received a Civic Award Certificate in tribute to their programming excellence."[103]

Beck vigorously promoted membership growth; for the first time the percentage of Fourth Degree members exceeded 15 percent of the total membership of the Order in 1992.[104] The fastest-growing jurisdiction in total membership as well as that of the Fourth Degree was the Philippines. At his 1996 visitation there, Darrell Beck was one of the principal participants in "wreath-laying ceremonies at monuments to Philippine patriots and war heroes and at the dedication of a memorial to unborn children,"[105] reported Virgil Dechant in 1996.

In the spirit of the Degree's foundation, the John W. McDevitt Fund for Religious Liberties was actively engaged in patriotic endeavors during the mid-1990s. In 1993 it was supportive of a project to help the bishops maintain public funding of Catholic schools in a Canadian province.[106] Funds also went to the plaintiffs of the Knights of Columbus of Trumbull, Connecticut, in St. Theresa Council No. 2961, which had been prohibited from placing a nativity scene on the town green.[107] With these McDevitt funds and another grant to this Connecticut council, it could afford to appeal the lower court's decision against the scene. That court vacated the lower court's decision, thereby instructing local authorities to allow purely religious exhibits if they also allow other seasonal exhibits.[108] In October 1996 another past State Deputy of Illinois, Charles H. Foos, became the Supreme Master, and he presided during its centennial year, which began on February 22, 2000.[109] At the 1999 meeting of the Supreme Council Dechant set the membership goal of the Fourth Degree for Jubilee 2000 at twenty thousand new members. Charles H. Foos reported to the General Assembly in August 2000 that the campaign actually fell short of the goal of twenty thousand by 1,247 new members, but the net increase was 8,255 Sir Knights, "which is 4,305 (109%) more than the previous year and the highest net increase, to my knowledge."[110] Under the leadership of Virgil Dechant and the Supreme Masters of the Fourth Degree, membership went from 185,000 in 1978 to 264,300 at the end of the centennial year.

In the year 2000, two patriotic programs were at the top of the Fourth Degree agenda: "aligned with older patriotic organizations the Fourth Degree is part of campaign to win congressional passage of a constitutional amendment restoring to Congress and the state legislatures power to enact laws banning the desecration of the American flag," stated Dechant.[111] In his 1995 Report to the Supreme Council, Virgil Dechant noted the criticism of the proposed amendment from "super-sophisticated quarters . . . all due respect to critics I believe they are missing the point. The amendment embodies a widely shared belief that the flag, as a concrete symbol of national unity and patriotism, deserves the protection of law that is now denied." Against those who sided with the Supreme Court on the ground that the amendment would be tantamount to denying free speech, Dechant said that despite the profound value of free expression, "it is not an absolute value, as laws against obscenity and libel make clear." He concluded that the decision over desecration of the flag "belongs with the national legislature."[112]

The other priority was announced as part of the February 22, 2000 centennial: that the U.S. Assemblies be committed to raising $500,000 for the World War II memorial in Washington, D.C.[113] (On Veteran's Day, 2000, President William J. Clinton formally broke ground for the monument, but in the court there are opponents to placing the monument on the mall.) The latter priority represents a period when the ideals of patriotism were flourishing; recall Timothy Galvin's World War II slogan, "We are fighting for God Given rights." This was an example of the Fourth Degree's commitment to good citizenship, a reminder to all who "believed in a personal God." The campaign to protect the flag from desecration symbolized the Fourth Degree's commitment to compete with those groups that perceived the flag as a sign of capitalism's oppression and of U.S. exploitation of the global markets. This was a struggle between patriotism based on idealism versus a new patriotism based on a realistic, or cynical, assessment of national power. There was also a countercultural critique of the flag by many artists who depicted it as one among many symbols of war, reminiscent of the desecrations of the flag by the anti-Vietnam War protestors. In this context the movement to protect the flag is what one historian refers to as "the new patriotism" determined to restore respect for the nation's patriotic symbols in a post-Vietnam world.[114]

The Fourth Degree's campaign for the constitutional amendment is in accord with this "new patriotism." However, the secular character of the era is of course in opposition to the spirit of the Fourth Degree. Hence, this book closes with the Fourth Degree in competition with those whom they perceive as undermining the idealism of a "nation under God," a nation based on rights endowed by "our Creator." This book began with the Fourth Degree's celebration of the Catholic foundation stories and of the Catholic contribution to the making of America: "the proudest boast is ours to make, 'I am an Catholic American citizen.'" It also ends with this refrain still echoing in the exemplifications of the Fourth Degree one hundred years later, a refrain that conveys the traditional idealism of patriotism and fraternalism in an era of pluralism and individualism.

Notes

Chapter 1
The Origins of Catholic Patriotism

1. Cynthia M. Koch, "Teaching Patriotism," in *Bonds of Affection: Americans Define Their Patriotism,* edited by John Bodnar (Princeton: Princeton University Press, 1996), 31. Albert J. Raboteau has noted that this scriptural language of "Redeemer Nation" has no application to African Americans, whose biblical imagery was related to the people in bondage yearning for the promised land. See Albert J. Raboteau, *A Fire in the Bones: Reflections on African-American Religious History* (Boston: Beacon Press, 1995), 28–36.

2. Cecilia Elizabeth O'Leary, "'Blood Brotherhood': The Racialization of Patriotism, 1865–1918," in *Bonds of Affection*, ed. Bodnar, 53. Also see John Bodnar, *Remaking America: Public Memory, Commemoration, and Patriotism in the Twentieth Century* (Princeton: Princeton University Press, 1992), "The Memory Debate: An Introduction," 14–20. For an excellent presentation and analysis of the liberal understanding of patriotism that is sympathetic to the Knights' claim for all to live by the ideals of the nation, see John Patrick Diggins, *On Hallowed Ground: Abraham Lincoln and the Foundation of American History* (New Haven: Yale University Press, 2000).

3. Donald L. Kinzer, *An Episode in Anti-Catholicism: The American Protection Association* (Seattle: Washington State University Press, 1964).

4. M. J. McGivney to "Reverend Pastor," April 1882. McGivney Papers, AKC.

5. Ibid.

6. Daniel Colwell, "Knights of Columbus," *Columbiad* 20 (January 1913): 12.

7. Ibid.

8. Dr. Mathew C. O'Connor's Recollections, handwritten text, AKC.

9. Thomas H. Cummings "Catholic Gentlemen in Fraternity," *Donohoe's Magazine* 33 (November 1895): 1240.

10. Introductory Matter, Minutes of the Supreme Assembly of the Fourth Degree, AKC.

11. O'Leary, "'Blood Brotherhood,'" 53.

12. Josiah Strong, *Our Country: Its Possible Future, Its Present Crisis* (New York: American Home Mission Society, 1885), 75.

13. Rogers M. Smith, *Civic Ideals: Conflicting Views of Citizenship* (New Haven: Yale University Press 1998), 355.

14. Ibid., 354.

15. Ibid., 85.

16. David J. O'Brien, *Public Catholicism* (Maryknoll, N.Y.: Orbis Books, 1996), 33.

17. Quoted by Gerald P. Fogarty, S.J., "Public Patriotism and Private Politics," *U.S. Catholic Historian* 4 (fall 1985): 4.

18. For a study of John England, see Patrick Carey, *An Immigrant Bishop: John England's Adaptation of Irish Catholicism to American Republicanism* (New York: United States Catholic Historical Society, 1982).

19. Fogarty, "Public Patriotism," 5

20. Rogers M. Smith, "The American Creed and American Identity: The Limits of Liberal Citizenship in the United States," *Western Political Quarterly* 41 (1988): 225–39. For the quotation of Hughes, see Smith, *Civic Ideals,* 208–9.

21. For a concise and comprehensive treatment of these topics, see John McManners, *The French Revolution and the Church* (London: SPCK, 1969).

22. Lawrence J. McCaffrey, *The Irish Diaspora in America* (Bloomington: Indiana University Press, 1977), 93. For an excellent study of how Catholicism functioned for Protestants, see Jenny Franclot, *Roads to Rome: The Antebellum Protestant Encounter with Catholicism* (Berkeley: University of California Press, 1994).

23. Wilfred J. Bisson, *Countdown to Violence: The Charlestown Convent Riot of 1834* (New York: Garland, 1989); and Jeanne Hamilton, O.S.U., "The Nunnery as Menace: The Burning of Charlestown Convent, 1834," *U.S. Catholic Historian* 14 (winter 1996): 35–66.

24. Ray A. Billington, *The Protestant Crusade, 1880–1960* (Chicago: Quadrangle Books, 1938).

25. Ibid.

26. Ibid.

27. Quoted by Fogarty, "Public Patriotism," 11.

28. For an excellent work on the Know-Nothing Party, see Tyler Anbinder, *Nativism and Slavery: The Northern Know-Nothings and the Politics of the 1850s* (New York: Oxford University Press, 1992).

29. John Carroll Noonan, *Nativism in Connecticut* (Washington, D.C.: The Catholic University of America Press, 1938), 190.

30. Quoted by Rogers Smith, *Civic Ideals,* 211.

31. Koch, "Teaching Patriotism," in *Bonds of Affection,* ed. Bodnar, 33.

32. One of the first scholars to discuss the origins of *Columbia* is Albert H.

Hoyt, "The Name 'Columbus,'" *N. E. Historical and Genealogical Register* (July 1886): 7. Also see John Alexander Williams, "The First American Hero" unpublished paper. Copy in AKC.

33. Jeremy Belknap, *A Discourse Intended to Commemorate the Discovery of America by Christopher Columbus* (Boston: Belknap & Hall, Apollo Press, 1792), 56–58.

34. Robert N. Bellah, "Civil Religion in America," in *Nationalism and Religion in America,* edited by Winthrop S. Hudson (New York: Harper & Row, 1970), 48–51. For an original work on *e pluribus unum,* see Martin E. Marty, *The One and the Many: America's Struggle for the Common Good* (Cambridge, Mass.: Harvard University Press, 1997).

35. Smith, *Civic Ideals,* 34.

36. Ibid.

37. For reports on the activities of St. Mary's YMTA, see the *Morning News* [New Haven], September 11, 1883. The most recent study of the Catholic temperance movement is Diedre M. Maloney, "'Combating Whiskey's Work': The Catholic Temperance Movement in Late Nineteenth Century America," *U.S. Catholic Historian* 16 (summer, 1998).

38. Joan Bland, *The Hibernian Crusade: The Origin of the Catholic Total Abstinence Union of America* (Washington, D.C.: The Catholic University of America Press, 1951).

39. Michael J. McGivney, "Connecticut Knights of Columbus . . . Objects, Benefits and Instructions for Forming New Councils." McGivney Papers, AKC.

40. Kinzer, *An Episode in Anti-Catholicism.*

41. "Secret Oath of the American Protective Association, October 31, 1893," in *Documents of American Catholic History,* edited by John Tracy Ellis (Wilmington, Del.: Michael Glazier, 1987), 484.

42. Ibid.

43. "Armed Know Nothings," *Connecticut Catholic* 17 (April 5, 1893): 4.

44. Thomas H. Cummings, "The Knights of Columbus," *Donohoe's Magazine* 29 (May 1893): 557.

45. Stuart McConnell, "Reading the Flag," in *Bonds of Affection*, ed. Bodnar, 113.

46. "William J. Coughlin addresses Council No. 72," *Columbiad* (January 1894): 1.

47. Ibid.

48. McConnell, "Reading the Flag," 110.

49. Mary Ann Clawson, *Constructing Brotherhood: Class, Gender, and Fraternalism* (Princeton: Princeton University Press, 1989), 124.

50. Cummings, "Catholic Gentlemen in Fraternity," 1243.

51. Mark C. Carnes, "Middle-Class Men and the Solace of Ritual," in *Meanings for Manhood: Constructing Masculinity in Victorian America,* edited by Mark C. Carnes and Clyde Griffin (Chicago: University of Chicago Press, 1990), 48.

52. Cummings, "Catholic Gentlemen in Fraternity," 1253.

53. "Knights of Columbus in Uniforms," *Connecticut Catholic* 10 (November 10, 1886): 4.

54. Editorial, *Connecticut Catholic* 10 (November 10, 1886): 5.

55. Ibid.

56. "How About a Uniformed Degree?" *Connecticut Catholic* 14 (July 1890).

57. "Christopher Columbus—Discoverer of the New World," *Connecticut Catholic* 17 (May 25, 1892): 4.

58. James E. Foley and Nicholas Virgadamo, eds., *The Knights of Columbus in the State of New York, 1891–1968* (New York: The State Council of New York, 1968), 19.

59. Ibid.

60. For an overview of the insurance reforms, see my revised edition of *Faith and Fraternalism: The History of the Knights of Columbus* (New York: Simon & Schuster, 1992), 142–50.

61. Fourth Degree Ceremonial, included in the "Minutes of the Supreme Assemblies of the Fourth Degree," February 22, 1900, AKC.

62. Ibid.

63. Ibid.

64. John Tracy Ellis, *The Life of James Cardinal Gibbons, Archbishop of Baltimore, 1834–1921* (Milwaukee: Bruce, 1952), 2:90. Also see Dorothy Dohen, *Nationalism and American Catholicism* (New York: Sheed & Ward, 1967). Dorothy Dohen, the last editor of *Integrity*, the journal that originated among first-generation activists in the Catholic Worker movement of Dorothy Day and Peter Maurin, is a sociologist who, though aware of the abiding anti-Catholicism during the period of the Spanish-American War, did not perceive it as a mitigating factor in her criticism of Cardinal James Gibbons and others for not assuming a prophetic mission to condemn this unjust war.

65. State Deputy's Report, Fourth Annual Convention, Maine State Council." Reprint, Supreme Council Proceedings 1899, 74, AKC.

66. "Editorial Notes," *Columbiad* 7 (April 1900): 5.

67. Ibid.

68. "The Fourth Degree," *Columbiad* 7 (April 1900): 5.

69. David I. Kertzer, *Ritual, Politics and Culture* (New Haven: Yale University Press, 1988), 9–10.

70. "Knights of Columbus, Fourth Degree Emblems," 1901. SC-9-0-003, AKC.

Chapter 2
Growth, Reform, and the Bogus Oath

1. Christopher J. Kauffman, *Faith and Fraternalism: The History of the Knights of Columbus*, revised edition (New York: Simon & Schuster 1992), 124–28.

2. Editorial Notes, "Joseph Scott," *Columbiad* 11 (February 1904): 18. For biographical material on Scott, see Francis J. Weber, "Joseph Scott," in *The California Encyclopedia of Catholic History* (Spokane: Arthur H. Krock, 2000), 159–60.

3. Joseph Scott, "The Mission of the Order in the Land of the Missions," *Columbiad* 11 (February 1904): 3.

4. Ibid., 4.

5. Ibid., 5.

6. Kauffman, *Faith and Fraternalism,* 138.

7. "Editorial Notes," *Columbiad* 7 (April 1900): 5.

8. James P. Monaghan, S.J., to the Editor, *Columbiad* 15 (August 1908): 8.

9. Maurice Francis Egan and John B. Kennedy, *Knights of Columbus in Peace and War* (New Haven: Knights of Columbus, 1920), 1:217–28.

10. "Notes from the Councils," *Columbiad* 14 (March 1907): 12.

11. P. H. Rice, "Fourth Degree in Georgia," *Columbiad* 13 (November 1906).

12. "Banquet to Honor Archbishop Blenk," *Columbiad* 13 (November 1906): 4.

13. Ibid.

14. "Archbishop Ireland Present, Delivered a Magnificent Address at Hennepin Council Anniversary Banquet," *Columbiad* 15 (July 1907): 6.

15. "Archbishop John Ireland's Sermon at the Solemn Pontifical," in *Centenary Celebration Souvenir, Events of the Catholic Congress of the United States* (Detroit: Van Hugh, 1889), 18.

16. "Archbishop Ireland Present," n. 14.

17. Ibid.

18. W. Bourke Cochran, "Father Hecker, The Citizen," *Columbiad* 18 (March 1910): 3–4. Also see David O'Brien, *Isaac Hecker: An American Biography* (Mahwah, N.J.: Paulist Press, 1994).

19. "The Missionary Congress," *Columbiad* 16 (January 1909): 7.

20. Ibid.

21. Angelyn Dries, O.S.P., *The Missionary Movement in American History* (Maryknoll, N.Y.: Orbis Books, 1998), 89.

22. *The First National Missionary Congress,* edited by Francis C. Kelley (Chicago: J. S. Highland Co., 1909), 443–44.

23. Ibid., 445.

24. Ibid., 158–59.

25. Ibid., 59.

26. Ibid.

27. John H. Reddin, *Fourth Degree Knights of Columbus: History—Activities—Aims—Accomplishments* (New Haven: Knights of Columbus, 1931), 6–10, AKC.

28. Ibid., 12.

29. Ibid.

30. "New Fourth Degree Appointments," *Columbiad* 17 (August 1910): 7.

31. Edward E. Grusd, *B'nai B'rith: The Story of a Covenant* (New York: Appleton Century Press, 1966), 20.

32. Ibid., 15.

33. Ibid., 150.

34. Kauffman, *Faith and Fraternalism*, 175–77.

35. John Higham, *Strangers in the Land: Patterns of American Nativism, 1860–1925* (New Brunswick, N.J.: Rutgers University Press, 1955), 134.

36. Ibid., 155–75.

37. Ibid., 176.

38. Ibid., 179.

39. Ibid.

40. Ibid., 179–80. Also see C. Vann Woodward's book, *Tom Watson, Agrarian Rebel* (New York: Oxford University Press, 1963; originally published by the Macmillan Company, 1938). On p. 424 Woodward reports that to raise money for his *Magazine* Watson wrote, "Remember, I am up against 263,000 Knights of Columbus who have sworn to put me out of business." On the same page Woodward tells about Watson's attempt to "get into a perfectly beautiful fight" with a man he knew was a Knight, by bumping into him and when the Knight "would demand an apology" Watson would refuse and thereby fight it out. "The man showed no resentment, however, and Watson's friends dragged him out of the hotel."

41. *The Menace*, March 4, 1913. SCII File 93, The National Archives, Washington, D.C..

42. Ibid.

43. Higham, *Strangers in the Land,* 181.

44. *The Menace* August 31, 1913. SCII File 93, The National Archives, Washington, D.C.

45. Leo Christopher Donohue, "The Alleged Fourth Degree Knights of Columbus Oath" (Ph.D. diss., Boston College, 1938), 43–44. For the alleged Jesuit oath, see Rev. William Livingston, Castilian Council No. 154, "The Knights and their Traducers," *Columbiad* 20 (January 1913): 3.

46. "The Knights of Columbus Oath," *The Menace,* July 13, 1912, made from the *Congressional Record* of the Sixty-Second Congress, Third session, for Saturday, February 15, 1913. This oath was submitted as evidence of slander in the case of Eugene C. Bonniwell, a member of Congress, against Thomas C. Butler, the Republican candidate who defeated Bonniwell for circulating the oath to disparage his opponent who was a Fourth Degree Knight of Columbus. This quote is from a copy in the AKC. Also *Faked and Bogus Oaths and Bogus Documents,* Our Sunday Visitor Press, in the papers of Bishop John Noll. PANT 6/07, Archives of the University of Notre Dame.

47. Donohue, "Alleged Fourth Degree," 43–44.

48. N. M. Phillips, "The Knights of Columbus," *The Menace,* October 12, 1912, p. 1. SCII File 93, The National Archives, Washington, D.C.

49. Ibid.

50. Ibid.

51. "Addresses Delivered at the Unveiling," *Columbiad* 20 (July 1912): 3.

52. Dennis A. McCarthy, "Unveiling a Magnificent Success," *Columbiad* 19 (July 1912): 3.

53. "Edward Hearn, Proud of His Knights," *Columbiad* 19 (July 1912). This irony was noted in "The Guardians of Liberty," *Columbiad* 19 (August 1912): 10.

54. Editorial, "The Guardians of Liberty," *Columbiad* 19 (August 1912): 10.

55. N. M. Philips, "The Knights of Columbus," *The Menace,* October 12, 1912, p. 1. SCII File 93, The National Archives, Washington, D.C.

56. Quoted in *Knights of Columbus vs. Libel and Malicious Bigotry* (New Haven: Knights of Columbus, 1914), 4.

57. Ibid.

58. *Faked and Bogus Oaths* (see n. 46 above).

59. *Knights of Columbus vs. Libel* . . . , 9.

60. "The K of C Inquisition," *The Menace,* March 8, 1913, p. 1. SCII File 93, The National Archives, Washington, D.C.

61. *The Menace* Publishing Company to Leroy N. King, March 5, 1913. Bogus Oath Files, SC-11-1-093, AKC.

62. "The Knights of Columbus Oath," *The Menace,* September 12, 1914. Bogus Oath Files, SC-11-1-093, AKC.

63. W. J. Smith To His Excellency the President of the United States, October 10, 1913. Woodrow Wilson Papers #281 Accession 109929. Manuscript Division, Library of Congress, D2.

64. A. A. Kaisse to Hon. Woodrow Wilson, President of the United States, March 4, 1913. Woodrow Wilson Papers #286 Accession 109931. Manuscript Division, Library of Congress, D2.

65. "Tumulty Holding Two Jobs," *The Menace,* a reprint from the *American Chicago,* January 11, 1913, pp. 1–2. Accession #109981, Manuscript Division, Library of Congress, D2.

66. On Tumulty's entrance into the Order, see John O'Neill to Joseph Tumulty, December 13, 1915. Copy in the Woodrow Wilson Papers, Manuscript Division, Library of Congress, D2.

67. "A Love of Socialism," *The Catholic Columbiad*, in *Columbiad* 20 (April 1913): 10.

68. Andrew P. Doyle, C.S.P., *Columbiad* 20 (August 1913): 4.

69. John A. Ryan, "The Legal Minimum Wage," *Columbiad* 20 (August 1913): 4.

70. Mary B. O'Sullivan, "The Child Labor Question," *Columbiad* 20 (May 1913): 7.

71. Doyle, 5 (see n. 68 above).

72. Ibid.

73. Philip Gleason, *The Conservative Reformers: German-American Catholics and the Social Order* (Notre Dame, Ind.: University of Notre Dame Press, 1968).

74. Philip S. Foner, *History of the Labor Movement in the United States* (New York: International Publishers, 1964), vol. III, *The Policies and Practices of the American Federation of Labor,* 116.

75. Higham, *Strangers in the Land,* 180.

76. John H. Reddin, "To Masters and Fourth Degree Officers" *Columbiad* 19 (December 1912): 6.

77. James A. Flaherty, "Supreme Knight's Report," *Columbiad* 20 (September 1913): 10.

78. Reddin, *Fourth Degree Knights of Columbus,* AKC. See n. 27 above.

79. David Goldstein, *Autobiography of a Campaigner for Christ* (Boston: Catholic Campaign for Christ, 1936), 143.

80. Ibid., 1–20.

81. Ibid., 49.

82. Debra Campbell, "'I can't imagine Our Lady on an Outdoor Platform': Women in the Catholic Street Propaganda Movement," *U.S. Catholic Historian* 3 (spring-summer 1986): 103–14. Also see D. Owen Carrigan, "Martha Moore

Avery: The Way of a Crusader" (Ph.D. diss., University of Maine, Orono, 1966); and Debra Campbell, "David Goldstein and the Lay Catholic Street Apostolate" (Ph.D diss., Boston College, 1982).

83. Goldstein, *Autobiography*, 51–55.

84. Ibid., 18.

85. Quoted by Foner, *History of the Labor Movement*, III, 120.

86. Ibid.

87. Ibid., 121–22. Speaking for Eugene V. Debs, the Socialist Party presidential candidate in 1912, his brother, Theodore Debs, caustically stated: "Collins is not worthy of a decent man's account" because Collins attacked Debs as having had his house built with scab labor (Theodore Debs to Carl D. Thompson, in *Letters of Eugene Debs,* edited by J. Robert Considine [Urbana, Ill./Chicago: University of Illinois Press, 1990]).

88. John H. Reddin, "The Free Lecture Movement," *Columbiad* 21 (March 1914): 1.

89. Ibid.

90. Peter W. Collins, "Socialism and the Labor Movement," *Columbiad* 20 (May 1913): 7.

91. "Goldstein's Catholic Lectures," *Columbiad* 21 (July 1914): 5.

92. Goldstein, *Autobiography,* 145.

93. Higham, *Strangers in the Land,* 183.

94. Ibid., 185.

95. Ibid., 186.

96. Ibid.

97. "Supreme Knight's Report," *Columbiad* 21 (September 1914): 11.

98. Ibid.

99. P. H. Callahan, "Introduction to an address by Washington Gladden 'Patriotism,'" reprinted in *Columbiad* 24 (February 1917): 4. Also see Washington Gladden, "Anti-Papal Panic," reprinted in *Columbiad* 21 (August 1914): 4, 13.

100. Joseph E. Green, "Patrick Henry Callahan (1866–1940)" (Ph.D. diss., Catholic University of America, Studies in Sociology 54, 1964, 57–58. Also see William E. Ellis, *Patrick Henry Callahan (1866–1940): Progressive Catholic Laymen in the American South* (Lewiston, N.Y.: Edwin Mellen Press, 1989).

101. *Report of the Commission on Religious Prejudices* (Davenport, Ia.: Knights of Columbus, 1916), 6; also in *Columbiad* 23 (October 1916).

102. P. H. Callahan to Woodrow Wilson, June 1, 1916. Woodrow Wilson Papers #281 Accession 1995, Manuscript Division, Library of Congress, D2.

103. Quoted in *Report of the Commission on Religious Prejudices,* 6; also in *Columbiad* 23 (October 1916).

104. *Report of the Commission; Columbiad* 23 (October 1916): 5–9.

105. P. H. Callahan to John H. Reddin, August 11, 1916, 110051. Copy found in the Woodrow Wilson Papers, Manuscript Division, Library of Congress, D2.

106. Ibid.

107. Ibid.

108. Ibid.

109. *Report of the Commission on Religious Prejudices* (New Haven: Knights of Columbus, 1917), 3–5.
110. Ibid
111. Ibid.

Chapter 3
War and the Tribal Twenties

1. The title of this chapter is taken from John Higham's chapter "Tribal Twenties," in *Strangers in the Land: Patterns of American Nativism 1860–1925* (New Brunswick, N.J.: Rutgers University Press, 1955), 264–99. See also Lynn Dumenil's article "The Tribal Twenties: Assimilated Catholic Response to Anti-Catholicism in the 1920s," *Journal of American Ethnic History* (fall 1991); Christopher J. Kauffman, *Faith and Fraternalism: The History of the Knights of Columbus,* revised edition (New York: Simon & Schuster, 1992).
2. Higham, *Strangers in the Land,* 267.
3. Ibid., 277.
4. Cecilia Elizabeth O'Leary, *A Nation to Die For: The Paradox of American Patriotism* (Princeton: Princeton University Press, 1999). Also see David M. Kennedy, *Over Here: The First World War and American Society* (New York: Oxford University Press, 1980).
5. Quoted by Sydney E. Ahlstrom, *A Religious History of the American People* (New York: Doubleday, 1975), 2:317.
6. Quoted by John Tracy Ellis, *The Life of James Cardinal Gibbons, Archbishop of Baltimore, 1834–1921* (Milwaukee: Bruce, 1952), 2:239.
7. Ibid., 2:240.
8. Martin E. Marty, *The Irony of It All: Modern American Religion* (Chicago: University of Chicago Press, 1986), 315.
9. Quoted by Ellis, *James Cardinal Gibbons,* 2:240.
10. James A. Flaherty to Woodrow Wilson April 17, 1917. War Activities File, AKC. This letter is also quoted by D. J. Callahan to Joseph Tumulty, July 24, 1917. Woodrow Wilson Papers #286, Manuscript Division, Library of Congress, D2.
11. Ibid., May 23, 1917.
12. "Knights on Border Service," *Columbiad* 23 (August 1916): 11. Also see Frederick Kath, "Pancho Villa and the Attack on Columbus, New Mexico," *American Historical Review* 83 (February 1978): 101–30. For the border work of the Texas Knights, see William H. Obereste, *Knights of Columbus in Texas, 1902–1952* (Austin, Tex.: Knights of Columbus, 1952): 207–12. For the border "Huts program," also see Maurice Francis Egan and John B. Kennedy, *Knights of Columbus in Peace and War* (New Haven: Knights of Columbus, 1920), 1:201–10.
13. Remarks of Bishop Muldoon at Meeting of Supreme Board of Directors, May 26–27, 1918. Copy, War Activities File, AKC.
14. John Reddin, Supreme Master's Report, Supreme Assembly Meeting 1918. Minutes of the Supreme Assembly, AKC.
15. Ibid.

16. P. H. Callahan to *Post Standard* of Syracuse, reprinted in Callahan's own newsletter which he published, *The Good of the Order* 14 (August 1, 1919): 5.

17. Ahlstrom, *Religious History,* 2:376.

18. John F. Noll, "Dear Archbishop" form letter. Mundelein Papers 230, Archives of the Archdiocese of Chicago.

19. Elizabeth McKeown, "World War I and American Catholics," in *Encyclopedia of American Catholic History,* edited by Michael Glazier and Thomas J. Shelley (Collegeville, Minn.: Liturgical Press, 1998), 1519. Also see eadem, *War and Welfare: A Study of American Catholic Leadership* (New York: Garland, 1989).

20. Elizabeth McKeown, "The National Bishops Conference: An Analysis of its Origins," *Catholic Historical Review* 66 (October 1980): 565–83. Also see Douglas J. Slawson, *The Foundation and First Decade of the National Catholic Welfare Council* (Washington, D.C.: Catholic University of America Press, 1992).

21. Kauffman, *Faith and Fraternalism,* chapter 9, "Serving the Servicemen in World War I."

22. "The Proposed Statue at Metz," *Columbiad* 26 (September 1919): 8; also see the Metz File that contains John Reddin's unpublished diary, AKC.

23. "The Audience with the Pope," *Columbiad* 26 (October 1919): 16.

24. Ibid., 17.

25. John W. Maynard and Carlo M. Ferrari, *The Methodist Episcopal Church in Rome* (Rome, 1930).

26. "Extracts from letter of European Commissioner Edward Hearn," Received in the Supreme Office August 1, 1921. Roman Playgrounds File, AKC.

27. H. O. Wittpenn to Joseph Tumulty, August 2, 1919. Woodrow Wilson Papers, #110429, Manuscript Division, Library of Congress, D2.

28. Higham, *Strangers in the Land,* 237.

29. O'Leary, *A Nation to Die For,* 240–41.

30. Ibid., 240.

31. John Higham, *Send These to Me: Immigrants in Urban America,* revised edition (Baltimore/London: Johns Hopkins University Press, 1984), chapter 2, "The Politics of Patriotism," 29–70.

32. Judge Daniel Cohalen, "Obituary of Edward F. McSweeney," *Journal of the Irish Historical Society* 27 (1928): 426–29.

33. Lawrence McCaffrey, "Irish Nationalism," in *Encyclopedia of the Irish in America,* edited by Michael Glazier (Notre Dame, Ind.: University of Notre Dame Press, 2000), 644–49.

34. Cohalen, "Obituary of Edward F. McSweeney."

35. Edward McSweeney to Dermiad Lynch, June 27, 1922. Cohalen Papers, McSweeney Files 1922, Box 11, Folder 3, Archives of the American Irish Historical Society, New York City.

36. Edward F. McSweeney, *De-Americanizing Young America: Poisoning the Sources of Our National History and Traditions* (Boston: Friends of Irish Freedom, 1920), 2.

37. Ibid., 6.

38. McSweeney to Lynch, June 27, 1922; see n. 35 above.

39. Higham, *Strangers in the Land,* 280.

40. Ibid.

41. John Reddin, Resolution on the Historical Commission passed by Supreme Assembly, May 28, 1921. Historical Commission Files, AKC.

42. Edward F. McSweeney to Daniel Cohalen, mid-July 1921. Cohalen Papers, McSweeney Files, Box 11, Folder 15, Archives of the Irish American Historical Society, New York City.

43. McSweeney to Cohalen, August 21, 1921. Cohalen Papers, McSweeney Files 1921, Box 11, Folder 15, Archives of the Irish American Historical Society, New York City.

44. Kauffman, *Faith and Fraternalism*, 263–64.

45. "Knights Correct False Impression," *The Pilot* [Boston] 92 (September 24, 1921): 1.

46. Samuel Flagg Bemis, *Jay's Treaty: A Study in Commerce and Diplomacy* (New York: Macmillan, 1923), 270–71.

47. Kauffman, *Faith and Fraternalism,* 283–84.

48. Edward F. McSweeney to the Supreme Board of Directors, October 8, 1922. Historical Commission Files, SC-12-10, AKC.

49. Ibid.

50. Edward McSweeney to William McGinley, January 5, 1923. SC 12-023-02-AKC.

51. Ibid.

52. Report of Thomas P. Flynn, Vice Supreme Master, Marquette Province, 1921. Supreme Assembly Minutes, AKC.

53. Edward F. McSweeney, Address to the Supreme Council of 1922. Historical Commission Files, AKC.

54. John H. Reddin, "The American History Contest," *Columbia* 1 (September 1921): 23.

55. Higham, *Strangers in the Land*, 20.

56. Edward F. McSweeney, "Racial Contribution to America," *Columbia* 3 (June 1924): 8.

57. Higham, *Strangers in the Land*, 124.

58. Ibid., 124–25.

59. Quoted by Higham, *Send These to Me*, 209.

60. Ibid., 211.

61. Quoted by Higham, *Send These to Me,* 213.

62. Edward F. McSweeney, L.L.D., "The Racial Contribution Series," an introduction to *The Gift of the Black Folk: The Negroes in the Making of America,* by W. E. Burghardt DuBois, Ph.D. (Harv.) (Boston: Stratford Publishers, 1924), 1.

63. Ibid., 28.

64. DuBois, "Foreword," in *Gift of the Black Folk,* iii.

65. Ibid., iv.

66. Stephen J. Ochs, *Desegregating the Altar: The Josephites and the Struggle for Black Priests* (Baton Rouge, La.: Louisiana State University Press, 1990), 233.

67. Ibid., 236.

68. Cyprian Davis, *The History of Black Catholics in the United States* (New York: Crossroad, 1990), 235–36.

69. Herbert Aptheker, ed., *The Correspondence of W. E. B. DuBois* (Amherst: University of Massachusetts Press, 1973), 1:311.

70. George Cohen, *The Jews in the Making of America* (Boston: Stratford Publishers, 1924).

71. Frederick Franklin Schrader, *The Germans in the Making of America* (Boston: Stratford Publishers, 1924).

72. "Knights of Columbus Reconstruction Program." Luke E. Hart Papers, AKC.

73. Quoted by McSweeney in his "Memorandum for a Special Committee, May 5, 1923." Historical Commission, AKC.

74. Supreme Master's Report 1925. Proceedings of the Supreme Assembly, July 29-31, 1926, AKC.

75. Leonard J. Moore, *Citizen Klansmen: The Ku Klux Klan in Indiana* (Chapel Hill/London: University of North Carolina Press, 1991), 3.

76. David M. Chalmers, *Hooded Americanism: The History of the Ku Klux Klan*, 3rd edition (New York: Franklin Watts, 1981), 28–30.

77. Ochs, *Desegregating the Altar.*

78. "Ku Klux Salesmen circulated a forged oath of Treasonable and Murderous Obligations. They say Knights take . . ." *The World* [New York] 62 (September 14, 1921): 1.

79. John B. Kennedy, "The Profits of Prejudice," *Columbia* 1 (October, 1921): 13.

80. John M. Mecklin, *The Ku Klux Klan: A Study of the American Mind* (New York: Harcourt Press, 1924), 124–25.

81. Robert Alan Goldberg, *The Ku Klux Klan in Colorado* (Urbana, Ill./Chicago/London: University of Illinois Press, 1981), 34.

82. Ibid., 32–33.

83. Ibid., 33.

84. Kathleen M. Blee, *Women of the Klan: Racism and Gender in the 1920s* (Berkeley/Los Angeles/Oxford: University of California Press, 1991). Blee refers to the bogus oath on p. 87.

85. Report of the Hennepin Province, Master of West Virginia, M. J. Cullinan. Minutes of the Supreme Assembly 1924, AKC.

86. Ibid.

87. A. H. Bell, "The Knights of Columbus Unmasked," *Rail-Splitter* 8 (July 1923): 1. Bogus Oath Files.

88. William Lloyd Clark, "The Ku Klux Klan," *Rail-Splitter* 8 (July 1923): 4, AKC.

89. Copy of Hart's letter (March 20, 1923). William Lloyd Clark's response to a handbill presented by The *Rail Splitter* Press. "Knights of Columbus Exposed" in the Clark Case, Bogus Oath File, AKC.

90. Ibid.

91. James Malone to Luke E. Hart, June 26, 1923. Clark Case.

92. Hart to Malone, June 28, 1923. Clark Case.

93. Douglas Slawson, "The Attitudes and Activities of American Catholics Regarding Proposals to Establish a Federal Department of Education Between

World War I and the Great Depression" (Ph.D. diss., The Catholic University of America, 1980).

94. Leslie Woodcock Tentler, *Seasons of Grace: A History of the Archdiocese of Detroit* (Detroit: Wayne State University Press, 1990), 444–49.

95. Report of Hennepin Province, John J. Donovan, Vice Supreme Master's Report, Minutes of the Meeting, 1926. Supreme Assembly, 1–2, AKC.

96. Sir Knight Murray of Blue Grass Assembly in Lexington, Ky., Minutes of Supreme Assembly, 1926, 8, AKC.

97. Quoted by Kauffman, *Faith and Fraternalism,* 299.

98. Quoted by Michael Williams, *The Shadow of the Pope* (New York: McGraw-Hill, 1932), 193.

99. "Governor Smith's Answer to the Religious Bigotry of the Presidential Campaign, September 20, 1928," in *Documents of American Catholic History,* edited by John Tracy Ellis (Wilmington, Del.: Michael Glazier, 1987), 2:616–20.

100. For this symbol of white purity I am indebted to John Higham, *Send These to Me,* 19–97.

101. Dumenil, "The Tribal Twenties," 21–22.

102. John H. Reddin, "Silver Jubilee of Fourth Degree," *Columbia* 4 (July 1925).

Chapter 4
The Great Depression to Postwar Anti-Communism: From the 1930s to the 1950s

1. Francis J. Weber, "Joseph Scott," in *Encyclopedia of California Catholic History* (Spokane: Arthur H. Clark, 2000), 158–59.

2. For works on the politics of the 1930s, see Alan Brinkley, *Voices of Protest: Huey Long, Father Coughlin and the Great Depression* (New York: Vintage Books, 1983); Anthony Badger, *The New Deal: The Depression Years* (New York: Alfred A. Knopf, 1989); Terry A. Cooney, *Balancing Acts: American Thought and Culture in the 1930s* (New York: Twayne, 1995); William A. Luechtenburg, *Franklin Roosevelt and the New Deal* (New York: Harper & Row 1963); Arthur M. Schlesinger, Jr., *The Politics of Upheaval* (New York: Houghton Mifflin, 1966).

3. "Supreme Knight's Report." Proceedings of the Supreme Council, 1931, 21, AKC.

4. Ibid.

5. "Supreme Knight's Radio Message," *Columbia* 12 (May 1932): 28.

6. On John A. Ryan, see Francis L. Broderick, *Right Reverend New Dealer—John A. Ryan* (New York: Macmillan, 1963); idem, "The Encyclicals and Social Action: Is John A. Ryan Typical?" *Catholic Historical Review* 55 (April 1969): 1–6; Joseph M. McShane, *Sufficiently Radical: Catholicism, Progressivism and the Bishops' Program of 1919* (Washington, D.C.: Catholic University of America Press, 1986). On Catholics and the administration of Franklin D. Roosevelt, see George G. Flynn, *American Catholics and the Roosevelt Administration* (Lexington: University of Kentucky Press, 1968); idem, *Roosevelt and Romanism: Catholics and American Diplomacy, 1931–1945* (Westport, Conn.: Greenwood Press, 1976); David J. O'Brien, *American Catholics and Social Reform—The New Deal Years* (New York:

Oxford University Press, 1972); idem, *Public Catholicism* (Maryknoll, N.Y.: Orbis Books, 1996), chapter 6.

7. Quoted by Flynn, *American Catholics*, 17–18. On James Gillis, see Richard Gribble, *Guardian of America: The Life of James Martin Gillis* (Mahwah, N.J., Paulist Press, 1998).

8. John Reddin, *The Fourth Degree Knights of Columbus: History—Activities—Aims—Accomplishments* (New Haven: Knights of Columbus, 1931), 28.

9. Ibid., 29.

10. Quoted by O'Brien, *Public Catholicism,* 165.

11. Reddin, *Fourth Degree Knights,* 26.

12. "Ludendorf, Erich," *Encyclopedia Britannica* (Chicago/London/Toronto/Geneva: Encyclopedia Britannica, 1962), 14:479.

13. Reddin, *Fourth Degree Knights,* 27.

14. Quoted by Joseph P. Chinnici, *Living Stones: History and Structure of American Catholic Spiritual Life in the United States* (Maryknoll, N.Y.: Orbis Books, 1995), 167.

15. Ibid., 158.

16. Ibid., 160.

17. Ibid., 162.

18. Reddin, *Fourth Degree Knights,* 31.

19. Chinnici, *Living Stones,* 167.

20. Reddin, *Fourth Degree Knights,* 30.

21. Debra Campbell, "Part-time Female Evangelists of the Thirties and Forties: The Rosary College Catholic Evidence Guild," *U.S. Catholic Historian* 5 (summer/fall 1986): 372.

22. Reddin, *Fourth Degree Knights,* 34.

23. Ibid., 27.

24. Ibid., 31.

25. Ibid., 32.

26. Ibid., 18.

27. O'Brien, *Public Catholicism,* 169–70.

28. Ibid., 170.

29. For a detailed account of the Knights and the Mexican crises, see my chapter on the topic in *Faith and Fraternalism: The History of the Knights of Columbus,* revised edition (New York: Simon & Schuster, 1992), "The Knights Crusade in Mexico," 302–29; E. David Cronon, "American Catholics and American 'Anticlericalism,'" *Mississippi Valley Historical Review,* 1933–1936, 45 (September 1958): 206–19; John W. F. Dulles, *Yesterday in Mexico: A Chronicle of the Revolution 1916–1929* (Austin: University of Texas Press, 1965); Daniel James, *Mexico and the Americans* (New York: Praeger, 1963); Octavio Paz, *The Labyrinth of Solitude, Life and Thought in Mexico,* translated by Lysander Kemp (New York: Grove Press, 1985); Robert E. Quirk, *The Mexican Revolution and the Catholic Church, 1916–1929* (Bloomington: Indiana University Press, 1973); Paul V. Murray, *The Catholic Church in Mexico: Historical Essays for the General Reader* (Mexico City: Editorial E.P.M., 1965).

30. For this period leading up to the *modus vivendi* of 1929, see Harold Nicholson, *Dwight Morrow* (New York: Harcourt, Brace, 1931), 319ff., Quirk, *Mexican*

Revolution, 219–20; Francis Clement Kelley, *Blood Drenched Altars: Mexico Study and Comment* (Milwaukee: Bruce, 1935). On Kelley during this Mexican crisis, see James P. Gaffey, *Francis Clement Kelley and the American Dream* (Bensonville, Ill.: Heritage Foundation, 1980), 2:3–103.

31. Quoted by Cronon, "American Catholics and Mexican 'Anti-clericalism,'" 206.

32. Ibid.

33. Martin Carmody, "Supreme Knights Condemnation of the American Government," in *The Record. Religious Liberty: The Mexican Government* (New Haven: Knights of Columbus, 1935), 5, AKC.

34. Robert R. Hull to Luke E. Hart, August 16, 1935. Mexican Files, AKC.

35. "Editorials," *Columbia* 15 (October 1935): 13.

36. Quoted by Flynn, *American Catholics*, 166.

37. Kauffman, *Faith and Fraternalism,* 325–29; also see Cronon, "American Catholics," 328–30; and Flynn, *American Catholics,* 191–94.

38. Thomas F. Mahony, "Economic Place of Mexican Welfare Problems in Colorado," Meeting of the National Council of Catholic Women, September 2, 1930. Mahony Papers—MAH 3/ Archives of the University of Notre Dame (hereafter AUND). Included in these papers is correspondence between John H. Reddin and Thomas F. Mahony.

39. Ibid.

40. Ibid.

41. "Twelfth Annual Report of the Mexican Welfare Committee of the State Council," Knights of Columbus, May 26, 27, 1928. CMAH 3/2, AUND.

42. Ibid.

43. John A. Ryan to Thomas F. Mahony, July 30, 1929. CMAH 3/2, AUND.

44. Thomas F. Mahony to John Reddin, February 21, 1928. CMAH 1/6, AUND.

45. Howard Gidd Powers, *Not Without Honor: The History of American Anticommunism* (New York: Free Press, 1995), 134.

46. Martin Carmody, "Knights Crusade—Your Part," *Columbia* 16 (February 1937): 14–15.

47. *Encyclical Letter of His Holiness, Pope Pius XI (Divini Redemptoris) Atheistic Communism* (New Haven: Knights of Columbus, 1937).

48. *Knights' Crusade for Social Justice: Council Schedule and Organization* (New Haven: Knights of Columbus, 1937).

49. Mary Herman Corey, S.N.D., "Young Christian Students: Historical Treatment on the Foundation in Toledo," *U.S. Catholic Historian* 9 (fall 1990): 141–42.

50. Steven M. Avella, *This Confident Church: Catholic Leadership and Life in Chicago, 1940–1965* (Notre Dame, Ind.: University of Notre Dame Press, 1992). Also see Jeffrey M. Burns, *Disturbing the Peace: A History of the Christian Family Movement, 1949–1974* (Notre Dame, Ind.: University of Notre Dame Press, 1999).

51. For works on Coughlin, see Mary Christine Athans, "Charles E. Coughlin," in *The Encyclopedia of American Catholic History,* edited by Michael Glazier and Thomas J. Shelley (Collegeville, Minn.: Liturgical Press, 1997), 385–87; eadem, *Father Denis Fahey, C.S.P. and Religious Anti-Semitism, 1936–1942* (New York: Peter Lang, 1991); Markus Sheldon, *Father Charles E. Coughlin : Tumultuous Life*

of the Priest of Little Flower (Boston: Little, Brown, 1973); Charles J. Tull, *Father Coughlin and the New Deal* (New York: Syracuse University Press, 1965). Donald Warren, *Charles Coughlin: The Father of Hate Radio* (New York: Free Press, 1996).

52. Athans, "Charles E. Coughlin," 387.

53. Leslie Woodcock Tentler, *Seasons of Grace: A History of the Archdiocese of Detroit* (Detroit: Wayne State University Press, 1990), 327.

54. Ibid., 328.

55. Ibid., 340–42.

56. This letter is included in the "Minutes of the Supreme Board of Directors," October 17, 1938. Copy, Luke E. Hart Papers, AKC.

57. Quoted by David J. O'Brien, *The Renewal of American Catholicism* (New York: Oxford University Press, 1972), 126.

58. Patrick McNamara, "A Study of the Editorial Policy of the Brooklyn *Tablet* Under Patrick F. Scanlon, 1917–1968" (M.A. thesis, St. John's University, New York, 1994). Also see Alden V. Brown, *The Tablet: The First Seventy-Five Years* (New York: *Tablet* Publishing Co., 1983).

59. Helen Baldwin Krippendorf to Bishop John Noll, November 1, 1937. CNOL/NOLL correspondence of Misc. subjects A-B Box 7, AUND. Also see Thomas L. Blantz, C.S.C., *George N. Shuster: On the Side of Truth* (Notre Dame, Ind.: University of Notre Dame Press, 1993).

60. For a biographical sketch of John H. Reddin, see "A Pioneer of Knighthood," *Columbia* 25 (January, 1942): 1.

61. Flynn, *Roosevelt and Romanism,* 64–65.

62. Ibid., 65.

63. For information on Murphy's political involvement, see Tentler, *Seasons of Grace,* 484–88.

64. Flynn, *Roosevelt and Romanism,* 89.

65. Timothy Galvin to Luke Hart, September 3, 1941. Hart Correspondence, August September SC 5-6-0733, AKC.

66. Hart to Galvin, September 4, 1941. SC5-6-0733, AKC.

67. Galvin to Hart, September 15, 1941. SC5-6-733 AKC.

68. Flynn, *Roosevelt and Romanism*, 88.

69. See the Hart Correspondence, World War II Files, AKC. Also see Rita L. Lynn, *The National Catholic Community Service in World War II* (Washington, D.C.: Catholic University of America Press, 1952).

70. *War Services of the Canadian Knights of Columbus* (Montreal: Knights of Columbus, 1948), 5.

71. Ibid., 198–99.

72. Timothy Galvin to the Most Reverend Francis McIntyre, February 14, 1942. Copy in the Luke E. Hart Papers, January–March 1942. SC5-6-0734, AKC. Clarence Manion, who worked in the K. of C. Huts program in World War I, was strongly pro Joseph McCarthy and a notable Catholic anti-Communist.

73. "It Need Not Be a Civil War," *New Haven Journal Courier,* June 25, 1942. Copy in Luke E. Hart Papers (see preceding note).

74. Quoted by Flynn, *Roosevelt and Romanism,* 193.

75. *Peace Program Proposal by the Knights of Columbus* (New Haven: Knights of Columbus, 1943), 3. World War II Files, SC-16-3-028, AKC.

76. Quoted by George Hermann Derry, "Our Columbian Peace Crusade," *Columbia* 23 (April 1944): 1.

77. William Mulligan, Report to the Supreme Assembly, August 23, 1946. Minutes of the Supreme Assembly, AKC.

78. Ibid.

79. Ibid.

80. Ibid.

81. O'Brien, *Public Catholicism,* 200; also see Patricia McNeal, "Catholic Conscientious Objectors and the Second World War," *Catholic Historical Review* 61 (April 1975): 220–42.

82. Quoted by James Hennesey, *American Catholics: A History of the Roman Catholic Community in the United States* (New York: Oxford University Press, 1991), 282. Also see O'Brien, *Public Catholicism,* 201.

83. David F. Crosby, S.J., *God, Church, and Flag: Joseph R. McCarthy and the Catholic Church 1950–1957* (Chapel Hill: University of North Carolina Press, 1978), 8.

84. "Testimonial to Supreme Knight," *Columbia* 25 (March 1946): 15.

85. "Report of the Supreme Knight," *Columbia* 26 (October 1946): 56.

86. Ibid., 16.

87. Ibid.

88. Ibid.

89. Ibid.

90. "Report of the Supreme Knight," *Columbia* 27 (October 1947): 14.

91. "Report of the Supreme Knights," *Columbia* 28 (October 1948): 5.

92. This article by Rubin and a rejoinder are in "Truth Makes Commie Squad," *Knights of Columbus News*, March 10, 1947, p. 1.

93. "Supreme Knight's Report," Supreme Council Proceedings, 1947, 135–36.

94. Steven M. Avella and Elizabeth McKeown, *Public Voices: Catholics in the American Context* (Maryknoll, N.Y.: Orbis Books, 1999), 238. This is one of a nine-volume series in the *Documentary History of American Catholic Identities,* General Editor, Christopher J. Kauffman.

95. Crosby, *God, Church, and Flag,* 56.

96. Ibid., 90–92. Father John F. Cronin was a major force as an anti-Communist activist in postwar Baltimore labor unions. He was "the conduit between the Federal Bureau of Investigation (FBI) and Richard Nixon during the Alger Hiss Case, and in the 1950s was Nixon's chief speech writer and a 'one-man brain trust.'" Labor historians Joshua B. Freeman and Steve Rosswurm, conclude this commentary: "Thus for over a decade Cronin was a linchpin in the triumphant cold war consensus, linking together anticommunist forces in the Catholic Church, business, government, and the labor movement." Joshua B. Freeman and Steve Rosswurm, "The Education of an anti-communist: Father John F. Cronin and the Baltimore Labor Movement," *Labor History* 33 (spring 1992): 218. For a history of the Sulpicians, see my book *Tradition and Transformation: The Priests of St. Sulpice in the United States since 1791* (New York: Macmillan, 1988).

97. William Buckley and Brent Bozell, *McCarthy and His Enemies* (Chicago: Regnery, 1964).

98. The most recent conservative interpretation of McCarthy is Arthur Herman,

Joseph McCarthy: Reexamining the Life and Legacy of America's Most Hated Senator (New York: Free Press, 2000). For a critical evaluation of this book, see Sam Tanenbaum, "Un-American Activities," *The New York Review of Books* 47 (November 30, 2000): 22–27. Also Crosby, *God, Church, and Flag,* 235.

99. William J. Mulligan, "Our Fourth Degree Golden Jubilee," *Columbia* 29 (February 1950): 1.

100. Ibid.

101. "Supreme Knight's Report," The Supreme Council Proceedings, AKC.

102. Quoted by Martin E. Marty, *Modern American Religion: Under God Indivisible, 1941–1960* (Chicago/London: University of Chicago Press, 1996), 287.

Chapter 5
New Forms of Anti-Catholicism, A Catholic President, the New Patriotism, 1950–2000

1. Quoted by Albert J. Menendez, *John F. Kennedy, Catholic and Humanist* (Buffalo: Prometheus Books, 1978), 24.

2. Ibid.

3. Harold E. Fey, "Can Catholicism Win America?" *Christian Century* (November 29, 1944): 1378.

4. Ibid.

5. Ibid., 1379.

6. Ibid.

7. Ibid., 1380.

8. Ibid.

9. Ibid.

10. C. C. Goen "Baptists and Church-State Issues in the Twentieth Century," in *Civil Religion: Church and State,* edited by Martin E. Marty (Munich: K. G. Sauer, 1992–93), 121.

11. Leonard Curry, *Protestant Catholic Relations in America: World War I through Vatican II* (Lexington, Ky.: University of Kentucky Press, 1972), 43.

12. Goen, "Baptists," 118–22.

13. "To Protestants and other Americans," *Columbia* 20 (February 1940): 1.

14. See "Editorials," *Columbia,* 1948 and 1949.

15. "On Church and State," reprinted in *Columbia* 20 (October 1940): 11.

16. On John Courtney Murray, see Joseph Komonchak, "Catholic Principle and the American Experiment: The Silencing of John Courtney Murray," *U.S. Catholic Historian* 17 (winter 1999): 28–44.

17. John Courtney Murray, S.J., *We Hold These Truths* (New York: Sheed & Ward, 1960).

18. Walter M. Abbot, S.J., ed., *The Documents of Vatican II* (New York: Doubleday, 1966).

19. Quoted in "Editorials," *Columbia* 26 (March 1947): 43.

20. *Church and State Newsletter*, "Compiled and circulated by Protestant and Others United for the Separation of Church and State" [Washington D.C.] vol. 1, no. 2 (July 10, 1948). Noll Papers, PANT, Anti-Catholicism 1/01, AUND.

21. "Old Forgery Resuscitated," *Church and State Newsletter* 4 (November 1951): 5. Noll Papers, PANT, Anti-Catholicism 6/01, POAU, AUND.

22. "Popular Demand Causes Extended Blanshard Tour," *Church and State Newsletter* 5 (February 1952): 6. Noll Papers, PANT, Anti-Catholicism 6/01, POAU, AUND.

23. Barbara Welter, "From Maria Monk to Paul Blanshard," in *Uncivil Religion: Interreligious Hostility in America,* edited by Robert N. Bellah and Frederick Greenspahn (New York: Crossroad, 1987), 43–71.

24. Paul Blanshard, *American Freedom and Catholic Power,* 2nd edition (Boston: Beacon Press, 1951), ii.

25. Quoted by John T. McGreevy, "Thinking on One's Own: Catholicism in the American Liberal Imagination, 1928–1960," *Journal of American History* (June 1997): 97.

26. Blanshard, *American Freedom,* 48.

27. Ibid., 42.

28. Ibid.

29. Ibid., 336.

30. Ibid., 333.

31. Ibid., 334–35.

32. David O'Brien, *Public Catholicism* (Maryknoll, N.Y.: Orbis Books, 1996), 203.

33. Jay P. Dolan, *Transforming Parish Ministry* (New York: Crossroad, 1993), 289.

34. Robert S. Ellwood, *The Fifties Spiritual Marketplace: American Religious in a Decade of Conflict* (New Brunswick, N.J.: Rutgers University Press, 1997), 52.

35. Ibid., 58.

36. Luke E. Hart, "Supreme Knight's Report," Supreme Council Proceedings, 123, AKC.

37. "God's Country," *Time,* May 4, 1953, pp. 57–58.

38. Dwight D. Eisenhower to Luke E. Hart, August 6, 1954. Quoted in Hart's "Supreme Knight's Report," Supreme Council Proceedings, 1954, 318, AKC.

39. Luke E. Hart to Members of the Supreme Board of Directors, Hart papers, AKC.

40. Ibid.

41. "Supreme Knight's Report." Supreme Council Proceedings 1957, 43, AKC; also see "Tito, Stay Home," *Time* (February 11, 1957): 6.

42. "Our Great Day," *Columbia* 37 (May 1957): 4–5.

43. "Busy Brotherly World of the Masons," *Life* 41 (October 8, 1956): 104–22.

44. "Knights of Columbus in 75th Year," *Life* 42 (May 27, 1957): 54–66.

45. Interview with George Hyatt, a past Grand Knight of Havana Council, who emigrated to Miami when Castro turned toward the Communist left and later was employed by the Order in New Haven as head of the Spanish desk.

46. Richard Patee, "Report on Cuba," *Columbia* 39 (March 1959): 6, 10–12, 34, 44.

47. Thomas A. Tweed, "Diasporic Nationalism and Urban Landscapes: Cuban Immigrants of a Catholic Shrine," in *God of the City,* edited by Robert Orsi (Bloom-

ington: Indiana University Press, 1999), 132–54. Also see *¡Presente! Latino Catholics from Colonial Origins to the Present,* edited by Timothy Matovina and Gerald E. Poyo, in collaboration with Jamie Vidal, Cecilia Gonzales, and Steven Rodriguez (Maryknoll, N.Y.: Orbis Books, 2000).

48. Quoted by Mark Massa, *Roman Catholics in American Culture* (New York: Crossroad, 1999), 141.

49. Massa notes that Peale was a friend of Nixon (*Roman Catholics,* 140).

50. Quoted by Massa, *Roman Catholics,* 141.

51. Paul Blanshard, *Communism, Democracy and Catholic Power* (Boston: Beacon Press, 1951). For his final words on religion and democracy, see his autobiography, *Personal and Confidential* (Boston: Beacon Press, 1973).

52. Paul Blanshard, *God and Man in Washington* (Boston: Beacon Press, 1961).

53. William F. Buckley, Jr., *God and Man at Yale: The Superstition of "Academic Freedom"* (Chicago: Henry Regnery, 1951).

54. Paul Blanshard, *Classics of Free Thought* (Boston: Beacon Press, 1969).

55. Quoted by Massa, *Roman Catholics,* 141.

56. Ibid., 138.

57. Ibid.

58. Lawrence H. Fuchs, *John F. Kennedy and American Catholicism* (New York: Meredith Press, 1967), 187.

59. Luke E. Hart to John Gillis, May 31, 1960. Luke Hart Papers, AKC.

60. "Injunction issued against circulation of a [Fourth Degree] Bogus Oath of the Knights of Columbus," *Columbia* 40 (October 1960): 16, 38.

61. "The Fake Oath," *Time,* August 22, 1960.

62. Luke E. Hart to John J. Gillis, May 31, 1960. Hart Papers, AKC.

63. Luke E. Hart to John J. Gillis, July 25, 1960. Hart Papers, AKC.

64. "The Supreme Knight at the White House," *Columbia* 42 (November 1962): 4, 43.

65. Luke E. Hart, "Christopher Columbus and Our American Ideals," copy of the radio address of October 12, 1962, *Columbia* 42 (November 1962): 11–12.

66. Luke E. Hart, "The Death of the President . . . A statement by Supreme Knight Luke E. Hart," *Columbia* 43 (December 1963): 1.

67. Luke E. Hart, "A Year of Progress . . . with a Sorrowful Chase," *Columbia* 44 (January 1964): 16.

68. Ibid.

69. Newspaper clipping, *Chicago Daily News.* Luke E. Hart Papers, AKC.

70. Newspaper clipping, "K of C Chief would air Membership," *Catholic Chronicle* [Toledo, Ohio], January 22, 1964. Luke E. Hart Papers, AKC.

71. John W. McDevitt, Supreme Knight's Report, Supreme Council Proceedings, 1964, 44–45, 138–40, 1960. AKC. I also benefited from interviews with John W. McDevitt, 1977–1980, when I was researching and writing *Faith and Fraternalism.*

72. John W. McDevitt, Supreme Knight's Report, Proceedings of the Supreme Council, 1966, 173, AKC.

73. Ibid.

74. Patrick W. Carey, *The Roman Catholics* (Westport, Conn.: Greenwood Press, 1993), 112.

75. Avery Dulles, *Models of the Church* (Garden City, N.Y.: Doubleday Image Books, 1978), 95–108.

76. John McDevitt, "The Crucible of Changing Times," *Columbia* 48 (October 1968): 21–22.

77. John W. McDevitt, "The Crisis in Authority," Supreme Knight's Report 1966, *Columbia* 46 (November 1966): 6.

78. Ibid., 7.

79. John McDevitt, Supreme Knights' Report, Proceedings of the Supreme Council, 1968, 189, AKC.

80. Press release quoted by John W. McDevitt, Supreme Knight's Report, Proceedings of the Supreme Council 1967, 51, AKC.

81. Luke E. Hart, Supreme Knight's Report, Proceedings of the Supreme Council, 1963, 43, AKC.

82. John W. McDevitt, Supreme Knights' Report, Proceedings of the Supreme Council 1964, 46, AKC.

83. John W. McDevitt, "In God We Trust," *Columbia* 55 (November 1975) 23.

84. Ibid.

85. Minutes of the Supreme Assembly, 1964, AKC.

86. Minutes of the Supreme Assembly, 1966, AKC.

87. Garry Wills, *Under God: Religion and American Politics* (New York: Simon & Schuster, 1990), 80–81. Wills quotes one Christian Pledge of Allegiance "we pledge allegiance to the Christian flag, and to our Savior, for whom it stands . . ." (p. 81).

88. George Lipsitz, "Dilemmas of a Beset Nationhood: Patriotism, the Family and Economic Change," in *Bonds of Affection: Americans Define Their Patriotism,* edited by John Bodnar (Princeton, N.J.: Princeton University Press, 1996).

89. Wayne Gollipoli, "Fourth Degree Milestones," *Columbia* 60 (February 2000): 18.

90. Ibid.

91. Virgil C. Dechant, Supreme Knight's Report, Proceedings of the Supreme Council, 1987, 53–54.

92. Virgil C. Dechant, Supreme Knight's Report, Proceedings of the Supreme Council, 1991, 62.

93. Lee A. Iacocca to Virgil C. Dechant, March 9, 1983. SC1-12-03-020-001, AKC.

94. Ibid.

95. Virgil C. Dechant to "Worthy Faithful Navigator," September 11, 1985. SC-1-12-03-020-001, AKC.

96. "Liberty Centennial Celebration, New York Harbor, July 3, 4, 5, 6, 1986." Copy of the first two pages, SCI-1-12-03-020-007, AKC.

97. Gollipoli, "Fourth Degree Milestones," 18.

98. Virgil C. Dechant, Supreme Knight's Report, Proceedings of the Supreme Council, 1987, 54.

99. Virgil C. Dechant, Supreme Knight's Report, Proceedings of the Supreme Council, 1988, 44.

100. Virgil C. Dechant, Supreme Knight's Report, Proceedings of the Supreme Council, 1989, 30.

101. Christopher J. Kauffman, interview with Hilary Schmittzehe, October 2, 1999.

102. Virgil C. Dechant, Supreme Knight's Report, Proceedings of the Supreme Council, 1992, 63, AKC.

103. Ibid., 82.

104. Ibid., 64.

105. Virgil C. Dechant, Supreme Knight's Report, Proceedings of the Supreme Council, 1996, 64.

106. Virgil C. Dechant, Supreme Knight's Report, Proceedings of the Supreme Council, 1994, 24.

107. Ibid.

108. Virgil C. Dechant, Supreme Knight's Report, Proceedings of the Supreme Council, 1995, 37.

109. Virgil C. Dechant, Supreme Knight's Report, Proceedings of the Supreme Council, 1997, 48.

110. Charles H. Foos, Report of the Supreme Master, Assembly Meeting, August 3, 2000, AKC.

111. Virgil C. Dechant, Supreme Knight's Report, Meetings of the Supreme Council, 1995, 37.

112. Ibid.

113. Charles H. Foos, Supreme Master's Report, Special Centennial Meeting of the Supreme Assembly, February 22, 2000, AKC.

114. Lipsitz, "Dilemmas of a Beset Nationhood," 270.

INDEX